"Global business is an arena where human beings [...] challenges, and yet, the importance of authentic l[...] long been deserving the deeper approach it now f[...] Koestenbaum's work, an approach that should free the creative leadership in those willing to take advantage of it.

Nothing is more liberating for me as a business leader than to be able to leave behind the useless simplistic how-to recipes I have been used to getting from consultants, and learn to consciously deal with the hard truths of business from an adult perspective, recognize my subjectivity, dare to look for the right questions to ask when things get 'stuck,' accept to walk the tightrope in polar situations where a problem does not have any definitive solution, face the consequences of tough decisions, and throughout all of these maintain integrity and hope."

Michael Cimet, Electronic Data Systems,
President for Latin America

"We live at a time that requires of leaders both competence and authenticity. We face both business issues and character issues. In becoming a leader, all of us must display both wisdom and business skills. What Peter Koestenbaum does in *The Philosophic Consultant* is not only to integrate wisdom into leadership, which is what you would expect of a philosopher, but he is also very pragmatic and applies this new thinking directly to the crucial strategic marketing needs—something that is essential for a company's very survival."

Dan Werbin, President and CEO,
Volvo Cars of North America, LLC

"*The Philosophic Consultant* redefines the way managers must think about their organizations, people, and markets to be successful both in business and in life. It calls each of us to understand that ethics in life and in business may be your most important concerns. By helping the reader focus on implementation decisions, choices, and commitment, Peter Koestenbaum points the way for responsible and effective management in a world where trust seems to be challenged on every front."

Otis W. Baskin, Ph.D., special advisor to the president and CEO of the Association for the Advancement of Collegiate Schools of Business, International; professor of management and former dean, Graziadio School of Business Management, Pepperdine University

"After a decade of often excessive superficiality in management theory and practice, Peter Koestenbaum's refreshing book, *The Philosophic Consultant,* provides answers for leaders and organizations in search of deeper meanings. The author's philosophical roots are clearly visible in the new work on enlarging the dimensions of leadership. His most significant insights are the importance of freedom, the choice to be ethical, and the acknowledgment of our boundaries."

Tomas Sattelberger, executive vice president, product and service, member of the board of Lufthansa German Airlines; vice president of the European Foundation for Management Development

THE PHILOSOPHIC CONSULTANT

THE PHILOSOPHIC CONSULTANT

Peter Koestenbaum

REVOLUTIONIZING ORGANIZATIONS WITH IDEAS

Foreword by Warren Bennis

JOSSEY-BASS/PFEIFFER
A Wiley Imprint
www.pfeiffer.com

Published by Jossey-Bass/Pfeiffer
A Wiley Imprint
989 Market Street, San Francisco, CA 94103-1741   www.pfeiffer.com

ISBN: 0-7879-6248-1

Library of Congress Cataloging-in-Publication Data
Koestenbaum, Peter.
The philosophic consultant: revolutionizing organizations with ideas/Peter Koestenbaum.
  p. cm.
Includes bibliographical references and index.
ISBN 0-7879-6248-1 (alk. paper)
 1. Management—Philosophy. 2. Leadership. 3. Business consultants.
I. Title.
HD30.19 .K64 2003
001—dc212002005155   2002005155

Jossey-Bass/Pfeiffer books and products are available through most bookstores. To contact Jossey-Bass directly call our Customer Care Department within the U.S. at 800-274-4434, outside the U.S. at 317-572-3993 or fax 317-572-4002.

Jossey-Bass/Pfeiffer also publishes its books in a variety of electronic formats. Some content that appears in print may not be available in electronic books.

Acquiring Editor: Josh Blatter
Director of Development: Kathleen Dolan Davies
Developmental Editors: Susan Rachmeler and Leslie Stephen
Editor: Rebecca Taff
Senior Production Editor: Dawn Kilgore
Manufacturing Supervisor: Becky Carreño
Interior and Cover Design: Bruce Lundquist
Illustrations: Lotus Art

Printed in the United States of America

Printing 10   9   8   7   6   5   4   3

DEDICATION

For Peter Block, who taught me the meaning of generosity.

CONTENTS

Part 5 Appendices: Using the Total Diamond

LIST OF FIGURES, TABLES, AND EXHIBITS

FOREWORD

TODAY'S WORLD REQUIRES broader and deeper ways for leaders to understand reality and find new tools with which to build a future. The big issues begin with the digital divide, pitting communities with access to modern technology and medicine against villages without telephones or potable water. We witness the standoff between democracies and brutal dictatorships. We stand by helplessly in confrontations generated by ethnic hostilities and terrorist upheavals. And we find abuses in our own midst —hindrances to basic human honesty in a capitalistic economy.

The terror of 9/11/01 directed the American economy to a more sober, balanced, and especially deeper focus. There is a call for less greed and more morals, less beating up of employees and more compassion, less concern with building a business or career and more openness to home life. Our values have tempered. The human factor is trying to reemerge.

Peter Koestenbaum's new book fits in with this new need, although in a possibly unexpected way. He attempts to deepen the face of leadership—and the professions that counsel and support it—through philosophy. He correlates philosophical deepening with business effectiveness. I think that basically he is right, for he is no romantic. He is not one who went from business to philosophy and exhorts others to follow him. Quite the contrary, he migrated from philosophy to business, determined to make succeed in the toughest arenas of modern life what he learned about the human mind, the human heart, and the human body in his years as a philosophy professor. And it is here where he exhorts others to consider doing likewise.

Peter's model of leadership is based on understanding more profoundly the underlying dimensions of human nature. It gives issues like freedom and ethics, anxiety and guilt, evil and destiny a new meaning and urgency. These are larger themes than we are accustomed to think of in business—much less to act on—but we have to do just that. We are fortunate to have this book for a guide, for it is like listening in on a coaching conversation with Peter. You will find vital help here no matter where you fit in the equation—whether you are the "philosophic consultant" or a leader in business or government, education or healthcare, entertainment or community service.

Georges Braque wrote, "The only thing that matters in art is the part that can't be explained." Peter understands that the self is bigger than any theory about it, and so is the world. Nevertheless, he has consolidated his philosophic insight into a series of formal propositions. He has called his compendium of leadership consciousness the Leadership Diamond®. In this book he has simplified his earlier versions of it, making it more intelligible and practicable. His experience in business shows.

What I think is strongest here—at the same time ancient and original—are several sensitive analyses, grounded in a philosophy of existence, of a type not seen today in books on management and leadership. One is the recurring examination of freedom and free will. Another is his scrutiny of the decision to be ethical and of how ethics is grounded on free will. There are great insights here into courage, which he interprets as the merger of free will and anxiety. For Peter, courage means not only to make tough choices, but literally to be willing to risk your honor and, what's more, your life for them. The will is the capacity to transform negative energy into positive, intention into action, abstractions into reality. It was the message of Descartes, the founder, four centuries ago, of modern Western thought. Descartes translates doubt into certainty, questions into answers, and also, in the end, despair into hope.

Peter is concerned with the questions of power and anxiety, roots and responsibility, identity and human relationships. But perhaps his preeminent concern—as with philosophers as divergent as Bertrand Russell and Elie Wiesel—is the problem of evil. Ethics—and how we all have a responsibility to participate in the creation of an ethical world—is his ever-present theme.

In describing the human condition, we do not use the concept of "evil" frequently enough. Peter reemphasizes duty and obligation in ethics: service above self-interest, concern for others over concern for self. He raises the question of motivation not from a psychological perspective, but from a philosophical one: The motivation to be ethical is based on the choice to be motivated by conscience and moral sentiments. He makes the point, much needed in a decade of greed, that after all there exists a conscience.

I met Peter for the first time at American Medical International in 1986, when I was dean of their leadership program. He was on the faculty, having come fresh from Ford Motors in Detroit. What I first noticed was that he was kindly, attentive, sharp, and innocently passionate—but also somewhat anxious and shy. As much as he tried sincerely to be a patriotic American, he clearly had a European mind. That became obvious when he showed how uncompromisingly serious he was about philosophy. For him, devotion to philosophical reflection makes life worth living. Today, to many of us, philosophy is dry and abstract. To Peter it has always been a realistic sensibility, rich with concrete ways to shape and elevate our motives and goals in daily life.

Peter is not a social reformer. But he does challenge the ethical conscience in us. He is convinced that there can be no humane society unless we sustain, single-handedly and from the core of our being, the ethical conscience of mankind. He wants to help people face the relentless toughness of life, never losing their capacity for compassion. This clearly is what the post 9/11 world needs from philosophy, and not only theoretically but also practically. Here is where application of philosophy to daily business life makes sense.

No human being can live without learning to rummage around in the deeper regions of the soul. In truth, the more profoundly we discover ourselves the more powerful we become. What is unique here is how these thoughts are brought into business, how they are applied to the spectrum of commercial activity, from motivation and culture to helping employees adapt to the agonizing difficulties of contemporary corporate life and to pervasive entrepreneurial anxiety.

As promised in its subtitle, Peter's book is indeed a blueprint for revolutionizing organizations with ideas. It offers deep and practical advice for any leader engaged in shaping the future of our businesses and institutions and for the consultants and coaches who support them.

Every once in a while, a book comes along that illuminates the darkness and genius of our time. This is *the* book for our time.

Warren Bennis

ACKNOWLEDGMENTS

THIS BOOK OWES MUCH *for its existence to Roland Sullivan. I shall always be thankful to him for his enthusiastic support. I received a great deal of on-target help from two excellent minds: William Rothwell and Kristine Quade. The staff at Jossey-Bass/Pfeiffer has been impeccable in their standards and most loyal in their commitment: Susan Rachmeler, Dawn Kilgore, Josh Blatter, Kathleen Dolan Davies, Ashley Greer, Jeanenne Ray, Jin Im, and Leslie Stephen. My wife, Patty, her loyal support has made all the difference.*

Peter Koestenbaum
Carmel, California
July, 2002

PART ONE

Context

CHAPTER 1

Introduction

As a Phoenix Out of the Ashes,
Greatness Grows Out of Anxiety

IN SEPTEMBER OF 2001, *not long after the terrorist attack on the New York World Trade Center, I received a call from* Fast Company, *the magazine for the New Economy. Their question: "After this great catastrophic event, all else seems so insignificant. How can we get back to doing what we do—competing, strategizing, working effectively, making deals—without forgetting or trivializing this global tragedy?"*

Our problem was that we had already trivialized work, because we had trivialized existence itself, reducing life to greed, narcissism, and entertainment. We had ignored that we were meant to complete a task greater than ourselves. Human beings need meaning and significance, to make a difference and to be devoted to values so that their consciences are clear and so that they can feel proud, honorable, and worthy.

We had forgotten. We needed a reminder. And we got one. It turned out to be the "mother of all reminders"! And we knew that if we did not listen this time, as we had not listened many times before, the next reminder would strike us with even more fury, if that were possible.

The cry for greatness that arose out of the disaster had always been there. We had just shouted it down with the din of our irresponsibility. We can now return to work, knowing that our strength lies in the character and the prosperity of the nation, in the degree to which we exhibit our values of decency and rationality, in the extent to which we arrive at effective solutions, and in how well we act on our terms and not react in the terms of those who would destroy us.

Here was not a temporary political event but a gaping hole revealing ultimate eternal reality.

This is our issue in this book: how to seize the greatness of our lives, honor it, and make it come to life in how we do business and in how we work. But *we do this in line with business purposes, for bottom-line results*. Too often management is alienated from the workforce and, in the spirit of "reciprocity," the workforce is alienated from management. Greatness is not bigness; it can be very small, like lovingly raising a baby, or taking pride in quality work that may never sell at higher margins. However, it also could be to move nations and markets.

We Are All Needed to Install Overarching Greatness

We are all responsible for industry creation and for nation building. Greatness in the workplace is the kernel of a nation's response to assault. For we meet terror with resoluteness to make the nation great, to be economically strong—stronger than ever—and to be able to meet her world leadership obligations. All of which is to be consonant with the universal values of freedom, equality, dignity, and justice.

Who will uphold our values if it is not we? When will we uphold our values if it is not now? Such is the nature of the world.

At the heart of what this book needs to say lies this theme of extreme personal responsibility.

Organizations Owe Their People Shelter, a Place for Security and Meaning

Organizations need to help their people find real meaning in work. They need to help them participate in the greatness objectives of the organization and make a contribution that will dignify both themselves and the company. Work can never again be trivial, and companies need to take responsibility to create a culture and an atmosphere in which destiny and dignity both become palpable realities.

Employees Owe Their Organization Full Understanding and Support in Its Strategic Objectives

In no way are employees off the hook. Employees need to make the business objectives their own. Employees must take care of their own issues with commitment and greatness, with dignity and self-esteem.

The bond established between the objectives of the business and the values of the people impacts massively both the fate of the company and the future of the employees.

The Leader in You Wrests Victory out of the Jaws of Defeat

There is a situation that demands special attention. What if either side does not meet its leadership obligations, which is probably more the rule than the exception? What if there is no family feeling in this company; it is a jungle instead, a merciless free-for-all? The truth then is how to cope with defeat; it is how to maintain authentic and civilized comportment in an exploitative, insensitive, and unscrupulous environment; it is to uphold the needs of all the stakeholders even though they may be no better than vultures. To be a moral giant is then the fate of many a hero in today's workplace.

Heroic Leadership

Leadership blends business (competence) and character (authenticity). We thus need to distinguish between *competence* and *authenticity*, the two vectors whose sum is leadership (see Figure 1.1).

Competence is to apply profound insights about what it means to be a person to the daily strategic marketing and selling needs of an enterprise. This is an exceedingly pragmatic undertaking. How do you design an attractive product? How do you structure an effective sales talk?

Authenticity is to deal with greatness. How does one make enormous decisions, such as going to war or not? How does one manage defeat with dignity? What is our best response to evil? To great fear? How does one cope? These are the farther reaches of leadership concerns.

These two approaches, authenticity and competence, are light years apart, yet mastering one is prerequisite for succeeding in the other.

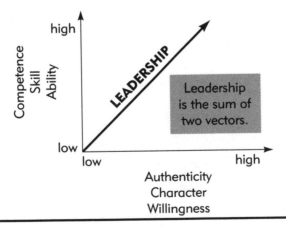

Figure 1.1. Leadership as a Vector Sum

The Leadership Diamond

The basis of our discussion is the Leadership Diamond® Model (see Figure 1.2), which provides the framework and the language in terms in which leadership discussions are expected to be carried out. The premise is that the model will give individuals and organizations credibility in what they do and speed in getting to the high-leverage issues for effectively managing today's two big business topics: *change* and *innovation*. The model looks dry and abstract, but through the analyses in this book, it will become animated and alive, like a warming burst of sunlight. The themes are big, representing different ways in which human beings look at the world: ethics and all the concerns of human relationships; courage and learning how to make the tough choices; reality and coming to terms with that which we cannot change; and, finally, vision, the capacity to use our minds to the farthest reaches of possibilities.

The Clients for Diamond Interventions Are Line Executives and Support Consultants

In applying Diamond Theory to organizations, we address two sets of employees: those who do the work, the so-called line people—CEOs, executives, and managers, on the one hand—and those who support them with counsel—consultants, trainers, organization development and human resource professionals.

This occurs on two levels. One is pragmatic, with emphasis on techniques, tools, systems, behaviors, and things to do. The other is what we here call philosophical, where depth is what matters. We believe that the more profoundly we discover ourselves the more powerful we will also become. The first concerns behaviors—how to conduct a meeting. The second concerns experiences—exploring the revelations of anxiety. The first is to design a new product. The second is to know the price of not feeling accountable for the whole organization.

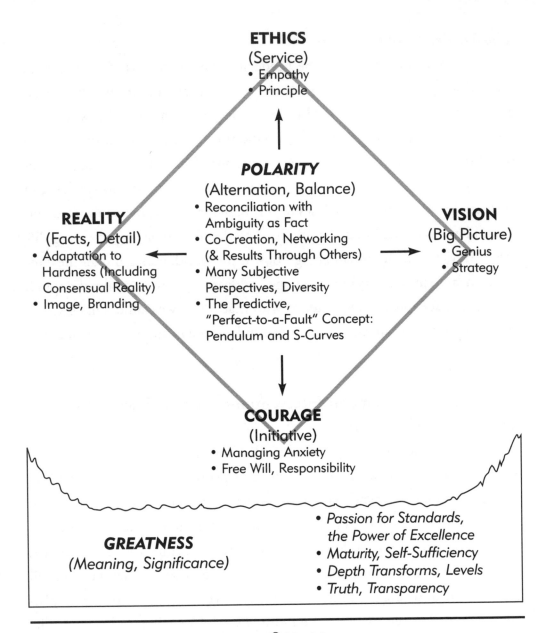

ETHICS
(Service)
• Empathy
• Principle

POLARITY
(Alternation, Balance)
• Reconciliation with
  Ambiguity as Fact
• Co-Creation, Networking
  (& Results Through Others)
• Many Subjective
  Perspectives, Diversity
• The Predictive,
  "Perfect-to-a-Fault" Concept:
  Pendulum and S-Curves

REALITY
(Facts, Detail)
• Adaptation to
  Hardness (Including
  Consensual Reality)
• Image, Branding

VISION
(Big Picture)
• Genius
• Strategy

COURAGE
(Initiative)
• Managing Anxiety
• Free Will, Responsibility

GREATNESS
(Meaning, Significance)

• *Passion for Standards,
  the Power of Excellence*
• *Maturity, Self-Sufficiency*
• *Depth Transforms, Levels*
• *Truth, Transparency*

Figure 1.2. The Leadership Diamond® Model

Serving Your Clients Is to Flow from a Coal Through Intense Stresses to Become a Diamond

We use a diagram, called the Leadership Diamond®, which is an image of your client—an atlas of where your client wants to be. The Diamond describes in business-biased terms your customer at the high end of Maslow's hierarchy of needs. People are eager to have these needs fulfilled, a condition that is essential for surviving with integrity. You help them achieve this fulfillment with the kind of business that you conduct.

There is a second figure—the coal, the shadow, the deficit. That's where your customer is currently.

Central to this change management intervention and support is to move people from shadow to leadership, from coal to diamond, from deficit to fulfillment, from needy to satisfied. This is the key business application of the Diamond. It is a theory that needs to be understood and a technique that can be learned.

Your business is the activity that transports your customer from unhappy to happy, from needy to satisfied, from empty to full, through the use of your products and services, through your customer's contact with you and your organization. Your genius is to connect your products and services with the Diamond needs of your customers: How can you meet their needs of mastering reality, for example? How can you help them improve their personal relationships? That opportunity is so important to your customer that the client is willing to compensate you handsomely for your help.

This is our conceptualization of the nature and function of business. This is what commerce today is all about. Figure 1.3 illustrates this point.

We Bring About Culture Change Through a New Language

The Diamond is a language that can be taught and learned, used and measured. The strategy is to translate ordinary and non-leadership conversations into positive and strong leadership ones. To teach this skill is a major part of

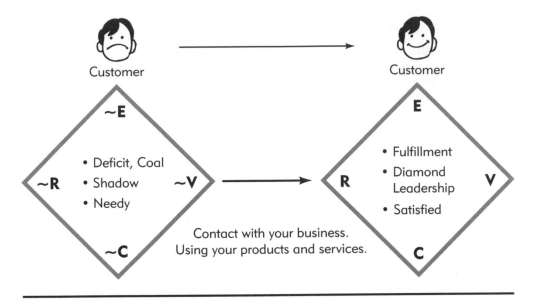

Figure 1.3 Transforming Customers

what we do in Diamond technology. The new language is the language of the Leadership Diamond®. Its goal is to change the organizational culture. And since culture implements strategy, changing the culture is an organization's critical success factor.

There Needs to Be an Anchor!

Language changes culture only if language becomes anchored in experience and takes root in the soul, so that both attitudes and behaviors are also changed. That is far from easy. There is magic in changing ideas into reality. A central insight in the philosophies of the world is how an abstract idea can be embodied and become a physical act.

This magic is *free will,* the mysterious decision-making capacity of human beings. It is courage and commitment, integrity and authenticity. That is how greatness in organizations transforms from cerebral theory to dynamic fact, and *you* can make it happen!

In returning to doing great things, we have come full circle.

Audience

This book is for coaches and consultants and for the leaders whom they serve. It also is to help leaders identify qualified philosophically oriented coaches. It focuses on change management and innovation. Understanding philosophy adds a dimension of depth. It functions to ground both theory and practice for organization development practitioners. This material should deepen and render more effective the work of leaders, change agents, and, in particular, the human resource community that serves them. But this book is also for CEOs and high-level line managers. Companies spend millions on expensive consultants. Do they get their money's worth? The chances are better if they look for those who are philosophically inclined and who respond to the more deep-seated and profound concerns of their clients.

How this Book Is Organized

This is a preview of what this book hopes to help you achieve. The next chapter in Part One presents many of the necessary philosophical underpinnings related to the Diamond and to great leadership. Part Two presents a simplified overview of the Leadership Diamond® model. Then, in Parts Three and Four, each dimension of the model is discussed at length and illustrated with business situations. Part Five provides activities and tools to help you apply a philosophic approach to leadership.

> For more information, go to www.PiB.net and take the leadership quiz.

CHAPTER 2

Your Heroic Journey

ALIENATION IS AN UNADORNED FACT *with which we need to live, and it is not easy to be a responsible person in the midst of a disempowering environment.*

Companies no longer take care of their people, and employees no longer care about the fate of their employers. Companies and workers exploit each other. Not that they are evil. In a world with global business and global terrorism, alienation is part of what it means to exist as a responsible human being and a responsible organization. Today's leader squarely faces this ambiguity. The deeper answer is to see life as a journey.

It is both touching and useful to help people see life as a journey—as a process, as something in time, as an experience that continues, something that brings good times but also bad times, and we pass and transcend them all. This shift of world from thing to time, from stasis to continuity, is the heart of grasping the power of transformation as a solution to human problems, as the vestibule to the deep roominess of the soul. Here is where the leadership language is designed to guide you. Above all, on our journey we face tests, some incredibly tough. But we can have the faith that they are there for a purpose, to build character, and the good news is that we are equipped to pass each and every test. But the learning, well, that may have to be monumental!

On this journey, the Diamond is the Atlas of the leadership mind, the continents and seas you traverse in order to get full command over what's available to you, and possible—your tools and your powers to achieve what business demands and what leadership can be.

Starting Off

Early on, we as human beings face the future. It is the task of coaches and OD consultants to frame life in the soothing terms of a journey, to find the language of myth and archetypes, and help their clients in the throes of change to see failure and frustration simply as necessary tests for the eventual authentication of life itself.

Clients will be confronted with *tests,* perhaps "dragons." Each test they pass advances them to the next, which is even harder. All tests are alike: making exceedingly difficult *choices.* In addition, they make a *second decision,* a decision about previous decisions, to continually revitalize the first. If they choose the high road, then they continue to choose the high road. If they decide to expand their businesses, then they continue to choose, daily, the energy and enthusiasm for the details, and to be persistent for years to come. The same holds for changing jobs. If they choose partners, they make decision number one. Decision number two is to make the partnership work, daily and indefinitely. Henry Kissinger is reported to have said, "Each success only buys an admission ticket to a more difficult problem."

First on the heroic journey clients will meet a *wizard,* who advises them. The wizard gives them a magic "*Diamond,*" with four facets, each of which reflects a different color from the sun: yellow, red, green, and blue. As the client rubs each surface, it summons a different *helper*: the yellow facet summons the *healer,* the red the *warrior,* the green the *merchant,* and the blue the *seer.*

We call these four faces of this Diamond, respectively, *ethics, courage, reality,* and *vision.* Wisdom lies in knowing *which* helpers to call, and *when,* and *how long* to use them. And your power lies in having all of them always at your beck and call.

Figure 2.1 illustrates the journey.

Becoming Unstuck

If you think you are failing in business and don't know why—we call it "being *stuck*"—it may well be that you do not call the right helper or you overuse one helper at the expense of another (see Figure 2.2). For example, if you are too kind to your employees (overusing the healer) instead of confronting your employees (using the warrior), you will never get action (1)! This is typical. Is that why you are "stuck"? If you are too people-oriented (again overusing the healer) at the expense of strategy (not using the seer), then you cannot reach your distant goals (2). If you are too realistic (overdoing it with the merchant and looking only at quick fixes and the numbers) at the expense of vision (forgetting the seer, who represents the company mission), you will become boorish, dull, and unimaginative (3)! And if you are too realistic (excessively the

THE HERO
Greatness

**(The Heroic Journey
of Your Life Begins)**

THE WIZARD
Polarity

THE HEALER
Ethics

THE MERCHANT   **THE SEER**
Reality   Vision

THE WARRIOR
Courage

Figure 2.1. The Heroic Journey

merchant) at the expense of courage (ignoring the warrior), then you fall into
the trap of thinking that citing numbers and presenting facts will actually
motivate people. This is "throwing money at a problem" (4). You cannot live
life without courage, no matter how many facts you know and how many people you love. Courage cannot be delegated. No matter where you are on the
organizational hierarchy, you contribute significantly to what Peter Block calls
"creating an organization of your own choosing."

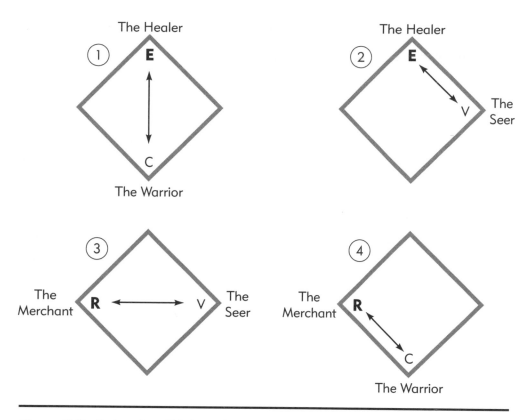

Figure 2.2. Balancing "Helpers"

Transformation

The tests along the way are meant to teach you the *meaning of life,* which is *transformation.* Before transformation you have problems. After transformation they go away. It sounds simplistic, but it is not. That is how deep coaching works, when it touches the unconscious. Why were you born? To serve, to make a commitment to the well-being of others, to realize that what matters is *character* over pleasure, *meaning* and *significance* over authority and dominance, and *growth* over security. That was the message of Socrates: to become a more substantial human being.

> Aristotle said that it is better to be a Socrates dissatisfied than a
> pig satisfied, and if the pig is of a different opinion then that is
> because it sees only one side of the picture!

A mature person intuitively understands the priority of character, meaning, significance, and growth over pleasure, authority, dominance, and security. A person not yet fully mature simply does not have the saturated experience of both sides.

The wizard's Diamond gives you access to helpers to manage your journey. Thus equipped, you will find that as you progress on your journey, and if you listen attentively, you will hear the *universe respond.* The silence *will* be broken! That is the formidable truth, waiting for you to discover it!

Returning then to the home you had left, you teach what you have learned, you help people remember what they themselves unconsciously know already. You can't go home again, said Thomas Wolfe, but you can see your old home with new eyes. Then you are a leader.

Here are questions for your clients.

- What language would you use to help them?
- What have been *your* tests?
- How have *you* responded?
- What are the ones still to come?
- How will you measure up? What helpers will you call?
- What will be the conclusion?

In real life, your most important and perhaps hardest choices are

- To maintain your *dignity in defeat* and
- To take *individual responsibility for the effectiveness and the welfare of the whole.*

You *cannot feel sorry for yourself* but each time rise to the occasion, measuring up to the task, taking care of your own feelings.

You honor the fact that you exist—never taking life for granted.

Raising the Questions

Results in managing and effectiveness in coaching—an executive's and consultant's daily work—depend on addressing the daily *stuck points* intelligently. The following examples can be read from two points of view. If you are an employee, this may be how you feel. If you are an OD consultant, this is how your clients may feel.

> You need urgently to talk to your boss but find him arrogant and uncooperative, difficult to reach. You have a problem and he does not care. Nevertheless, he will judge and punish you if you fail. You are frustrated, upset, angry, and rejected. You are so upset that managing your own employees, dealing with disgruntled clients, and making sales calls are now for you virtually impossible. You try to talk your way out of it, but, like whistling in the dark, you are just rationalizing.
>
> *How do you recover your composure, steady your nerves, regain control over your life? How do you restore your dignity? How do you understand what is really happening to you? What is the ethical response? What is a healthful action plan for you? What's the right perspective?*

> Your company's stock is dropping and, embarrassingly, you don't know what to do. Your reputation is at stake, the expensive measures you have taken have had no lasting effect, you have hired an expensive consulting firm to help you reengineer the corporation, raised your revenues by acquisitions, and taken a charge two years in a row. The stockholders are rebelling. It's getting ugly.

Do you have the inner strength and the strategic genius to address these issues? Can you face your loneliness. Are you losing face? Can you let go and accept defeat? Do you envy those who succeed? Will you get physically ill? How would a great leader manage your crisis? Can you recover?

You are measured by the quality of the team you manage. Your team is disorganized, not dedicated, and always late. Your people do not respect you and do not care about company strategy. They do not pay attention to your instructions, are not interested in their work, and do not take it seriously. You are at the end of your wits, discouraged and depressed, losing your nerve.

What steps can you take to get past this stuck point? As things are going from bad to worse, how do you manage the stress? What are the root causes? The solutions? How good are you at co-creation? How much empathy can you muster for your workers? How hardy are you?

You are in the middle of reshaping your team, barely half finished with creating your legacy. You are proud of what the team has accomplished. As happens often, you are recognized and promoted before you are ready. The CEO wants you overseas, which is for you a major step up. No matter how much the CEO protests to the contrary, she really doesn't want "no" for an answer. However, if you leave, you will let your people down, breaking promises you have made to them.

Do you want to do that? What is the right decision? What acts of courage are required of you? How will you manage the damage you will cause (for either way there will be complications)? How will you reinvent yourself?

You are a successful young executive, making more money than you thought possible. You live in an intensely performance-driven corporate culture.

Being bright, disciplined, and loving competition, you thrive under these conditions. But you feel viscerally the loss of other values. Your conscience draws you to your children and your spouse, and you miss the strong and healthy body you had while on your college tennis team. You want it all.

What are your options? Rein in your ambition for wealth and sacrifice for the future of your family? Expect more of your family and let them know that you are an example of how to be a hero, for them to model? Announce that you can't take it any more and have a nervous breakdown? Rev up your energies and smarts to a new level, telling yourself you can dare to have it all? Are there new ways of being in business that foster both wealth and love? Can you break through your paradox between values and strategic thinking to the genius level? Can you avoid the heart-rending choice among your conflicting values and self-concepts, the needs of your family and of your personal ego?

You are firmly convinced that the organization's strategy is seriously flawed.

Should you be a good soldier and implement what in your heart you feel is wrong? Should you keep a low profile and perform as best you can? Or is this the time to resign in protest? Or go into business for yourself?

A prominent government official complains about the pressures on the public sector: the tribal behavior of political organizers; the increasing specialization of community stakeholders; and the macho solution mentality. Politics can be overwhelming: it seems so unfair, so full of rage, and so irrational!

Is there anything more difficult than being in public life? How do you steel yourself against attack? How do you balance opposing political agendas? How do you deal with outrageous pathological projections on you? How do you hold on to your principles and values with integrity? What higher ideals are you realizing through public service?

Your company's advertising is outdated. You need imagination and impact.

How can you increase the creativity that your company now so urgently needs? How can you achieve inventive breakthroughs? What might an Einstein have done? A Jack Welch?

You feel guilty for being materialistic, working only to support your family and raise the market value of your company. You ask, "Where is the effervescent idealism of my youth?"

Should you commit to improve the state of the world, one company at a time? Is instituting sustainability, for example, the primary direction to take your team and your company?

You are an organization development professional. The economy is in a recession. You are "fat" and in the frenzy of cost-cutting you will be first among the downsized. You also know that OD experts never are considered for CEO positions.

What can you do to change the perception of your profession? How can you let people know how important what you do really is? How can you make it clear to stockholders that dealing with the people, especially in hard times, is everyone's primary task?

All these are *stuck points,* dilemmas without easy answers, moral crises, stressful emotional conflicts. They make or break organizational success. They make or break personal lives. They make or break families.

How much effort do you spend thinking through these concerns? How can you fortify your sense of self? How does one address quickly issues that are more likely to respond to slow and fundamental changes in attitude and self-concept than to routine analysis and speedy problem solving? How does one manage the conflicts among the deeper values and the deeper structures of human existence that are evoked at these moments of crisis? What is guilt? What is authenticity? What makes you really happy? What are your obligations? What makes you feel proud? How do you follow your conscience when under the pressure of performance?

From the perspective of leadership training and leadership coaching, what is a promising and effective way to address these pervasive and damaging problems? What would be deep and enduring rather than a superficial and temporary?

Addressing the Questions

Most organizational change movements fail. People get angry and proffer profound explanations as to why. Nothing gets done. Everyone ends distressed and depressed. Change is too important to allow it to be "talk without walk," "rhetoric and no action." Leadership is about implementation and results. How do we mobilize such motivation? We have to connect with the seat of the soul, the zone where the real choices are made. We connect the tree's flowers and branches, via the trunk and roots to the soil; the horizontal needs to become vertically grounded. *Thought, which is theory, becomes action, which is you.* This concept is illustrated in Figure 2.3. It goes beyond language and is therefore the secret of implementation, for this magical transformation from idea to reality can be brought about only by a mysterious act of free will.

Perhaps a stronger metaphor than leaves, trunk, roots, and soil for the groundedness of implementation is a blueprint for a house. For it contains everything you find in the house, without exception, but for the reality of it. Even though the blueprint may be complete, you can neither live in it nor can you buy or sell it. The all-important difference is to transform a concept into a real object. That is done by the person, the instrument of implementation. To grasp this non-verbal action point, and to see it as a mystery, and to know that it is you at your core, that is what leadership is.

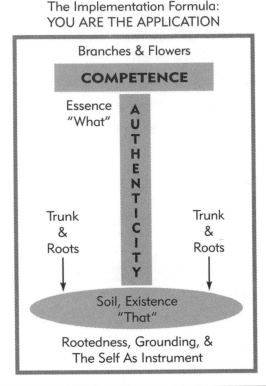

The Implementation Formula:
YOU ARE THE APPLICATION

Branches & Flowers

COMPETENCE

Essence
"What"

AUTHENTICITY

Trunk
&
Roots

Trunk
&
Roots

Soil, Existence
"That"

Rootedness, Grounding, &
The Self As Instrument

Figure 2.3. The Tree As Metaphor

Motivation and Engagement

Implementation is based on motivation. Motivation leads to action. Action is a decision. There can be no implementation strategy. There are only implementation decisions, choice, and commitment.

If you are looking for implementation as a competence, you are ignoring the non-rational and non-formulaic aspects of actual human existence.

All formulas and all descriptions are concepts, ideas, words, theories. What makes them real is your involvement, your commitment, your life, your engagement. And that is a choice that you make with your whole being and not a system that an organization puts in place to achieve results automatically. The theory and concepts you wish to make real and the you that actually exists—and is the self as instrument—belong to two different realms of being: that which can be described and that which exists, the *what* and the *that*. This is an ancient and crucial and insightful philosophic distinction—as obvious as it is hard to grasp conceptually. It is not a concept. It is the living act. How often have you seen a plan that makes sense but no one adopts it? Because human beings are not ideas but they are alive. And what is alive goes dead when it becomes solely an idea.

The key to business effectiveness is to make it happen, that is, implementation. We have instead consulting theory. That's great. But only *you* can make it work. No one can force you. No one can seduce you. You must choose. And that is up to you. It is called free will.

That is why making things happen—not just talking about them—is the most difficult thing to do on the surface of the earth! You act and you co-create.

The Leadership Diamond® is an orderly, simple, relevant, logical, and hard-hitting methodology whose deliverable is to find those key points of effectiveness that have demonstrated themselves to make the leadership difference.

The Diamond provides the language of depth. All we can teach is language. Language is important. It guides you. It gives you a voice. It helps you express yourself. Through it we communicate. Through it we relate. Without you there is nothing. To substitute for you a theory or a computer program is to miss the point entirely of leadership and of making things happen through leadership.

This is the heart of leadership.

The Resistance to Action

You want people to act? Then ask: Why do people not act? In psychiatry this is known as the resistance. Why do people resist, fight, what they want most? You want to finish your project, but you procrastinate instead. The answer that works is not to try harder but to ask yourself why you procrastinate. What does it gain you? Then you have an insight that can leverage you into action.

People like to talk about science and technology, about techniques and plans. But when one touches on the true issues of implementation under adversity, then the topic is summarily ignored.

What are these issues? Here are some:

- Why do people resist facing the truth? Why do people check out or become angry when you disturb their comfortable world view? What are they defending? What are their weaknesses? Why, when you make some rather obvious points of depth, do people stare at you in total incomprehension?

- "We must find out what makes people tick," you hear. "Is it genetics or is it socialization and culture?" A common question indeed, and a reasonable one. Now, what if someone were to ask, "What about free will? What about personal responsibility and accountability? What about individual initiative? What about self-definition? Are these not motivations also? Or is free will but another cultural or genetic determinant?" Questions such as these will be interpreted as disruptive—as stopping the proceedings and the conversation. The metaphysical shock is too dramatic.

- Free will may be dismissed with some platitude like "This is the province of philosophy and theology," or "We have established long ago that free will is an illusion," or "It does not help us to bring in this abstract issue; we are here dealing with pragmatic propositions," or "The ideal that you should think for yourself is one more cultural bias and indoctrination." And so it goes. Destroy the core. Stay on the surface. Forget the center, stay on the periphery. This type of thinking is the disease, the static that clouds the implementation.

Going into Depth

The language of the Leadership Diamond® helps your clients move into the depth where the real solutions exist. It is all about protecting people from the dangers of being superficial and thinking they have solved problems when all they have done is deny and repress them.

The following questions can be used by OD professionals and consultants to help their clients work through important business decisions:

- What do you feel when you are defeated? How much is denial, and how much do you allow yourself to learn about the regions that the facts and emotions of defeat reveal to you? How do you tolerate defeat? How do you overcome it? How do you get past it, not by repressing its pain but rather by being fertilized through it?

- Why should people be loyal? What does it mean to make a commitment?

- Why do some face opposition with resolve whereas others run away?

- What is a resistance to free will? Do we realize that we choose our resistances and are responsible for not doing what pieces of us say we should do?

- Does your dogmatism turn people off? Are you cynical and naive, as others may think, rather than smart and onto the truth, as you yourself may think?

- What about self-sacrifice? Is that genetic? Is that cultural? Or is that a matter of individual responsible decisions based on ethical principles that are not cultural but endemic to human existence anyway? Are these principles discovered by your conscience?

- The possibility that there may exist a separate reality to which you do not attend—be it God, or the collective unconscious, or the ancient memory that Plato says we all tap into, or simply your individual unconscious—is a necessary pursuit to touch the complete human. It is also a striking source of strength. The idea of a separate reality is not an incidental thought but a fundamental shift in your view of human nature.

The Two Worlds of Leadership

Depth is critical for leadership success. Only to the degree that you reach profoundly into the inner self can you also be effective in leading organizations. The OD professional and organization consultant is accountable to support that inner depth into becoming outer reality. It is precisely here at this point of insisting on thinking and feeling that philosophy has a role in business change and innovation.

Philosophy

Flying from Chicago to Los Angeles, I sat squeezed into the middle in a row of three. On my right, Joe, a slick and know-it-all young aspiring American businessman, and, on my left, Manuel, a shy Mexican farm laborer, speaking no English. Both asked what I was writing. When I told them I worked in philosophy, Joe reacted quickly. "Oh!" he said, "*phailosophy* is too abstract. It's no concern of mine!"

I panic when anyone says "*phailosophy*," as I do when they ask a friend of mine if he is "*Aitalian*"! Or when people talk about the political situation in "*Airan*"!

"*Phailosophy* has nothing to do with me," continued Joe. "I am real. I am a pragmatist. And I play golf!"

So much for revealing his metaphysical position!

Manuel also took the initiative: "Isn't philosophy when you close your eyes," he said as he held his hands over his face, "and you look inside and pay attention to what you see?" He went on, in Spanish, "And then you use what you find and bring it into your business to support your family better."

I was stunned! Either he had secretly read Plato, or both Plato and Jung were right, in that we are born with a collective unconscious, a body of philosophical knowledge, so that learning is but remembering. While Joe was blinded by contemporary materialism, Manuel could see the necessity and sanctity of inner truths.

The Eye

To help empower managers and consultants to install change, they need metaphors to understand the contrast between the inner and outer worlds. The eye is perhaps the best!

The ego is like an eye. You see the objects in the world—houses and trees, automobiles and airports. The ego sees also inner "objects": You *think* ideas and you *feel* emotions, all of which are "inner" things. You *long* for your dreams and you *fear* your worries, *pine* for your vacation and *fret* about your child's schoolwork. But you never see the eye itself. It is hidden, perhaps unknown. However, without the eye the world is extinguished (see Figure 2.4).

The inner eye is your zone of freedom, where you make your choices, the true you that you can't see. It is the authentic you, which you do not sense, the healthy heart that beats silently. It could also be the cancer in your liver, still painless. Your freedom is who you truly are, the source of your power and the origin of your dignity—but also the seed of your vulnerability and the basis of your anxiety. That is the inner eye. *There you find the tools of leadership.*

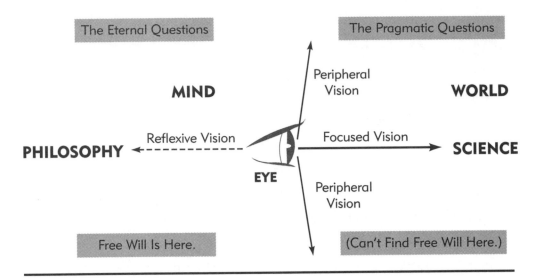

Figure 2.4. The Eye

The insights you need to lead successfully in the outer world have their origin in explorations of the inner world. That is why authentic leaders understand the two worlds in which the true drama of business plays itself out.

Eight Steps to Apply Philosophic Insight to the Real World

There is a growing interest today in spirit and spirituality in business. It's a way to bring religion into the life of commerce. Leadership consultants need to be able to deal with that topic. Some leaders find the entry of religion into the workplace exceptionally important, and even though they often are shy, they welcome introducing it. Others are disinterested or even hostile and adopt an attitude that human beings can go it alone in this world. Coaches cannot make judgments about the religion of their clients. We are dealing here with First Amendment rights. They need a language for depth no matter where the client's metaphysics may be. Philosophy in the Western world really began with Plato. He posited the existence of two worlds, the inner and the outer, the world of consciousness and the world of matter. And this idea never really left Western thought. It is not a religious distinction, nor is it anti-religious. It applies across the spectrum of human beliefs. It is part of cultural literacy to be comfortable in both realms, the inner and the outer.

Following are some characteristics of the two-world theory. It is prerequisite to be able to deepen one's leadership conversations—even for the most mundane business and bottom-line results-oriented dialogues.

1. There is an *inner* universe as much as an *outer* universe. Space and time are not only of the external world, but they are in every way also of the inner world. The door connecting the two is "*my-body*," the body-as-me, the *body-mind,* the complete mind-body oneness. That is the existing and living we touched on in the first chapter, the "I AM experience." Your business and your career are the vehicles through which you as the "I Am" exist. You and your business are an outer world, an inner world, and a body, your body, connecting the two. And it is in your body that you live as executive and as consultant.

2. I am the only interface between the inner and the outside worlds that I know. You are to me part of my outer world. My thoughts and feelings are inner objects of my experience, and not part of you. I am different from others, because I am the only ego I know. Yet equality is my basic value. I think of all other persons as being the same, that is, being like me, even though I experience only my feelings and my perceptions. This is the paradox of leadership! It is the source of my sense of responsibility for other persons, for those I coach and those I lead, and those who are my customers.

3. Going from the outer to the inner world is *perception.* A piece of real estate in external space becomes a replica of itself in inner space. A house you see. But you can also think the house. When you live there you see it. When you are away you think it. The house got into your mind by perception. You saw it first in outer space. But if you want to build a house, it starts as an idea in inner space and then, as you build it, through willing it becomes a house in outer space. And then you can either live in it or sell it. That is how inner and outer spaces are related.

Volition, that is, willing, is the opposite. An idea in inner space becomes an event, a result, in outer space.

There is also the unknown, deep behind the ego, in the inner world, and far out in dark space, on the outer side. This arrangement, illustrated in Figure 2.5, makes for fascinating symmetries!

4. Leadership is to take the "insights" from the inner world and make them work as the "outsights" of the outer world. Deep inside me I discover free will, self-chosen energy, initiative, power, ethics, and self-authentication. I make that work in my business, far in the outer world. I cannot use these truths without access to the inner world. Change in business occurs in the outer world. I can succeed as an executive only if I reach the values of the inner world. (See Figure 2.6.)

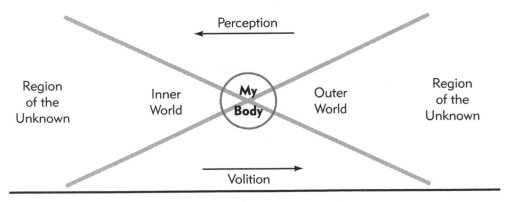

Figure 2.5. The Two-World Universe, Part I

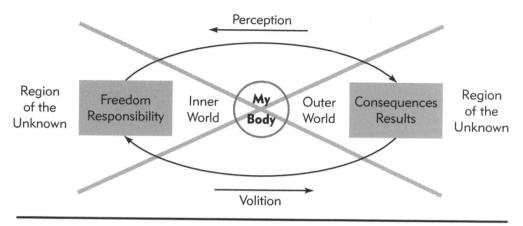

Figure 2.6. The Two-World Universe, Part II

The answers to leadership questions are in the inner world. But they are needed in the outer world. Authentic CEOs must understand both worlds. Trainers need to teach how to bring the inner world into the outer world. We call that "crossing the line," for change agents exist at this point of intersection, giving them their unique edge.

5. There is a connection between the two worlds. Having studied both physics and philosophy, I find it rather stunning that words like *space* and *time,* as well as *energy, force, power, light, illumination, darkness, infinity,* and *laws,* have meaning and application in both realms—the outer world and the inner truth. There must be a connection. That is our-body.

When you try to describe how it feels to be a body, or to "have" a body, you see how different is the perception of one's own body as compared to the bodies of others. This peculiar phenomenon of our-own-body is what exists at this intersection. In order to meet, the two worlds go through my-body. This is the seat where the transformation to leadership and implementation actually occurs. And it is you. This is a "leverage producing insight," which, once understood, empowers us to effective leadership.

6. In the world in which we live—and which we consider real—there are deeply embedded cultural biases. We live today in a world clashing through its metaphysics, its theologies. Are today's larger geopolitical issues the strife of Islam against Christianity? Are both poised against scientific materialism and atheism? More than ever do we need to understand the unity of these worlds. The authentic leader does not live in the inner world alone, nor in the outer world, but comfortably in their intersection! *Do you?*

7. "Measurement" is an art. How do we *measure* the inner world? What gets measured gets done. But it is also true that if we use outer constructs to measure inner realities then what gets measured gets destroyed.

I remember a lecture before a delightful and responsive audience of academic support staff, having been asked to start them with an "inspirational" talk. I spent the evening becoming acquainted with participants, their issues, dreams, needs, their connectedness, and how graciously they smiled when introduced to one another. I hoped they would develop some trusting familiarity with me.

Nevertheless, the next morning, the group, sitting around a host of tables, was large and impersonal. As we were about to start, attendants appeared conspicuously handing out to everyone "FORM NO F-14750 © SCANTRON CORPORATION 2000. INDIVIDUAL SESSION EVALUATION." Obviously the time for measurement had arrived before the greetings had even started.

The instructions read, "Please fill out the bubbles completely, using a blue or black ink pen or a pencil. Please DO NOT use a RED ink pen. Do not make any marks inside the lines." The questionnaire, mass produced, one-size-fits-all, bought off-the-shelf, obviously designed to get to the very heart of this meeting, included such penetrating philosophic gems as (one of only four questions) "Quality of session handouts and materials."

I couldn't help but spontaneously exclaim, undiplomatically, "To start us like this is an instant turnoff! What a way to jump-start our relationship!" This gathering is about contact and alliance and rapport, I thought to myself, about people meeting people, and hearts touching hearts. It's about connecting rather than observing, participating rather than judging, getting closer in an alienated world, and not "co-dependently" colluding in exacerbating an already painful alienation. I thought even of the meaning of a "marriage." You do not enter a marriage throwing an evaluation form at your spouse! Marriage is about co-creation and commitment, about giving and love and generosity, not about grading coarse and visible behaviors based on someone else's standards. A fleeting thought it was, perhaps, but I felt it was worth some notice.

The inner world and the outer world can both be measured. And they should be. But they require their own version of the scientific method. Inner space and inner objects are measured by feelings and intuitions, whereas external space and external objects are measured with rulers and timers. We run into deep trouble when we use rulers and timers to measure the inner states of consciousness, and, correlatively, we run into difficulties when we use feelings and intuitions to measure the dimensions and stresses of a suspension bridge crossing a river (see Figure 2.7).

The "X"s in Figure 2.7 indicate that you cannot measure across realms or worlds: Measures for the outer world do not apply to the inner world, and conversely, how you measure the inner world does not apply to the outer. You do not measure feelings in inches, nor altitudes with descriptions of anxiety.

In confusing categories, we sabotage what we wish to accomplish, no matter how well-intentioned we may be. When it comes to practical matters such as performance evaluation and sales strategies, where we require both subjective and objective measures, then mastering the art of appropriate measurement becomes the litmus test of success.

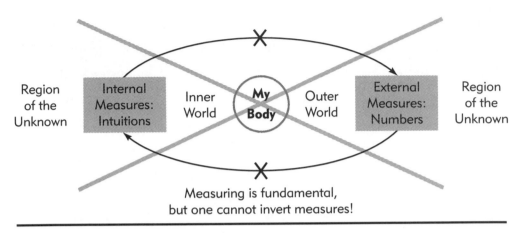

Figure 2.7. The Two-World Universe, Part III

8. Problems arise when we think that one region is superior to the other. It is just as harmful to think that the world is exclusively material. Then we do not understand the inner realm of leadership, and, basically, we are permanently paralyzed. Similarly, if we think the only reality is the inner world, then we will never be able to do serious business, because we cannot live a committed life in the external realm of matter where the real world exists. Then the inner world is but an escape from the often bitter struggles for survival.

Living in Two Worlds

There is a second illustration of the power of the two-world concept that came to me as a genuine spiritual insight on a trip to South Korea—for the inner world is explored intensely in the meditation practices of the philosophies of the Orient.

My Korean friend took me to see the largest Buddhist building in Asia, at the southern rim of JeJu Island, the southernmost tip of South Korea.

The awesome Buddha there has a jewel embedded in his forehead, symbolizing the Third Eye. On seeing this enormous icon, one is quite convinced that this precious stone indeed is the luminosity emanating straight from the inner realm.

And there is a story that goes with it. The original Buddha prayed one million eighty thousand times to obtain enlightenment, which is the comprehensive, clear, and permanent vision of the infinite inner world. Anyone can become a Buddha, so upstairs in this temple there is a virtual sea of Buddhas. There are on display exactly one million eighty thousand small golden Buddha statues, each with a protrusion on its forehead in the form of a jewel. The presumably real worldly Buddhas, when they die, are *cremated.* The fully enlightened ones *leave behind in their ashes, not consumed by the fire, an actual and real jewel!* True or not, it is a spine-chilling image! These rare jewels—visible, indestructible relics of real conscious egos—are collected, accessible only to the monks, and shown to the congregations on special holidays only. This tale struck me as evoking profoundly the primacy of the inner world so characteristic of Oriental philosophies.

And what do the faithful pray for? They ask for pragmatic results in the outer world: "Please get my child into a good university," "Please let me get pregnant," "Please let my family be in good health," "Please let us have more money," and "Please let our business prosper."

It became crystal-clear to me that here was a culture totally aware of the two worlds. It showed itself in their pragmatism, their business orientation, in emphasizing the *practical prayers.* And, as the economic powerhouse South Korea has been, the culture was actually living in these two worlds.

This is leadership: drawing from the wisdom of the inner world and applying it to the necessities of the outer world.

To achieve in the outer world presupposes that we connect first with the inner world. That is why we live at the intersection, in the zone of *engagement,* of "embodiment" and, in Latin, of "incarnation."

> Standing in that Buddhist temple on the southern tip of JeJu
> Island, I saw that all the tools of leadership are found in this real
> inner Diamond that has withstood the fire of cremation: not only
> freedom, responsibility, initiative, determination, managing anx-
> iety, and benefiting from guilt, but also big-picture thinking,
> choosing to care, sustaining genuine hope, being of service, and
> making commitments.

As Manuel said above, take what you find inside and make it work in the outer world. Plato's truth at the dawn of Western civilization was no different from the image of the luminous jewels that are the indestructible inner eyes of the authentic Buddhas. This is spirituality in business today.

Having set the stage, it's time to look at the Diamond. Dante begins his *Divine Comedy* with the sentence that in the middle on the road of life he found himself in a deep forest where he had lost the right way. This is the midlife crisis, which in thoughtful and ambitious people occurs daily. Equipped with the insights that there is an inner and an outer world and that life is a journey, the consultant is ready for in-depth support of leaders. For that purpose the Leadership Diamond® exists, as the language of a humanistic view of life, biased toward business applications.

PART TWO

The Diamond at a Glance

CHAPTER 3

The Change Agent's Diamond

WARREN BENNIS DISTINGUISHES BETWEEN *"once borns"* and *"twice borns."* *"The once born's transition from home and family to independence is relatively easy. Unsatisfied with life as it is, [twice borns] write new lives for themselves" (Bennis, 1993, p. 2). The Diamond is the generalization of this principle.*

As a "twice born," I am in charge of my life. The difference between the inauthentic and the authentic me, the true and the false self, is the extent to which I take full responsibility for what I do, who I am, and who I become. This is the alpha and the omega of leadership. Like first love, it is an old story but it is always new.

For implementation in business, that is, results, both managers and change consultants will find it helpful to start with a solid image of what it means to be an authentic human being. Here are the models we use, one positive—the Leadership Diamond®—and one negative—the Shadow Diamond (see

Figures 3.1 and 3.2). They represent the essentials of the language of leadership, drawn from the history of the humanities, coupled with current research in psychology and OD, and biased toward business applications. They are worth examining, since models should speak for themselves.

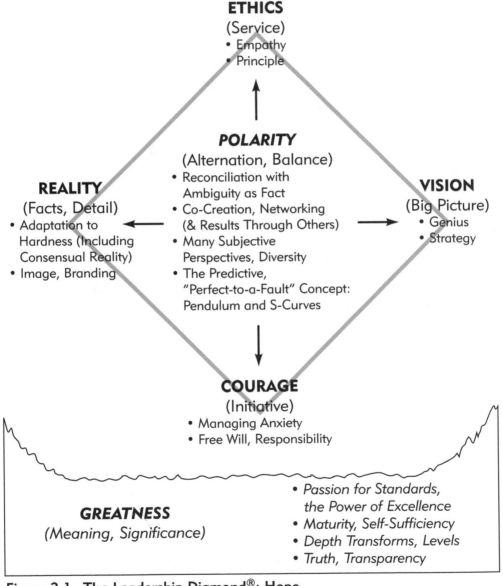

ETHICS
(Service)
• Empathy
• Principle

POLARITY
(Alternation, Balance)
• Reconciliation with
  Ambiguity as Fact
• Co-Creation, Networking
  (& Results Through Others)
• Many Subjective
  Perspectives, Diversity
• The Predictive,
  "Perfect-to-a-Fault" Concept:
  Pendulum and S-Curves

REALITY
(Facts, Detail)
• Adaptation to
  Hardness (Including
  Consensual Reality)
• Image, Branding

VISION
(Big Picture)
• Genius
• Strategy

COURAGE
(Initiative)
• Managing Anxiety
• Free Will, Responsibility

GREATNESS
(Meaning, Significance)

• Passion for Standards,
  the Power of Excellence
• Maturity, Self-Sufficiency
• Depth Transforms, Levels
• Truth, Transparency

Figure 3.1. The Leadership Diamond®: Hope

The Diamond represents both individuals and organizations. It is useful to think of the Diamond as sketching your customers' basic desires and wants, and deficits on the upper reaches of Maslow's hierarchy of needs. It is the role of good business to meet and fulfill these needs through products and services,

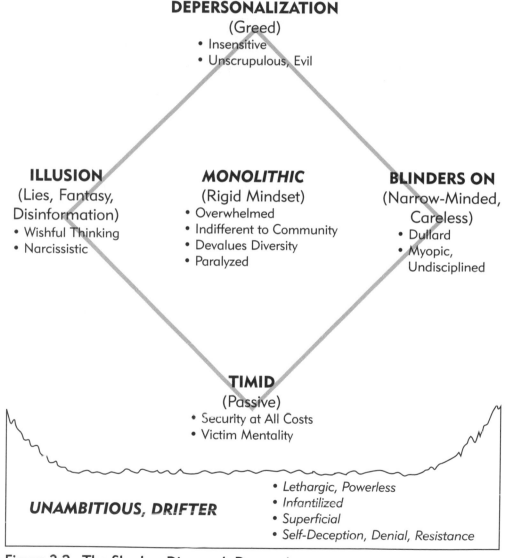

DEPERSONALIZATION
(Greed)
• Insensitive
• Unscrupulous, Evil

ILLUSION
(Lies, Fantasy,
Disinformation)
• Wishful Thinking
• Narcissistic

MONOLITHIC
(Rigid Mindset)
• Overwhelmed
• Indifferent to Community
• Devalues Diversity
• Paralyzed

BLINDERS ON
(Narrow-Minded,
Careless)
• Dullard
• Myopic,
Undisciplined

TIMID
(Passive)
• Security at All Costs
• Victim Mentality

UNAMBITIOUS, DRIFTER

• *Lethargic, Powerless*
• *Infantilized*
• *Superficial*
• *Self-Deception, Denial, Resistance*

Figure 3.2. The Shadow Diamond: Depression

including leadership coaching. Your business objective is to help your clients move from the Shadow to the Leadership Diamond® by their association with you and your organization, your products and your services, and, above all, your people.

Where are you and where is your organization on the Shadow-Leadership-Diamond continuum?

The heroic journey introduces you to this model. The two worlds, inner and outer, are required in order to make full use of the philosophic base. And the Diamond does not intend to compete with alternative views but rather to be seen as support to them, for the role of philosophy has been traditionally to encourage and enrich what science and religion, literature and politics, and business and commerce are trying to achieve.

If you know these concepts well, you will be able to make quick and insightful diagnoses of any employee, executive, customer, or board member, of any company or competitor, and of any action, service, or product. You will also be able to create an action plan based on these principles. Because we are grounded on the conviction that effectiveness requires depth, results can be achieved by reaching into the roots of the human condition.

A mutual fund advertises with children on a fence looking far away toward the horizon. A consulting firm advertises with a young executive looking out of his office window to a taller building in the distance, which becomes the center of a bull's eye. These are images of vision, of filling a universal human need. An accounting firm shows a huge Godzilla cleaning its teeth after a meal, with the caption, "The markets have consumed many a CFO without a sound financial strategy"—bringing in the guilt of not achieving your potential and of ridicule. You get people's attention through their Diamond points.

Before 9/11, executives and consultants could get away with superficial conversations. After the terrorist attack, individuals and organizations have been required to speak more deeply about leadership. The objective is not to promulgate some absolute "truths" about leadership or condense best practices into a magic formula, but to promise improved effectiveness in leadership conversations. That is the way for an organization change consultant to actually intervene in the system. You must be prepared to manage situations like these:

- How would you coach to improve the life of the angry wife of a former Enron employee who is bitter over the fact that she and her husband have lost their retirement?

- How do you help managers of a tobacco company to cope meaningfully with the plethora of ethical issues with which they are confronted?

- What is humane downsizing?

- How would you have coached Bill Clinton if he asked you for personal help in his relations with Congress after the Monica Lewinsky scandal broke?

- What would you say if asked to discuss with Kenneth Lay, the former Enron chairman, how to manage his painful personal position when questioned before Congress and berated for a motionless and respectful hour?

- How do you discuss with your employees the significance for their way of doing business resulting from the 9/11/01 terrorist attack?

The Diamond in Full

Following are preliminary descriptions of the four corners of the Diamond.

Ethics

Ethics here means first and foremost understanding in your gut the importance of people. Life is all about people, period. Then one gets practical. Ethics is *managing people relations successfully.* In your heart you know the meaning of dignity and of respect, and that people do not exist in and of themselves but in relationship. You affect them and they affect you. You are what you are *together,* connected, interactive. You never define a person without referring to the observer: Is this person who addresses you about to take a test? Is this person interviewing you? Selling you something? Are you friends having an honest conversation? Is this a therapy session? How is this moment co-created? In physics it is the Heisenberg Uncertainty Principle. In philosophy it is the Platonic dialogue.

Ethics also means commitment, and no one said it better than Alphie Kohn (1993):

> Do rewards work? . . . Research suggests that, by and large, rewards succeed at securing one thing only: temporary compliance. When it comes to producing lasting change in attitudes and behavior, however, rewards, like punishment, are strikingly ineffective. . . . They do not create an enduring commitment to any value or action. Rather, incentives merely—and temporarily—change what we do. (p. 55)

Compliance means to sell your soul. But commitment is an ethical response!

> For purposes of teaching, ethics consists of a definition and two components. The definition is *service*. The components are *empathy* and *principle*.
> - *Empathy* means being heard, valued, and included.
> - *Principle* means earning *trust*.
> Business is all about keeping *promises* and telling the *truth* and *respecting* persons. To be ethical is to be motivated by that principle.

Finding the feeling of having reached that region of the self and then lead-ing from within that inner truth are the authentic ways to intervene in a sys-tem. It is the role of OD practitioners, trainers, and HR professionals to facilitate this process of self-discovery and to make it operational throughout the organization. That is how change and innovation are achieved.

Courage

Courage likewise consists of a definition and two components. The definition is *initiative*. The components are *managing anx-iety* and *freedom* and *responsibility*.

- *Managing anxiety* is to see negative experiences as con-ducive to strength and health and not illness.
- *Free will, or freedom*, and *responsibility* mean that first and foremost we are decision-making beings, and we make a full commitment, wishing to be held accountable for our choices.

You are mature the day you discover that life cannot be lived without courage. Courage means autonomy, being a self-starter, and it is a non-nego-tiable resolute way in which your mind needs to think to make any serious progress in your business and your consulting. Courage is a heightened state of being aware and alert. *Do you talk to your clients like that?*

Anxiety

Anxiety is not a disease, but the normal feeling of transitions. To underscore this point in your consulting you might say, "Making decisions produces anx-iety. One cannot ignore this anxiety but should rather welcome it as a sign of one's leadership growth. Anxiety, guilt, defeat, conflict, polarity, and even death are normal anxiety-producing aspects of business life. They strengthen us. We are well-equipped to deal with these negatives and there is no reason to either fear them or avoid them. You will deflect them when you can, but they are far from damaging, and actually can be invigorating and give you meaning!"

One of the big problems after the terrorist attack on September 11 was management's uncertainty on how to deal with the anxiety of the workforce, not to speak of their own. A common response was therapy. *The Wall Street Journal,* in an editorial, "Good Grief: Don't Get Taken by the Trauma Industry" (2001), was negative about therapy. Corporate Counseling Associates of New York retorted, "Since Sept. 11, we've been inundated with requests from our clients asking us for emotional support and counseling for those traumatized by the terrorist actions." The question is, will these negatives strengthen you and make you into a leader or will you collapse and need nurturing? Here is where the deeper side of courage comes in. Are you always ready for the worst or do you have to be eased into it or tranquilized after it has happened? That is the big question.

Free Will and Responsibility

This is the key and much misunderstood concept indispensable for grasping and mastering your business life. Related concepts, growing organically from the inner world to be applied in the outer world, are "freedom," "consequences," "responsibility," and "accountability," in the sense of "being held accountable" all the way to the synergistic notion of "*choosing* accountability" for the sake of dignity and self-respect. We call this the Leadership Ladder (see Figure 3.3). It is the comet's trail that the idea of free will leaves in the sky of being. Fundamentally, they are all synonyms.

The ladder represents steps from the deepest insides of the soul, the place where your free will dwells, as it moves out to the world, ending not just in

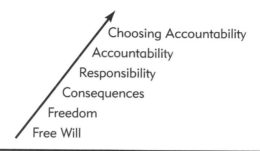

Figure 3.3. The Leadership Ladder

accountability, where you will be held responsible for the consequences of your choices, but actually wishing and willing to be so held accountable, as the ultimate expression of the power of your dignity.

Bringing these insights to the level of leadership language might prompt you to say things such as, "Whenever I am conscious I know that there is some part in me that always chooses. The feeling of making decisions all the time, big ones and little ones, never leaves me."

You constantly ask yourself, "How much energy shall I display at this meeting? How much shall I challenge the workers? How much empathy and compassion should I show? Should I be natural or should I think about my presence?" These are examples of the continuous choices that we make in our organizational lives, where managers and consultants must always be ready to make far-reaching choices. To be human is to make choices non-stop.

Reality

Reality also is described in three ways.

> The definition of reality is reliance on facts. The components are adapting to hardness and image and branding:
> - *Adapting to hardness* is to know that there are forces surrounding us, from illness to bankruptcy, that we do not

control but that control us; no amount of fighting, pleading, or cunning changes that. The good news is that we can adapt and make value out of it. Adapting to hardness is facing it, tolerating it, and coping with defeat. A long-time client of mine never tires of saying, "Life is hard. If I must, I can be hard also—but that is not the essential me."

- *Image and branding* mean awareness of one's public image. The image may not be accurate, but it is essential nevertheless that we know it. You will be treated as you are perceived, the latter being as much a diagnosis of the observer as of you. This can become exceptionally frustrating. The HR department of a large European bank displayed these signs in their offices:

   "When people judge us they reveal more about themselves than about us."

   "People act on their perceptions, no matter how they came by them. Neither I nor my organization can ever ignore these harsh facts."

When dealing with reality, we focus on facts, data, numbers, on what is called sometimes simply "the Other"—that which *you need, is not you, is not under your control, but nevertheless impacts you massively.* The key message is to avoid the temptations to sentimentality and wishful thinking. That is the definition. For the realist, facts are king.

Vision

The definition of vision is *the "Big Picture,"* that is, big picture thinking. The components are *genius* and *strategy.*

- *Genius* means creativity and intellectual brilliance. It means to have deep respect for the improvement of the mind's creative thinking capability. In this organization intellectual prowess is celebrated.

- *Strategy*—as the word is used here—means that your culture supports a strategic thinking organization. It means to build an organization, a place where participating in the imaginative invention of strategy is a key part of the culture. This is the learning organization, where the future promise of the company is judged by the employees' interest in strategic issues. The visionary mind, statistically speaking, also gets the greatest financial rewards.

Polarity

Polarity is at the center of the Diamond Model. The latter is a polarized symbol, in which each corner as well as the relationships among them is best understood as polarized. Between your vision for your client and the reality, there is a gap. That is the tension of polarity. Between the kindness and consideration you want to show toward your client, which is ethics, and the mercilessness with which you approach the need for profits, which is reality, there is a gap. This gap is the tension of polarity.

The general meaning of polarity as used in Diamond Theory goes something like this:

Do ask for answers, always, but also be fully prepared for frustratingly ambiguous responses. And these responses do not necessarily come from inauthentic people. They simply reflect that nature of life. And there is nothing wrong with us being confronted with life in the raw.

Polarity itself is not a Diamond corner in its own right but instead is a mode of mastering all the intelligences, the four Diamond points: ethics, courage, reality, and vision. Polarity is the vibrancy of life, the need for alternation and ultimately for balance.

> The definition of polarity is *alternation* and the need for *balance*. It has four components: *reconciliation with ambiguity, co-creation and networking, the primacy of the subjective perspective*, and *prediction*, such as S-curves.
>
> • *Reconciliation with ambiguity* means holding and accepting opposites concurrently as an axiom of existence.
>
> • *Co-creation and networking* mean to have a social conscience, working through others, building teams.
>
> • *The primacy of the subjective perspective* means to always ask, "From whose point of view is this analysis?"
>
> • *Prediction* is attention to being perfect-to-a-fault, as well as to the pendulum effect and S-curves, which are ways to forecast performance.
>
> An S-curve stands for the shelf life of a product; it starts slowly, grows in momentum, matures, and then goes downhill. Companies need to learn to innovate before the curve hits its peak, so that the company can survive the attrition of one product by substituting it with the next.

Ask for clarity but accept ambiguity, demand certainty, but adapt to surprises. You tell your stakeholders that you have given up the need to resolve every contradiction that stands in your way. As would a parent of many children, you too function well with seemingly incompatible demands. You can live with chaos and uncertainty, just as you can live with the facts of an economic recession and your ineluctable mortality. At first, accepting ambiguity and contradiction as real is counterintuitive. Systems thinking, quantum physics, and relativity theory were all counterintuitive when first introduced. So was modern art. Now they are commonplace. We are used to them. And we are better for it. So it is with reconciliation with polarities.

Executives are measured by the teams they build. Organization change consultants support them. We think not only in isolation; we think also as partners.

Currently, your markets are volatile. Should you take a few risky but bold steps and capitalize on the downturn, picking up cheap blue chips? Or should you retrench and consolidate, retraining employees while waiting for an economic upturn? Before you answer, think of subjectivity. *Who* wants this answer? And *when* and *where*? The stockholder? The employee? The boss? The public? Headquarters in New York or the branch in Hong Kong? The analyses are not the same. As consultant and executive, you choose an attitude being comfortable in the environment of chaos and paradoxes. And then you address your client from his or her perspective.

"High tech, high touch" is as true today as it ever was. Business is alternation, a wave phenomenon, not linear. Look at the stock market's performance. We exist with sequential S-curves and pendulum events. The future is like the past, only in its variations. In 1999, business went only up; companies were extravagantly overvalued on vacuous promises. At the end of 2001 the economy was in a funk and the dot-com bubble had burst. Yesterday your client was eager and interested in your proposal; today telephone calls are not returned. This is normal, sound, and healthful. Knowing this can alert one to unwarranted expectations and serious planning mistakes.

Greatness

Greatness is the overarching theme, the conclusion.

You strive to be part of something greater: something that existed before and will continue after you. Greatness is steadfastness of purpose and the euphoria of hope. It is the demand that work have meaning and significance. Your business becomes your opportunity for greatness. When you see greatness in your work, nothing is boring nor causes you stress.

A family business, for example, is an heirloom, a legacy. The family is a dynasty and the business their vehicle. Ford, Carnegie, and Mellon left behind major foundations bearing their names. That was their greatness. The auto worker takes pride in craftsmanship and the prestige of the company. The family is a third-generation union member. That is their security—and their greatness.

What is your greatness in your business? What would you like it to be? Go and create it!

The opposite is being numb, unaware of possibilities, bereft of ambition, closed to excitement and adventure. You have not yet been exposed to all the continents of the leadership mind, and you have been discouraged by the frustrations of business life.

> *Greatness* is *meaning* and *significance*; its components are *passion for standards, maturity and self-sufficiency, depth transforms,* and *truth and transparency.*
>
> - *Passion for standards*: "Our passion for standards is Olympian," you exclaim. It means you can mobilize your own ambition and enthusiasm, an attitude that becomes contagious.
>
> - *Maturity and self-sufficiency:* We value *character and adult behavior.* Excellent leadership is based on sterling character. We search for the wisdom that will in the end honor our parents, people, country, and God for having given us life.
>
> - *Depth transforms:* There are levels at which people think. Some are on the surface and others can go to profound wisdom. Organizations today demand deep change.

- *Truth and transparency*: There is no self-deception, there is full awareness of the resistance to knowing who in truth I am.

In every enterprise there are *business issues* and *character issues.* We need to devote time to both. They are interrelated and interactive. Business without character is not credible and character without business means it is never applied.

Greatness is not one of the corners. It is a way in which all of the Diamond corners must be approached: greatness in ethics, in courage, in realism, and in vision. Greatness in ethics is greatness in virtue. Greatness in courage is exhibiting great valor. Greatness in reality is to truly have your eyes open. And greatness in vision is to recognize the full scope of what is possible. This is indicated on the model by placing greatness outside the Diamond. Greatness is not merely one chess piece, but it is the chessboard itself.

True self-discovery work is to be aware of the resistances and the strategies we put in place to hide from ourselves the truth that deep down we fully understand. This is the beginning of wisdom.

The Philosophers
People ask how the Diamond is connected to philosophy and who these philosophers are.

For example, in Diamond Theory the principle of polarity is a major factor for exploration. It refers to many things, including the ambiguity of most business situations right in the midst of strident demands for clarity and simplicity. Much of what we call modern philosophy begins with the thoughts of René Descartes (1596–1650). He developed the method of systematic and universal doubt, which was his way of reaching the ultimate truth. That certainty is difficult to come by and that doubt and confusion are the order of things were his fundamental insights. He is the philosopher of polarity.

Descartes taught us that extreme doubt is the only way to full certainty, just as the tragic sense of life is the only way to earn one's worth, which, in turn, is the only form of true happiness. Friedrich Nietzsche was the philosopher of greatness, elevating the person to supreme status in the universe. Thomas Hobbes was the philosopher of realism, raising the brutal state of nature as the state of affairs to which we all must adapt. The French Nobel laureate novelist and philosopher Jean-Paul Sartre was the theorist of freedom and free will and of total responsibility. The Dane Søren Kierkegaard was the philosopher of the dominance of anxiety. The Jewish theologian Martin Buber was the philosopher of love, intimacy, empathy, dialogue, and relationship—not to speak of the profound foundation teachings of the New Testament. Epictetus, Marcus Aurelius, Baruch Spinoza, and Immanuel Kant were the great ethicists, the philosophers of duty and rectitude, reason and principle. Plato was the philosopher of the great vision, creating one of the most inspired comprehensive views of human beings, world, and cosmos—a view of the greatness of the human mind that transcends virtually all else ever done in the history of humanity. It is not without reason that Alfred North Whitehead said all of Western thought was a footnote to Plato. Socrates was the great teacher, informing millennia after him that true education is the self-discovery of one's own inwardness, from which we draw the strengths that see us through even the most difficult times. This is the paradigmatic philosophy of life. We are a powerhouse of leadership resources. Through the Socratic method we find them and through the Socratic challenges we use them. The Diamond is rooted in history but addressed to modern business.

Putting It All Together

You have four primary concepts or tools in terms of which to organize your leadership thinking: ethics, courage, reality, and vision. And you have two ways to master them: polarity and greatness. These six items together comprise what we will refer to as the deep structures. A map of that benchmark is laid out in Table 3.1. CEOs, managers, change consultants, and OD practitioners can now look at the model as a checklist outlining success and warning of trouble spots.

Attending to these six deep structures of human existence, seeing to it that the culture represents them, and ensuring that the organization's language and behavior conform to them is perhaps as close as we can come to prescribing a formula for success. Conversely, if the organization is stuck, then one or more of these template points have been ignored.

Today, the world is governed by Wall Street. It was not always that way in the past. Too many key daily decisions are determined by where the Dow is that day! One large retail firm posted in the employee dining room a sign, "Today our stock is. . . . Tomorrow? It's up to you!"

In their choices of CEOs, boards are influenced by this current cultural hypnotic fixation on the stock market, often picking CEOs with unbalanced Diamonds. The CEOs may temporarily raise the stock, but do not do long-term honor to the institution of business. Only the boards can change this, and in so doing, they will have a *major* impact on the future of nations. For boards to lead companies in this new spirit, they must select leaders who are not just competent but also authentic. This, in turn, will make business *genuinely* profitable and make the economy *genuinely* attuned to the needs of humanity. For Aristotle, economy meant a fulfilled society. Money is the foundation, perhaps, but to turn the heart into a number is not everyone's idea of success. The bottom line is not *either* profits *or* people, but it is *both* profits *and* people.

Now that you have been introduced to the Diamond as a key leadership tool, it is useful to put it into practice. Do some journaling to connect your life, your business, and your professional practice with these leadership parameters. The activity beginning on page 59 can serve as a guide.

Table 3.1. The Leadership Diamond® Tools

	Ethics	**Courage**	**Reality**	**Vision**
Polarity	Recognizes that different people can have very different moral points of view and values that may appear alien. The great conciliator. Makes a good mediator. *Jimmy Carter, Archbishop Tutu, Kofi Annan*	Is able to make sometimes excruciatingly difficult decisions under conflicting circumstances. *Abraham Lincoln, Harry Truman*	Balance of power is a key policy. Finds it unwise to be consistently decisive because there are many aspects to the truth. Pragmatic and adaptable. Manages well with insufficient data and information. A survivor. *Henry Kissinger, Bill Clinton*	Sees the other side of any great vision. Balanced. Can be very fair, but may have difficulties making decisions. *Colin Powell*
Greatness	To be decent to and supportive of people is a career, a calling. Idealistic. Perhaps utopian. Sometimes a martyr, even a saint. *Gandhi, Mother Teresa, Eleanor Roosevelt, Martin Luther King, Jr.*	Fearless. Takes big risks. The type who could be a winner of the Congressional Medal of Honor. *General George S. Patton, Norman Schwarzkopf*	A cunning politician. Cold and calculating. Can be ruthless if needed. Sticks to the bare and brutal facts. *Bismark; Machiavelli;* U.S. presidents who managed *two* major tasks: *Washington* (War of Independence and building a nation); *FDR* (The Great Depression and WW II); *Dick Cheney*	A passionate visionary. A reformer. An ambitious person. *Napoleon, Julius Caesar, Florence Nightingale, Jack Welch*

◆ Activity

Journaling

This activity is designed so you can help your client understand the Diamond and construct a self-diagnosis.

Using Exhibit 3.1 as a framework, ask your client to inventory his or her personal Leadership Diamond®. Using additional paper as necessary, your client should use the following questions to assess each of the deep structures:

1. In your own words, what does each deep structure mean to you? How would you communicate it to a client and a co-worker? Give an example.

2. Is there someone in your organization whom you feel exemplifies rather well this character trait and overall attitude?

3. Is this trait and attitude a priority in order for you to perform successfully in your job? Explain that. As change agent, you have inside clients, and as executive you have employees and outside clients. As you go over each deep structure, ask yourself how important that particular trait is to perform effectively in your professional duties. What are some examples?

4. How would you rate yourself in each trait and attitude? What is the level of your own performance? Which one or two deep structures are salient in your behavior? Which do you think is proportionately weaker than the others?

5. Think of career implications. One role of the Diamond is to support you in becoming more marketable as a leader, a manager, and a professional. How important is this trait to achieve that objective?

Deep Structure	1. In Your Words	2. Your Example/ Model	3. Relevance to Results	4. Your Performance	5. Gain/Loss and Career Implications	6. Added Value
Ethics/ Service *Healer* • Empathy • Principle						
Courage/ Initiative *Warrior* • Anxiety • Free Will						
Reality/Facts *Merchant* • Adaptation to Hardness • Image, Branding						
Vision/ Big Picture *Seer* • Genius • Strategy						
Polarity/ Ambiguity *Wizard* • Reconcil- iation • Subjective Perspective • Prediction						
Greatness/ Standards *Hero* • Passion • Maturity • Depth • Truth						
Action Plan: Stop Start Continue						

Exhibit 3.1. Personal Leadership Diamond® Inventory

6. What added value do you bring to your organization toward fulfilling its essential objectives?

7. Given what you've discovered about yourself and each structure, design an action plan of behaviors that you should start, stop, or continue in order to elevate your prowess for each structure.

CHAPTER 4

The Diamond at Work

IN THIS CHAPTER, *we go into greater detail on how to make the Diamond work in organizational line and staff functions—managers and executives, OD practitioners and organization change consultants—as they try to intervene in the system to bring about change and innovation.*

Managing Today's Alienation in the Workplace

Executives and consultants are charged today with an unprecedented demand: Achieve economic greatness in the era of terrorism. Too many in the population respond with mass hysteria and depression, adrift in business empty of meaning. Leaders, on the other hand, see this as an opportunity to do something significant with their businesses. Those overwhelmed are aliens. Leaders belong.

When we think globally in economic terms, we recognize alienation is not a question of right or wrong, of what is desirable or undesirable, but rather the result of being a responsible human and a responsible organization in today's world of commerce. Financial markets demand this, as do world politics. Today's leader squarely faces this ambiguity: people opposed by a string of new economies, confronted with stability versus permanence and change versus innovation.

It is not that companies produce alienation; it is the market speaking through companies that forces it. And human beings resist alienation: They are social, familial, gregarious. Leadership and leadership coaching are what is needed to manage well this acerbic interface. Figure 4.1 should illustrate this point.

> Leadership means to stand tall, ethically and financially, in the face of this change-innovation challenge. This shift is profitable to business because it replaces dependency with self-reliance, imitation with creativity, and narrow thinking with breakthrough breadth. In so doing, change and innovation exchange grumbling compliance for mature commitment.

Philosophy manages alienation through *character* and *maturity.*

We do business in a world where the everyday truth is a series of alienations, separations, enmities, and confrontations: employee against employer, worker against company, as well as employer against employer and worker against worker. And it is the company against the public and the public against the company, business against environmentalism, tax reduction against social responsibility, welfare caring against entrepreneurial greed. They are perforce *alienated* from each other—all noble protestations to the contrary notwithstanding. Consumers believe that airlines cancel flights to make certain that

Current Reality

- What do I need from the company that I am not now getting?
- What are my deepest needs that I expect my work to fulfill?

- What does the company need from its employees that it is not now getting?
- What does the market require of this company that employees are not now delivering?

Here is where
leadership is required.

Figure 4.1. Current Reality

each trip is full, that car rental companies make everyone check in at their stands, thus creating long lines, in order that clerks have a chance for a sales talk with the customer, the average additional sales thus generated being estimated at 20 percent. And airline fares are calculated on the profiles they have about the various segments of customers and their willingness to pay. In the not-too-distant future they will have a profile just for you, indicating the maximum that you are willing to pay, and invoice you precisely that. There is cynicism all around us.

We don't want it that way. We want love. But that is not what we find. The culprit is not a person nor is it a class of people, nor is it a government, but it is the *down-to-earth tough world,* today mostly in the form of the stock market. And the irony is that we all are the stock market. The stock market is the sum of us who complain about the power of the stock market.

But the stock market is also the expression of a fundamental value: freedom. In this case it is freedom in the marketplace. The stock price measures an enterprise's ability to withstand competition and to be perceived as financially promising: growth in earnings. And it is all based on respecting people's freedom in the wilderness of competition.

We all live in this jungle. We all contribute to it. And that is where we seek for opportunities to make a living and carve out significance. This jungle is not of our own making. It was born of the natural and well-intentioned passion for freedom, especially on the global marketplace. It is the result of liberating our institutions.

We, as human beings, all have the obligation to generate and uphold a *moral world order,* a civilized environment. The role of the organization change consultant is to help people respond to the cruel indifference of the stock market with both *the realism of guts and the nobility of heart.* Face the situation as it is: a cruel market, yet a market of opportunities, confronted with an unquestionable imperative for a higher moral order. That synthesis, seen not from the perspective of the dreamer but the realist, is today the nature of greatness!

Philosophy can help create a mature response, by all alienated people, to deal with their alienation, by creating a community of both ethics and realism, to have the vision that will make this possible and to have the courage to make it a reality.

Lack of a philosophic mindset and of high-enough expectations incapacitates us in a crisis. Results derive from early education in what is possible and from the ineradicable conviction that the power of your free will can liberate you from illness, ignorance, poverty, failure, and lack of personal significance. People who have done it are our heroes.

How much attention have you paid in your work life to this ancient truth in changing yourself and in changing organizations?

Using the Diamond in the Real World

The Diamond can be used in a practical and applied sense in several ways:

1. Strategy

The Diamond can be used for strategic marketing: developing new products, designing new sales tactics, energizing advertising, fashioning new consulting methodologies—capturing customers' attention and reaching their decision-making zones. Business strategy has to be built on understanding people. And philosophy has a long history of profound inner knowledge.

In the old days, consonant with Freudian psychoanalysis, an automobile was advertised with a bathing beauty on the hood. Today, more in keeping with the philosophical approach, automobiles are marketed with vision and courage as the Diamond associations that are encouraged. For in the knowledge society the decision to buy a car has more to do with the so-called philosophic "deep structures of human existence" than with sex.

There is great fear today of terrorism. While of course warranted and legitimate, fear of terrorism nevertheless is 10 percent reality and 90 percent unmanaged anxiety that's always been there. This is a one-to-nine anxiety management ratio—a bad prognosis. If we had managed that universal, normal, human, and essentially healthful underlying anxiety before, we would have responded to a world crisis with courage and determination and not with depression and sleep disorders.

Marketing and selling strategies in most industries orbit about the topic of managing the buying anxiety of the prospects. Mastering the art of intelligent leadership conversations on anxiety then becomes clearly a competitive advantage.

Consider real estate: buying and selling a home and purchasing loans. For the average buyer, these actions are fraught with anxiety. As a businessperson, realtor or banker, ask yourself, how well are your financial products tailored to help the customer from a 10/90 anxiety ratio to no more than a 50/50 ratio? Forty points will be released to cope with real issues and not squandered to hold in check unfinished childhood business. The customer's energy and good judgment for addressing the tough realistic part of the sale will have been raised from 10 to 50, which is a full 400 percent increase.

Required here is brand-new thinking about how to approach big-ticket sales resistance. It is achieved by distinguishing between authentic anxiety—which manages realities—and inauthentic anxiety, which mobilizes the residual repository of unexamined and unmanaged fear of venturing and dread of taking charge of one's business life. These latter stresses are to be managed before entering business negotiations so that they don't interfere with your economic progress.

The consultant's role in helping clients with strategy is to coach them in managing other people's purchasing anxiety—everyone's: salesperson, customer, advertiser, sales manager, marketing vice president. Marketing is to manage the subjective anxiety in a prospect who is choosing among risky alternatives.

2. Leadership

Leadership is the art of knowing where you are going and then getting there. Leadership is the secret of implementation. It is to build the team and to construct the culture. Some leaders may be born such, but not everyone is that lucky. Many have to learn laboriously. Principle, branding, genius, maturity, freedom—these are all great ideas. They are the raw materials to activate the heart and souls of people.

Leadership is needed to help make an organization a good place to work, to deal with internal conflicts, with difficult markets, and with high-maintenance clients. The Diamond is used to serve culture-building objectives. In the end, leadership is to inspire, and that requires acquaintance with vision and greatness, with courage and ethics.

The Diamond provides the key tools, in that it makes available the deepening language for such themes as commitment, responsibility, clearheadedness, perseverance, the long view, seeing the world through the eyes of the customer, and the like.

3. Coaching

Philosophy is the underpinning of coaching, even therapy. The Diamond is simply philosophy made accessible. As in archaeology, there are also in philosophy levels of depth in understanding people (see Figure 4.2).

We make the distinction between (1) *advice,* the most superficial, and then (2) consensual validation, social awareness, understanding what is appropriate (like not slipping ahead in a queue), which is *social appropriateness* and *social expectation* and stems from the pressure of society and culture. Advice is "You need more insurance." Social appropriateness is "You are violating my

Figure 4.2. The Archeology of the Self

psychological contract. You led me to believe I would get a meaningful job. I moved my family, and I find nothing but boring, repetitious, mindless, and unchallenging routines. I expect people to keep even their implied promises."

Then there are (3) *psychological* analyses of our actions. They touch the unconscious and point back to entrenched childhood habits. "You do not understand; your boss is not your parent but your customer. It is not your boss's role to make you happy, but your role to make your boss happy. That's why you receive compensation. You contracted to satisfy your customer. You never grew up as an independent person; you are still a dependent child!"

And then, beneath it all, is the (4) *philosophical* level, where you discover that your nature is to be free and alone, a self, a consciousness, confronted with a confusing world, out of which you are now expected to make sense and become an ethical and co-creating human being—wishing to build community. All that because the truth will make you strong.

Here is the philosophical leadership level, where it all begins. Here you find your power, your greatness, your love, your devotion, and your support. This is the *perennial philosophy*—it has always been true, always been known, always treasured. In practice, it has been mostly avoided. In theology, it is called the Fall of Man, the alienation from our own inner nature, shooting ourselves in the foot as it were. Philosophy wants to recover that inner deeper realm of authenticity. Philosophy is like a secular priesthood, as unorthodox and non-doctrinaire to use what we know about ourselves for the betterment of mankind.

Business is the vehicle, because the economy is the foundation of world health. The best way to fight terrorism is to make a nation economically strong. This requires authentic business leadership. For with that in place, all values can be realized. Absent economic health, no values can endure. It's a simple formula. It is not new. But to implement it, universally, is still far away from where we find ourselves today. This is where the free and autonomous free choice for ethics will make all the difference.

In coaching, you sit down with your client and connect that person's business with the deeper structures of the human psyche—from advice, to social expectations, to psychological insight, all the way to philosophy. It's the role of the HR change consultant and the role of the manager and executive, who are expected to achieve results through people.

Leaders suffer from situations that lead to intense frustration. "I will be fired! The end has come!" Look at it as a test on the journey of life. What are you meant to learn by this? What have you not yet understood about life itself that gets you into these crises? Can you translate the energy of the pain into the energy of going forward? Can you turn the anxiety of despair into the anxiety of hope? Both are stressful; one moves backward and the other forward. Your test gives you an opportunity to demonstrate to your children how one reacts heroically to defeat. These are privileges, blessings, invigorating turnarounds. Here is the cardinal role of the coach. The jewel is to help someone recover realistic hope.

4. Profession

Philosophy in business is a profession. Philosophy has traditionally supported the important disciplines. It started with theology, where philosophy gave religion its vocabulary and justification. It went on to political theory. The United States and large numbers of other democratic nations are living examples of philosophy's constitutional impact. The preeminence of science has been supported for at least two centuries by philosophical analyses. Then psychiatrists recognized that philosophic researches illuminated further the inner recesses of human nature. "You are responsible" is a philosophic assertion that resides in the kernel of psychotherapy. And today we talk about the philosophical buttresses for the practical as well as the greatness themes crying stridently for attention in contemporary business.

Some executives and OD professionals are interested in becoming philosophic business practitioners, developing subject-matter experts in their organizations. They choose to become leadership teachers and wish to ensure that key members of their team also grow into leadership teachers.

As for myself, after thirty-four years, I left teaching philosophy in order to submerge myself in the thoroughly practical applications of otherwise sterile abstract ideas. I have not been disappointed. It has been the most difficult, the most rewarding, and the most profoundly transforming activity I have ever attempted.

For me, the Leadership Diamond® is the heart of Philosophy-in-Business. That may be an exaggeration, but for me the full model has been the attempt to compress and consolidate into one reasonable useful mnemonic device what I have perceived over the years as the wisdom of philosophy—the philosophic insights about the structure of the human condition—which then make accessible to practitioners the tools available for truly effective coaching and consulting. These tools derive from the mind itself. Philosophers through the ages have found them and, as with repeatable scientific experiments, taught us how to recover them ourselves.

Business Applications Example I

The human resource department of a major tobacco company uses this model to transform a company dishonored and maligned by the population and the courts to turn itself around and become a valued member of the society of the future.

Here are their Diamond strides:

1. Clearly face the depression and the negative feelings about themselves and their company.

2. See them as messages that fundamental change and dramatic innovation are required—and possible.

3. View the emotional funk as a source of power and resolution, for it is a call to action, a call to arms, not an occasion for medication and absenteeism.

4. Recognize the ambiguity and conflict of it all: "I have over my work life constructed my business commitments loyally around a major industry with a noble tradition, and now I am told I am poisoning the population, having made the biggest mistake of my career!"

5. Activate all corners of the Diamond:

   - *Ethics.* Have compassion for the people damaged by smoking, have empathy for the workers at the company, make sure that you handle the problem of the company's business idea with principle and integrity, equally considering all the stakeholders involved.

   - *Courage.* Tough decisions are required. Perhaps the company should be closed, perhaps redefined. Whatever the decision, it will require uncommon courage, far more than mere business decisions—instead, a bold existential move.

   - *Reality.* Face the economic facts, the collapse of such a huge company has repercussions in the entire economy. Imports will simply replace the vacuum, with no gain in national health. Face the health facts: Illness cannot be promoted commercially. Face the psychological facts: The workforce is not equipped to handle being overwhelmed with so much moral chaos and financial uncertainty.

   - *Vision.* Have a plan. And make it a great one. This requires both genius creativity and a strategic thinking organization.

Once people see a way out, their energy is restored and hope reclaimed. Following are samples of proposed changes and innovations:

- Change course from promoting the use of toxic cigarettes to promoting their termination;

- Develop a non-toxic cigarette substitute;

- Make certain no other player replaces the business vacuum thus created;

- Become a forerunner in changing the nature of the business by significant diversification, such as foods, for example;

- Restore the dignity of the employees and managers of this institution; and

- Reestablish the reputation of the company in the public eye.

This is extreme change. It requires the capacity for innovation and an OD and HR department ready to lead the charge. And it needs executives and managers willing to "think outside the box" and take bold steps.

This task—which is both ethical and commercial—can be accomplished only if a critical mass of the managerial and employee population change their language from ineffective defensive conversations to effective, deepened, honest, and innovative leadership talk. For theirs is not only an economic issue; it is also a political, a social, and even an historical undertaking. When the stakes are high and society's basic values are at risk, philosophical deepening may be the only way to achieve the breakthrough that we all need.

> In being crisp about the strategy, the political risk may be great, because bureaucratic double-talk is always the enemy, and the spearhead of results will always be stunted by the granite of opposition. But the change is in willingness to risk. That needs to be celebrated.

Images of the Leadership Mind

To make the Diamond useful one needs to see its depth, which is its foundational character. We are not talking here of one more model, but of the philosophical foundations of all models. We are not competing but supporting. That is the intent. Our concern is attitudes that lead to behaviors, ideas that lead to action, understandings that lead to results. It's not that the Diamond is superior; it is that philosophy is undergirding. It is the philosopher in you that makes it possible for you to intervene effectively in organizations. The message is to go to root causes if you want lasting impact. It is important for consultants to be able to give their clients quickly an in-depth understanding of the Diamond themes. The same applies to leaders. They need to give to subordinates quick messages with impact and depth. The following metaphors can help.

The Diamond as. . .

> A computer chip in the mind
>
> An atlas of the inner landscape
>
> Light
>
> A springboard
>
> The subjective perspective for mind expansion
>
> Situational
>
> A vehicle or catalyst to get you from one place to another

All are metaphors symbolizing deep change and radical innovation.

The Diamond as a "Leader-Chip"

The Diamond is like a computer chip or a new operating system inserted into the mind—a leader-chip! Strictly speaking, it is the CPU, the central processing unit. The amateur is satisfied with operating systems and applications, learns them, and works with the PC. But the pro knows about the CPU. It is in that chip where the power lies and where new generations of leadership minds are created.

Greatness is the decision to insert that foundational "leadership chip" into your mind and brain. You will be a new person, seeing a new world, behaving differently, because you now think differently. *Where lies your interest? In applications only? Or do you also want a high-powered CPU?*

The Diamond as Atlas

The Diamond is also a complete map of the mind. It shows where you have been and where you have not, and can help you to realize that you may be on the wrong continent to achieve what you are after. It tells you where you are not living. And in describing the geography, we can tell you what you can expect where you are living and what you can expect elsewhere. There are unexplored "new worlds" where you can reside, and there business and organizations are very different.

The Diamond as Light

You are groping in the dark looking for essentials. You despair for you have no success. *You turn on the light!* You add nothing to the room, but the difference is that now you can see it. The Diamond insights do not give you anything new, nothing you did not already know. It shows what you have but had failed to notice. This is an exact parallel of what Plato taught at the dawn of Western civilization under the name of the Theory of Ideas or of Forms. You are born with leadership knowledge, and learning is but remembering. When it comes to leadership, you know more than you think.

In general, when people ask how to apply the Diamond, the answer is as simple as physical health. If you are ailing, you follow the rules for health and for feeling well. You gain health. To now ask how to *apply* health is meaningless. So it is with leadership health, philosophic health, achieving a fully developed mind. The question is not what do you do with health once you have it, but how to get to health when you don't have it. You know what to do: Do it!

My friend Peter Block puts it this way: "The answer to 'How?' is 'Yes!'"

The Diamond as Springboard

We start using the Diamond by isolating your stuck point. Where in business are you stuck? What is it that is no longer working, no matter how hard you try? The answer often lies in emigration and immigration. Leave your tired land and move to a fresh country. The idea of the New World took Europe by storm. The discovery of America led precisely to this river of humanity emigrating to the Promised Land, the New World, where the noble savage lived, the idolized and idealized Indian. The images of the pioneer, of the West, the Wild West, the hypnotic "Go west young man," the Oregon Trail, the Northwest Territory, all these idyllic images are places on the Atlas of the mind where hopeful answers are to be found to the stuck points of your business life.

The Diamond as Subjective Perspective for Mind Expansion

Another key factor here is to ask for whom you are doing this leadership analysis. A coach serves the client, not some other stakeholder. It is therefore important to determine from whose subjective perspective you are carrying out this analysis. This is a key point in the law and in psychotherapy. The attorney serves the interests and the rights of the client and is not concerned with the interests of the antagonist. That is the role of another lawyer. The United States was treated on television to a good example of this after the uncertain returns in the 2000 presidential election, where Bush and Gore received almost identical numbers of votes. For weeks the lawyers were on television arguing the respective merits of their clients. Often they were quite convincing. But it was clear that when Bush's lawyers defended the Republican interests in the outcome of the Florida election they presented the controversy from the latter's subjective perspective, and when the Democratic lawyers spoke they saw the same reality quite differently from the point of view of Gore's inner eye.

Next time someone asks you what is the truth, respond: "From whose point of view?" No matter how carefully we argue, in many instances the answer is based on who you are and what this universe is in which we live rather than an objective assessment of a state of affairs. This is both fortunate and unfortunate. It makes us responsible but it also causes problems with our need for absolute values.

Ignoring this principle is the source of misunderstanding and dead ends. On the Diamond, this insight is part of the Reality (branding), Polarity (subjectivity), and Ethics (empathy). And Courage (initiative) is required to cut through the Gordian Knot as there is no compromise solution. Many disputes lead to war because people see the same reality differently—be they you and your competition, people fired and hired, not to speak of Palestinians and Israelis, North or South Koreans, terrorists and their victims.

Ideally, one should let all speak their pieces. In this sense, some are open and some are closed. Some see the world only through their eyes, others automatically through the eyes of another. The first are arrogant and the second are timid. Authenticity is to do both.

> "Our stock dropped from 60 to 5 in six months. What is the right strategy in response?" Think of at least four stakeholders who would each give a very different answer to the same question once you ask, "From whose point of view are you talking?"

The Diamond as Situational

Leadership is mostly situational. This is a key insight. You construct your leadership mindset to suit the need. It is not true that one configuration fits all circumstances. The Diamond is also a *toolbox* and you do not use all your tools all the time. You have scalpels for delicate surgery and earth moving equipment for construction. When you do your accounting, you need to focus your mind on details. That means you turn on your *reality* headlights. When you take a walk to decide whether to embark on a new career, you need to shift your mind to *vision*.

The Diamond as Vehicle

Given the two-worlds principle, you are a consciousness, a free self that chooses an identity for yourself and your company with which to face the market. Think of a vehicle with a driver. The driver is you, always the same, but the vehicle can be many things: car, train, bicycle, roller skates, and more. You are a center of awareness, of free will and alertness.

In your search for greatness, you need to fulfill your destiny. You never do that in general, but you choose one specific *vehicle* through which you hope to attain your fulfillment and your greatness: You have a job, but not any job or every job. You believe in careers, but you commit to only *one specific career*. You could have taken another position, and done just as well or as poorly, or better. You have a degree in accounting or in marketing. You need a degree, but not any or all but rather this specific one. You need a taxi to go to your business appointment. Not any taxi nor all taxis, but this particular taxi in which you are now riding.

I remember the wisdom of my mentor, Rollo May: "The myth which brought you here may no longer be serviceable. Is it time to change myths?"

You need a new vehicle. The inner self you are is now ready for making radical change.

The vehicle metaphor will see you through some of your toughest times. Your vehicle can be destroyed, but you yourself cannot be defeated—unless you personally choose to be so. This is the meaning of steely determination, the confidence that you will find a way to prevail.

In Sum

One of today's most challenging changes is that workers find it more difficult to identify with their companies, that they have diminished interest in the fortunes of their employers, and that organizations do not render the loyalty to their employees that we think they used to. We have called this alienation. Much of that can be traced to the impersonality of the stock market and the severity of the competition, both natural phenomena. The change consultant's response is to strengthen people and organizations to be profitable and caring at the same time, to make companies a good place to work and at the same time fortify employees to prevail under new species of stress.

The answer lies in new dimensions of maturity, common sense, and reason that is demanded of the workforce.

However, many people let their anxieties get the better of them. During the anthrax scare of 2001, Sharl Roan (2001) reported in the *Los Angeles Times* that, "in Maryland, a deranged man sprays a substance inside a subway, and several dozen frightened passengers suddenly experience headaches, nausea and sore throats. . . . Anthrax cases have become a catalyst for what scientists call mass psychogenic illness, in which fear alone can trigger real symptoms in groups of people."

People can't go to work under these circumstances and pay attention to their responsibilities. The higher level of maturity required of them in this age of alienation is to manage their anxiety *before* a crisis by realizing that anxiety is normal and positive. When real problems arise, they will have the fortitude to solve them with courage rather than to feel justified in becoming dysfunctional.

Business Applications Example II

Sandra, the leader of an engineering design team at an aircraft company, complains to Kim, a consultant, "We have on our team a high-maintenance member, Dirk. We are all friendly, stick to our work, and out of nowhere he spouts off, 'We always meet like this and get nowhere!' adding sarcastically, 'I really don't know why we are meeting and why I'm here!' He is hostile and disruptive and gives everyone a headache."

"I get upset," Sandra continues, "I start shaking, and the day is wasted!"

"Yes," chimes in Deborah, her co-manager, "Dirk's outbursts bother me. In fact, I don't sleep well, and the work remains undone."

"Your emotions have been manipulated into being incensed," responds Kim. "People have free speech. And we must grant them the benefit of the doubt. Dirk may carry an important message after all. His problem is that he is rude, disrupts the work, upsets his co-workers, and blithely ignores his role in upsetting them. He creates chaos and takes no responsibility for it. There lies the problem: not taking responsibility for the consequences of his actions."

Dirk needs to be confronted with his non-leadership behavior. The crux of the matter is that he does not take responsibility for the effect his words have on his co-workers. He throws darts and daggers at people, and thinks nothing of it. This is being out of touch with reality. It is like crying "fire" in a theater and not assuming responsibility for the stampede that follows. Dirk seems to think that his crudeness is more than compensated for by his expertise. But there are no excuses for immoral behavior, inconsiderateness, and bad manners. There are crude and there are sensitive ways to deal with Dirk's behavior. The sensitive way is to bring this up generically before a meeting and then make it clear that you do not expect that this will happen here. If it does, one can gently point it out. Phase two is then direct confrontation: This behavior is not acceptable in our organization; you will be more comfortable elsewhere. It is the role of the manager in charge of the unit to take care of this issue for Sandra and Deborah. The boss offers the courage and the principle. The consultant clarifies the emotional and social realities of the situation. The employees benefit.

◆ Activities

Journaling Prompts

1. Think of an occasion at work when you were overwhelmed, frustrated, and became depressed—and received quality support. What was that like? What was done and how did it make you feel?

2. Do you agree fundamentally with today's reality of alienation? If not, how does your opinion differ?

3. Has alienation been part of your experience or that of your clients? If not, how is yours dissimilar?

4. Do you yourself support your employees and clients by being sensitive to their feeling of alienation?

5. Do you feel that you can help your *clients* cope with *their* alienation?

Metaphors

The metaphors for the Diamond are meant to underscore that it is central for leadership growth. Can you think of other metaphors, perhaps more imaginative and effective, that are better-suited to getting this point across to your clients?

CHAPTER 5

Secrets of
Implementation

"**W**HAT STEPS DO WE TAKE? *What do we do now? How do I apply it?*" *People always get these questions. Action plans and techniques do one thing: They inspire us, challenge us, and remind us that we are responsible, we are the agents, and we are the application, the self as an instrument. This confrontation invites us into a different realm of being: that of action as opposed to thought, of reality and groundedness rather than of speculation and abstraction. This is no longer another thought, another plan, another technique. This is now the real thing. And all one can do is to recommend actions that will leverage this realization. They are sparks to light the fire. Only you can do it! That is the foundation truth of the universe! And we don't want to know it. William Butler Yeats (Bartlett, 1992) wrote, "Education is not the filling of a pail, but the lighting of a fire."*

The Language of Leadership

We try to accomplish this deepening of the leadership experience by introducing a new language, rooted in a full picture of human nature, and then expecting that this language invites inner exploration—where many answers, like fossils in lava, lie buried—and outer action, where you find the applications.

If executives in their careers pay no attention to the need for depth, eventually they will get stuck and have no idea where to turn, degenerating into complaining and losing all meaningful efficacy. For unless we touch the hearts and the minds of people and we understand their legitimate fears of authenticity, we will never obtain their commitment nor their resolve.

In sum, depth is the answer, for it is when thought connects to feelings, to action, to choice, to attitudes, and to values, when thought takes root in the soul, that there is change in organizations, that teams and individuals move from compliance—which can be bought—to commitment—which is given freely.

You hear people say, "I'm tired of all the rhetoric. I want to see some action." True, but we cannot forget, can we, that when it comes to leadership, speech indeed can be action, words are behaviors: Signing a check is a linguistic act with great consequences. A judge who says on the bench: "You are sentenced to five years" creates an act, and the person who says, "I do" in a marriage ceremony has changed lives.

The Turning Point

What can you do to make the Diamond work in your team? When do you need the Diamond? You need Diamond thinking when you are at a turning point in your business career. Figure 5.1 dramatizes this point.

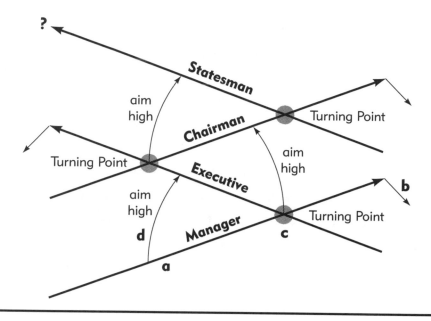

Figure 5.1. Turning Points

You cannot progress in your career in linear fashion alone. You cannot continue what you have been doing (a). You need to understand how the environment and your markets change. If you do not keep up with the times you go downhill (b). You cannot afford to forget that life is a sequence of S-curves. To protect themselves against the downturn, leaders innovate. In short, you reach a critical turning point (c). Promotions do not occur all by themselves. To *get* ahead you first *look* ahead, and aim high (d)! To be promoted from salesperson to sales manager you must extend the length of your view and be prepared not to sell but to manage the people who do the selling. This is a paradigm shift. It occurs *before* promotion, not after. You are promoted because your mindset has changed. If you continue as you had been doing, you will burn out, age, and become irrelevant. That's why we give attention to the turning point.

Carmel, California, is one of the nicest restaurant cities anywhere in the United States. There you find two types of restaurants: those that remain the same and are slowly going out of business, featuring a kind of food theme, such as an English breakfast or Country French home-cooked dinners. Their meals are simple and consistent, year after year, but the business is in danger. Then there are the more avant-garde restaurants, where as time moves on the menu becomes increasingly more varied, changes, becomes more cosmopolitan, and is truly innovative and inventive. The business results are measured in the lengths of the lines of hopeful diners waiting outside to be seated. In the former, you will always find a table without waiting. In the latter, you are lucky to obtain a reservation for the next day! And if you happen to own the business without the queues, you are probably sick with envy and anxiety!

To move to your next step in leadership there need to be drastic changes in your Diamond configuration: from running a restaurant to managing a chain, then becoming an investor in restaurants and a financier, and finally a consultant on how to innovate not only restaurants but businesses in general. Your income reflects this upward movement.

To repeat: You do not change when you have been promoted or have promoted yourself by redefining your business. It works the other way around: You first change how you think about leadership, and then the next step comes. This is a fundamental business and consulting principle. People do not get ahead because they do not change their leadership mindsets. If one change does not work, think again and think harder and try a second one. The days of crafts, where you do the same thing all your life and pass it on to your children, are gone. Today the new craft is change and innovation. Darwin was right: the future is not given to the intelligent or the strong but to those who adapt, those who deal well with the polarities of existence.

An Ongoing Diamond Audit

When preparing to use the Diamond Model in your or your client's organization, consider the following questions:

1. *What is available?* Which helpers can be called on? Is your team a complete Diamond?

2. *What is needed?* What does the market demand? Leadership is situational. Do you know which helper(s) to call? And do you know which ones should sit this one out?

3. *What is overlooked?* If even one of your Diamond corners is not available, then you can be sure that sooner or later there will be trouble ahead.

4. *What is the cost of any incompleteness or deficit in your Diamond?* In the worst case, the cost may be to lose the entire company. Any lost corner can do it: no *vision,* and the company will be gone; no attention to the future of the economy, that is, *reality,* and the company will die; inadequate attention to the people, that is, no *ethics,* and they will leave you, or, at best, practice "on-the-job retirement," even sabotage. And of course if there is no *courage,* then paralysis will ensue.

Intelligent Leadership Conversations and Strategic Intervention Moments

Of all the ways to apply the Diamond, the most systematic one seems to be to help people change the language they use. This can be taught and trained and measured. It can be formalized and made into a technique. In some respects this is questionable, for life is not reducible to mechanical techniques.

But in terms of what the OD market seems to want, this rigorous approach may be one of the best entries into companies that otherwise would close their doors to philosophical deepening. We can help people with the language they use and assure them that deepening is likely to occur, and with it enhanced credibility. And who can argue this point? Who wants to be less credible? This leaves open the kernel, the seed: changing words into action, thoughts into behaviors, bringing about implementation. Implementation is based on actions, and they are free. Implementation is a phenomenon of free will. It is a decision, and a decision that only the person proper can make. I can never make a decision for you. The operative term therefore becomes challenge: I can be challenged to act. You can challenge me to act, and I can challenge you to act. The language of information and the language of challenge: The former gives you the facts, the consensual reality, the inward truth, and the latter provokes you to do what only you can do, namely, to act. I believe that once the foundational parameters are clear, we have yet the very best chance for bringing into existence an empowered and effective organization.

So what is the *doable* secret of implementation? Change the language!

You transform Shadow Diamond language into Leadership Diamond® language. An implementation culture is one that gets things done, makes decisions, takes responsibility, in brief, cares for the organization, where people honor themselves by choosing to be held accountable. It is to build a culture where people reach to the core of their being, and then *dialogue* with others about it. Dialogue and language are the things to do to leverage the insights that invite action.

This proves you are grown up. You no longer postpone your moment of birth as a person, hoping to die before you wake up, for then you need not face the anxiety of being in business. That is the culture that motivates an organization for action, owning its strategies. The vehicle is not the stick and the carrot, but dialogue, what we call here Intelligent Leadership Conversations (ILC) at Strategic Intervention Moments (SIM).

We answer the questions of *when, how, what, who, where, whether,* and *why, which*—and then *act* on the answers! Acting is no longer a strategy point, or any concept whatever. It is an existential point, the precise locus where an abstract thought becomes concrete reality. And you, and only you, are the agent who makes it happen. If you don't then it will not happen. This is the truth about the human condition. The fate of the universe has come crashing down into the very center of your soul!

> Questions for a strategic intervention moment:
>
> - *When?* How soon must I talk with the supervisor?
>
> - *How?* What is the best way to approach the employee in this sensitive matter?
>
> - *What?* What is the purpose of this conversation?
>
> - *Who?* Who is the decision maker in this case?
>
> - *Where?* Where is it best to meet: over lunch, in the office, on the golf course?
>
> - *Whether?* Should we invest in this acquisition? Expand or contract?
>
> - *Why?* Is this meeting really necessary, or is it overkill?
>
> - *Which?* It is key to prioritize before the meeting!

Business is the language of effectiveness, the speech to get things done. Concepts such as marketing, investment, value migration, corporation, client system, SWOT analysis, earnings per share, productivity, core business, reengineering, and innumerable others facilitate obtaining results. They represent a "business approach" to the problem.

Below are some examples, taken from courage, that discriminate between negative and positive leadership language. Results are not automatic. The process works only to the degree that you consciously *want* to strengthen your leadership effectiveness. This means changing *language* to change *attitudes,* and then *behaviors.*

- "Here is why it happened. I can explain!" (*Diagnosis:* Negative in courage. *Rationale:* Announces an excuse, not a solution or act.)

- "I take responsibility." (*Diagnosis:* Positive in courage. *Rationale:* Is a positive action statement, a resolve to act with your freedom.)

- "I don't want to talk about it!" (*Diagnosis:* Negative in courage. *Rationale:* Avoids ownership.)

- "This is what I plan to do." (*Diagnosis:* Positive in courage. *Rationale:* Action statement.)

- "Of course it hurts! But I'm not stopping there!" (*Diagnosis:* Positive in courage. *Rationale:* Is aware of the need for action and makes an action promise—in spite of pain.)

- "I made you a promise and I am embarrassed to have to tell you that I will not be able to keep it. It makes me feel bad. Here's what I propose." (*Diagnosis:* Positive in courage. *Rationale:* Managing promises responsibly is a high sign of leadership authenticity.)

- I ignore something that I had told you I would do. I never bring it up again. I act as if I never said it. (*Diagnosis:* Negative in courage. *Rationale:* A cowardly evasion of mature behavior.)

- "My surgery? I knew that I had to do it. I had to go through anxiety and the pain, and the cost. I chose quickly to do it. It was worse than I thought, and am I proud that I did it!" (*Diagnosis:* Positive in courage. *Rationale:* I overruled my anxiety and chose the intelligent thing to do: Forge ahead!)

A common example of changing non-leadership to leadership language is in punctuality. "I am late because of the traffic; it's not my fault" is *not* a leadership statement. It discounts the choice component in every behavior. A leadership translation is "I am late because I chose not to make special allowances for traffic problems. I chose instead to finish my e-mail. The responsibility is mine." We acknowledge the pervasive existence of choice. Choice leads to owning our behavior. The point is not to be compulsively on time, but to take responsibility for what I do.

The IdeaBank™

The IdeaBank is a simple device, going back to Plato. For him, one of the founders of Western civilization, ideas were the main currency. Ideas exist on their own. You see them with the inner eye. They have always existed and always will. The soul lives among them before birth. Once on this earth, we forget them. Learning is remembering. We recognize things because they exemplify ideas.

We see with the inner eye the idea of "profit." But we cannot find the idea "profit" in the real, that is, outer, world, only objects that *exemplify* profitability, such as the competitor's profit and loss statement or the history of GE.

Collecting and working with ideas is one of the most powerful leadership tools at your disposal.

How does one do that? Use "Aha!" cards and automate the process. A good database will do. Record your ideas multidimensionally, as illustrated in Figure 5.2, file them, refer to them, edit them, organize them, do not lose the past, do not forget what you have learned, keep your brain active.

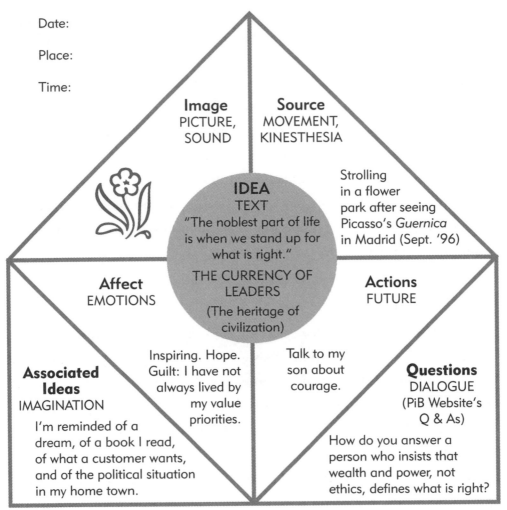

Date:

Place:

Time:

Image
PICTURE, SOUND

Source
MOVEMENT, KINESTHESIA

IDEA
TEXT
"The noblest part of life is when we stand up for what is right."
THE CURRENCY OF LEADERS
(The heritage of civilization)

Strolling in a flower park after seeing Picasso's *Guernica* in Madrid (Sept. '96)

Affect
EMOTIONS

Actions
FUTURE

Inspiring. Hope. Guilt: I have not always lived by my value priorities.

Talk to my son about courage.

Associated Ideas
IMAGINATION
I'm reminded of a dream, of a book I read, of what a customer wants, and of the political situation in my home town.

Questions
DIALOGUE
(PiB Website's Q & As)
How do you answer a person who insists that wealth and power, not ethics, defines what is right?

For Deepening Leadership Conversations and Feeding into the IdeaBank™

Figure 5.2. The "Aha!" Card

For example, I went with the participants of a banking workshop in Spain to view the 20th Century's most memorable work of art. I remember seeing Picasso's *Guernica* for the second time, in the Museo the Reina Sophia in Madrid, where it eventually landed after having been for years exhibited at the entrance of New York's Museum of Modern Art. There I saw it for the first time. The idea that struck me was how important it was to live by your values, no matter how hard.

The symbol that came to mind was a blooming daisy, a surge of hope. The day was gloomy, corresponding to the mood of the painting. And in some strange way it reminded me of my late mother, whom I had lost when I was fourteen, and often wondered what it would have been like to have had an aged mother.

As I revisit this idea I rediscover my conscience. I also ask, "Wouldn't it be interesting to set it to music, a kind of Richard Strauss tone poem?" I have neglected my music, I say to myself. And it hurts. All this is recorded on an "Aha!" card.

Maximize the generation of ideas. Brainstorming produces innovation. Teamwork helps. You work with your ideas. Use your imagination. Combine ideas, review ideas, modify ideas, create ideas about ideas, cluster ideas, invert ideas, expand ideas, contract ideas, rank ideas, compare ideas. This is how ideas proliferate.

The Diamond serves as a catalyst to generate ideas: What are the ethical, courageous, realistic, and visionary implications of an idea? And what have greatness and polarity to do with each idea?

Gary Hamel has a neat formula for teams: Start with one thousand ideas. Select one hundred for small seed money. Finance ten ideas with serious investment capital. Expect one to be a hit on the market.

Progress starts with mastering the art of generating ideas, collecting ideas, and then manipulating and working with ideas.

When you attend a lecture or read a book, it is constructive to take notes. Divide your page into three columns. In the middle, write down the content. After the experience, take ten minutes, using a different color, to clarify and amplify your notes. On the left, write a brief outline. On the right, reflect and comment on the content (see Exhibit 5.1). Ten minutes of this after each lecture and you will own, not squander, what you just learned!

If you work, for example, as manager in a chemical engineering or pharmaceutical firm, in studying beginning chemistry, you write in the middle what was said about the elements, valences, atomic weights, and the like. On the left is your outline of the main points: periodic table, and so forth. And on the right, your comments: "Mendeleev's periodic table and Kekule's benzene ring structure are fascinating," you say to yourself. "I wish also I could make discoveries of such genius."

This ten-minute methodology is well-suited for computers. Create your own Diamond Change Innovator, which should include your IdeaBank™. It enhances the joy of learning. The innovator is simply a database that you use for your ideas. You review it frequently to allow old ideas to spawn new ones, to modify and to combine ideas, to discard and replace them. Ideas as currency are your most precious possessions and your most valuable investments. The use of ideas as the basis of civilization started as we saw with Plato and his Theory of Ideas or Forms. You are an idea-generating organism. Your ideas

Outline	Notes Taken During Lecture or Reading	Comments
Periodic Table	• Mendeleer • Elements • Hydrogen	I want to become a researcher in chemistry

Exhibit 5.1. Note-Taking Format

will respect you as much as you respect them; they will do for you what you are prepared to do for them.

Diamond Reverse Engineering™

There is also the Diamond Reverse Engineering™ (D/RE) tool: We start with a business objective and work backward asking what else must occur for the goal to be reached (see Figure 5.3). This ultimately leads to the Diamond "chip" and how it is to be reconfigured in the minds of leaders and in the culture in general in order to reach the planned objectives.

For example, we may find that a lackluster insurance company emphasizes, externally, an unusual variety of products and, internally, a focus on employee benefits—reality and ethics, respectively. What this company needs to progress is courage and vision, guts for new strategies.

In practice, results usually exceed objectives. If the goal is to grow the business from half a billion to a full billion in two years, then, once accomplished, you find *also* a great increase in personal meaning, self-worth, pride,

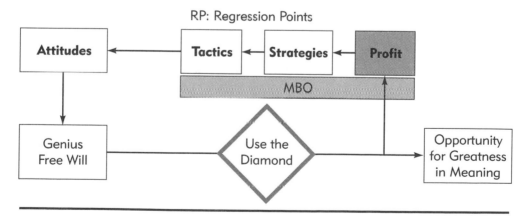

Figure 5.3. Diamond Reverse Engineering™

and marketability of the prime movers in this project. In retrospect, it is these latter values that become the true goals of the business thrust.

Advantages of Language Training

In Diamond Theory, we want to have something that is teachable, applicable, and measurable in simple and clear terms, even though the real world may not be that way. Consultants nevertheless need such tools. That is why we focus on language. We want to teach people to speak in leadership language terms. We want people to detect the use of non-leadership language. And we want people to be able to translate non-leadership expressions to leadership talk. Instead of saying, "You don't know what you are doing" or "You don't have your act together," we teach leaders to say, "I understand that this is not easy for you; perhaps we can find a better way." Instead of saying, "It's not my fault," we teach leaders to say, "No matter how it came about, I take responsibility." But we are not simple-minded either, recognizing that life and people are more complex.

The total Diamond package seems to have the following advantages:

- Language is easy to teach.

- Results will show themselves first in the language of managers, consultants, trainers, and employees.

- The expectation is that a deliberate effort is made to translate language into behaviors. From the point of view of technique, it is the simplest way to go.

- Attitude is in the end what matters, but language is behavior that can be measured. Many say that what gets measured gets done.

- The degree to which these six Diamond concepts become part of daily actions, that is, language and then behavior, predicts how far people will progress on their roads to success. It tells us whether managers and consultants obstruct or facilitate breakthroughs (see Figure 5.4).

- Conversely, being stuck in business can be traced to *not* using all six Diamond tools. Finding out which is missing, such as realism, and then activating that, becomes your solution.

- Diamond awareness is a root implementation mechanism. What we implement is strategy. Implementation is brought about by culture, the repository of the workforce's energy and commitment. And that is facilitated by judicious training in foundational leadership language. The goal of the Diamond is to remove the cap and allow the mind to explode to its full capacity.

In short, when we have leadership problems we know what to do: Activate the full six-point Diamond.

Those who do not manifest these core leadership traits, reflecting a Shadow Diamond, can be reliably predicted to have, at most, limited career success. Their business future will be capped. This is here viewed as a factual, causal connection. Choosing non-leadership yields negative outcomes. The right language will support you to the end of your ambition. And restricting yourself in your leadership thinking and speaking will handcuff your future.

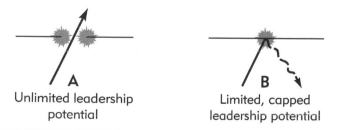

A
Unlimited leadership
potential

B
Limited, capped
leadership potential

Figure 5.4. Breakthrough Potential

Motivating

The question then of the leader is how does one motivate people. The first answer is radical and categorical: It simply cannot be done, not in any real sense. Human beings are free, and the sign of freedom is to take full responsibility for life. And that centrally includes being a self-starter at work, assuming full responsibility for results and for the success of the whole. The reason is built into the very structure of human existence, functioning as an axiom.

Carl Rogers, the great American psychologist from La Jolla, California, once told a group of students about a study showing that people who made a success of their lives were not those advantaged in childhood—with money and a good education—but, quite the opposite, were neglected children who knew early on they *had* to be free and responsible. Some who were rich as children are now in jail, and others, starting poor, won Nobel prizes. The differentiating insight was whether they knew about free will. If yes, they led authentic lives. If no, they became victims of false values.

> I cannot motivate you and you cannot motivate me, for it means to take over each other's freedom. I cannot choose for you and you cannot choose for me. That is a fact, and to try to run counter to this absolutely basic truth of human reality and human existence, this natural law, is of course the climax in naiveté.

It follows that the only way I can stimulate your motivation is to *create an environment* in which motivation would be for you a logical choice. That means

- I *expect* you to be free, autonomous, and responsible. You are caught in the web of my expectations. If you wish to be recognized in my circle, you need to demonstrate personal initiative, ownership, responsibility, and accountability. You work for your boss: The boss throws out a challenge and rewards with an acknowledgment. This is how you try to awaken the motivation in another.

- The final word is that *I motivate myself; you motivate yourself.* These are choices, fundamental, "archetypal" decisions of how much of a full human being you choose to become. There is no other way. *If there is anything else under the sun that can motivate me it is to see you freely take charge of your own motivation in your business life!*

This is modeling, inspiring by example. Aristotle said that children learn by imitation: "Mother, I fell down. Does this mean that I hurt?" Or the trite but cute, "Are we having fun yet?" The little boy sees his father kiss his new sister. He may be jealous, but he also learns that he loves his little sister.

Business leaders would do well to read biographies of successful business leaders. These are samples in recorded history of turning thought into reality and concretizing empty free will into the fullness of a business life. When you find leaders you can admire, it will be difficult not to choose yourself to be among them.

The Obstacles

Since Diamond effectiveness requires a transformation of how we think, we face the paradox of saying precisely what people do not wish to hear.

We tell the analytic mind to be intuitive and the intuitive mind to become analytical, the scientist to think like a poet and the poet to think like a scientist. We tell those who look at the outside world to explore their inner world, and we urge those who live mostly internally to find their truth on the outside. We are telling the Oriental mind to think like a Westerner, and we are telling the Western mind to think along Oriental lines.

We demand they stretch their minds and think as never before, while we realize how unfair, even impossible, this is. We give a formula to those who ask for a formula, while we know that formulaic thinking deflects people from the very changes they need to make. But also, we impart poetry and art, religion and coaching, to those who want depth and wisdom.

In short, we are asking people to be open to transformation, to the conversion to authentic leadership, when the transformation itself is that authenticity is all in their own hands, not in those of their teachers.

The mind is like a parachute. It works only when open.

The Standoff

Management wants more *accountability*. I once asked Harald Norvik, chairman of the Norwegian Statoil, what above all else he wanted from his people. His one word was "accountability." Before then, when at Ford, I had asked the president of the United Auto Workers what his union workers wanted from Ford. His answer was "empowerment." Management wants more *accountability*, and labor wants to be *empowered*.

Employees complain that members of management do not really walk their talk, that they don't mean what they say. Should you take management seriously and act on their challenges to empowerment, you will find out that you have made a bad career move.

Management complains that when they offer jointly to redesign the company's vision, instead of hundreds of volunteers, they find barely a handful. "Workers say that they want to be empowered," management grumbles, "but when you offer it to them they do not take it."

Here is the standoff! It's the "other guy's" fault!

If we do not change the culture, update and professionalize it, we will not have a company in the future. What's to be done? A credible chance of success requires a simple way to address fundamental problems not just surface issues. The solution is to correct both (1) ignorance about what it means to be a human being and (2) unwillingness to make the decision for authenticity.

◆ Activity

Intelligent Leadership Conversations for Trainers

Authentic executives discriminate among positive, neutral, and negative leadership conversations. You read examples previously in this chapter. Make a list of typical conversations in your workplace in need of repair, using the format in Exhibit 5.2. In one column, write a telling sentence from that conversation. In the second column, repair it, translating it from a negative or neutral sentence to a positive leadership sentence, such as from "I just work here" to "I am implementing our mission," from "I am here to make money" to "I am here to build a team," from "Now that I have been promoted, I want a bigger office" to "I wonder what kind of office I should move into in order to make for better employee morale?" In the third column, record which deep structure you used and why: "This is myopic and pedestrian and far from long-range and visionary language!"

Failed Conversation	Repaired Conversation	Deep Structure Utilized
It's your fault!	I shall help you fix it.	Ethics

Exhibit 5.2. Conversation Repair Format

PART THREE

The Main Body of the Leadership Mind

Four Intelligence Tools

ETHICS

We first crush people to the earth, and then claim the right of trampling on them forever, because they are prostrate.
LYDIA MARIE CHILD

Some day after mastering the winds, the waves, the tides, and gravity, we will harness for God the energies of love. And then, for the second time in the history of the world, man will have discovered fire.
PIERRE TEILHARD DE CHARDIN

Two things fill the mind with ever-increasing wonder and awe, the more often and the more intensely the mind of thought is drawn to them: the starry heavens above me and the moral law within me.
IMMANUEL KANT

The most momentous thing in human life is the art of winning the soul to good or to evil.
PYTHAGORAS

In spite of everything I still believe that people are really good at heart.
ANNE FRANK

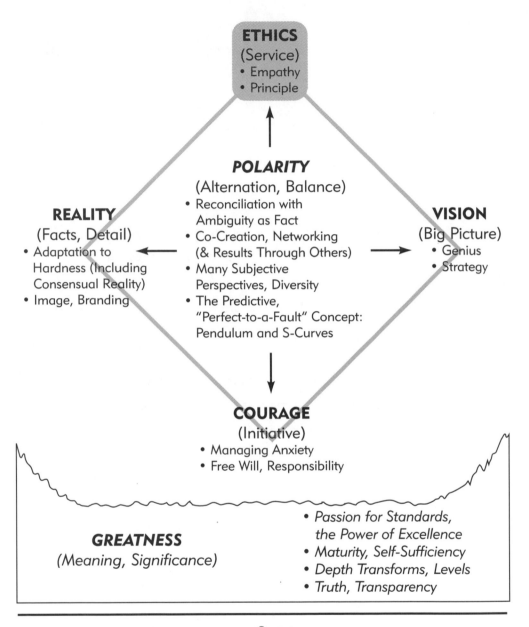

ETHICS
(Service)
• Empathy
• Principle

POLARITY
(Alternation, Balance)
• Reconciliation with
  Ambiguity as Fact
• Co-Creation, Networking
  (& Results Through Others)
• Many Subjective
  Perspectives, Diversity
• The Predictive,
  "Perfect-to-a-Fault" Concept:
  Pendulum and S-Curves

REALITY
(Facts, Detail)
• Adaptation to
  Hardness (Including
  Consensual Reality)
• Image, Branding

VISION
(Big Picture)
• Genius
• Strategy

COURAGE
(Initiative)
• Managing Anxiety
• Free Will, Responsibility

GREATNESS
(Meaning, Significance)

• *Passion for Standards,*
  the Power of Excellence
• *Maturity, Self-Sufficiency*
• *Depth Transforms, Levels*
• *Truth, Transparency*

Figure 6.1. **The Leadership Diamond®: Ethics**

CHAPTER 6

Ethics

DEFINITION: Service

ELEMENTS: Empathy, Principle

AFTER THE WIZARD GIVES YOU THE MAGIC STONE, *you embark on your voyage, and the first helper on whom you call is the healer. For the healer has great affinity to the inner realm, from where you draw your strength to be a leader.*

What Is Ethics?

Ethics is a complex topic in philosophy. But here it is used with a bias toward business. Ethics is empathy, which means service. It's an attitude of love and compassion, of caring, of including people, of valuing them, of hearing them, of suffering when they suffer, and of being proud when they succeed. It is soft. Ethics is also principle. This is hard. It is to know that there is evil and it is to live by the resolve that our destiny on earth is to struggle against evil and establish a moral order. If you are comfortable in these two zones of living, then you are a person well-developed in the region of the leadership mind called ethics.

Thus, ethics contains two important elements. One is the profound value of *empathy* and the other is the overarching power of *principle* (see Figure 6.1). Their opposites in the Shadow Diamond are being *indifferent* and being *unscrupulous.* Empathy is the *struggle* against emotional indifference. And principle is the *fight* against unscrupulous behavior.

The business bias of Philosophy-in-Business™ gets us into business ethics, the ethical role of business in the world situation. The larger social responsibility and goal of business is to fuel the economy. That grounds all human activity. Poverty is evil; a dysfunctional society is evil; the unfulfilled potential of a family or a people is evil. In a free economy, much of what is needed for a decent life with human values is made possible through a thriving economy.

Business is about people: by people, for people, and about people. On the feeling level ethical people deal with empathy, and on the rational level they concern themselves with principle. Both are necessary to know how to manage the people you require to run your business.

Business requires more than profits—it also requires compassion and integrity. Lacking the latter is true evil. Without values, society does not work. You cannot do business in a valueless society.

Consider these questions:

- People boycott products because they think they are harmful or antisocial. Cesar Chavez became famous for leading a boycott of California grapes as a protest against anti-union activity against farm workers in California vineyards. Was that ethical or was it not? How do you decide?

- Should you help SUV manufacturers, tobacco companies, and gun merchants create an honest and socially conscious business, or should you drive them out of business altogether with concerted class action suits?

- Who is more important to consider in the decisions you make, the stockholder or the employee?

As a leader, you are expected to think and talk intelligently on these matters. And OD practitioners and consultants need to help clarify these topics. It is people who make change happen in organizations and it is people who bring about innovation. Unless you can manage the people pathology to which these business efforts give rise, you do not have a productive organization.

Table 6.1 summarizes the various definitions we've discussed so far.

Table 6.1. Ethics

Deep Structure with Subsets	What It Is/Definition/ Description	The Shadow Against Which We Fight
Ethics	Being of service, which honors you; people matter	Abuse and exploitation of people; caving in to evil; unfairness, injustice
Empathy	Reaching out; understanding how others feel and caring about that	Indifference to the feelings of others; being an uncaring person; callous
Principle	Doing what is right, not necessarily what feels good; keeping promises; integrity; thoroughly trustworthy	Unprincipled; an opportunist; spineless; unreliable, untrustworthy, manipulative

Toward the end of Jack Welch's term, GE and Honeywell were thinking of merging. Some executives at GE argued vociferously against the merger. Many at Honeywell argued with equal vehemence in favor. But one attorney working on the case said, "The important people in this case are not those in favor or those against, but those who combat within themselves about which is the best solution." This attorney knows the difference between just plain ethics and the higher leadership posture of accepting the polarities of ethics. It is the latter that makes you authentically ethical.

For our journey into ethics we require an overview of the topics to which we will attend, the tourist stops we will make on our visit: What is evil? What is empathy? What is principle?

There is more: How do we make the decision to be an ethical person, and why should we choose that way? Tough questions indeed! And we want to get into the general area of duty. What is duty? What is reason in ethics? And what does it mean to be motivated by principle? The result should be the skill to have Intelligent Leadership Conversations on the topic of ethics and to apply what we have called Strategic Intervention Moments to specific business targets.

That is the process by which you can introduce ethics into the business context for business results. Without this capacity you have no credibility as a leader.

In the minds of most people, ethics is the central concern in life. How I am treated and how I treat others, the quality of my personal relationships, and how I stand vis-à-vis my conscience about being a worthy individual—these are for many people the things that matter most.

When we speak of ethics here, we are talking about that part of the mind, the leadership mind in particular—the map, the chip, the language, the behaviors, the attitudes, the illumination, or whatever metaphor suits you—that concerns itself with "people" issues. The questions for aspiring leaders are

- Do you want to live in that zone of the mind, ethics?

- Do you actually live there now?

- What can you do to migrate more wholeheartedly into that region?

- Are you interested in teaching others—in at least having the mindset to teach others—to be in that realm, to feel at home there, to have explored its every nook and cranny?

- Draw up a list of diverse values that people have held. Next to each state whether it is a value that, even though it is different from yours, you can accept. Finally, indicate which of these values are so outrageous that you cannot tolerate them and where you draw the line. Explain why.

Empathy and principle are very different. They represent respectively the emotional and the rational side of ethics. To be able to talk intelligently about them is the mark of a person who can influence employees and customers alike. It is not only the right thing to do, but from a business point of view it also gives you credibility and access to people, to your stakeholders.

Ethics is not just a matter of being nice to people. It is to understand human nature in depth and to see how critical that is to help along success in business.

Evil

To destroy the dignity of a human being is evil. To be indifferent to the feelings of others is evil. Not to support peoples' sense of self-respect is evil. Not to challenge people in becoming authentic is also evil. But the ethical component in all of this is the human contribution, the personal, freely chosen addition. For example, a natural disaster is in itself not evil. What introduces evil is when we do not approach a situation with all the tools at our disposal, namely using the self as instrument. *Ultimately, the source of good and evil lies in how we choose—from the depth of our freedom—what kind of a world we help create by the nature of our choices. That is the spring from which flows all good and all evil. And we are responsible.*

The Struggle

Ethics is fundamentally the struggle against evil, overcoming evil. Evil needs to be a separate and legitimized category of explanation of the world if the struggle against injustice and dehumanization is to be understood and make any sense.

Evil is in essence the disregard of human inwardness. It is to *not* value what it means to be a person. It is to *disregard* a person's dignity and self-respect. Evil is to degrade human beings, to humiliate them, to control them, to abuse them, to treat them like animals (not that animals should be treated that way).

Evil is not discussed in the sciences. And this is rather unfortunate, considering that the behavioral sciences dominate leadership work in business, and that without understanding evil, morality makes very little sense.

There is a *continuum* here: Disregard of a person's inner self can extend from a minor slight to a major rape. There is a point where you draw the line: Up to this level I can be tolerant, but beyond it there is war! Different people have different limits. In a well-run business people feel that their dignity is upheld. This is the responsibility of both managers and employees. It is to care about the feelings of others and it is to take care of your own feelings.

To repeat, the first point in ethics therefore is to take evil seriously and to see much of human life as the struggle against evil. Evil is rooted in human freedom, in the capacity to *not* care, the capacity to destroy human beings— not only physically but also emotionally and morally. Evil is when you suffer and nobody cares. Evil is when others suffer and you don't care.

That ethics is the struggle against evil is not an unimportant matter. Some people who compete with you in business—such as Larry Ellison at Oracle and Bill Gates at Microsoft—are, sadly, out to destroy the competition. There is, however, pushback in bringing up evil. There is much simplistic "positive" thinking that, like a drug, is "pushed" on the streets of our common culture. Even great persons fall prey to it. I once asked the gifted Finnish conductor Esa-Pekka Salonen—I was in Finland for a lecture and the maestro played a modern piece during the intermission—what was the greatest moment in his life. He said it was when he was deep in meditation with a piece he was conducting. I asked him then what had been his most difficult moment. He said, "I don't dwell on negatives and have already forgotten it." I asked General Colin Powell, two days after the inconclusive presidential election of 2000, what he thought about death. He said he doesn't think about it. His mind is positive and death comes when it comes and he will lose no sleep over it beforehand.

These anecdotes reflect the popularity of denying negative experiences. And yet these experiences are the source of our strength, our power, our character, and in the end of our "salvation" in a world surrounded with emptiness. "No pain, no gain." It's a cliché, but sadly true nevertheless.

Whenever someone sorrows, I do not say, "Forget it," or "It will pass," or "It could be worse"—all of which deny the integrity of the painful experience. But I say, to the contrary, "It is worse than you may allow yourself to think. Delve into the depth. Stay with the feeling. Think of it as a precious source of knowledge and guidance. Then and only then will you be ready to face it and be transformed in the process. Congratulations! God is smiling on you!"

Both great people, Salonen and Powell, sidestepped the tragic sense of life! As we descend into the depth of the soul, going past our innermost doubts, guilt, and anxieties, we discover our ultimate strength, our definitive power, the source of our free actions, and our joy, now richly earned. And that discovery is why we are alive—to discover some of the miracle involved in our own creation—as a thinking being, as a consciousness, as a person, as a leader in our own lives.

We have here a parade of ethical choices. There is a tragic element in life, and to recognize that (which is reality) and to choose to struggle against it (which is courage) is at its base the decision to be ethical. This is the highest and noblest calling of a human being. It does not produce pleasure or happiness nor profit, nor does it reduce pain, but it creates a sense of worth, the conviction of not having wasted one's life! Such behavior touches your conscience. A good coach learns how to touch the conscience of the client. And a good leader has a powerful conscience that warrants support.

Children became fearful after the terrorist attack. Parents did not know how to respond to a twelve-year old girl imploring, "Daddy, don't go to work. Don't fly to your meeting; I am afraid, stay home." It's of course OK to respond to your daughter, "Flying today is extra safe." But down deep somewhere you must know, and your daughter must hear from you when she is ready, that her father is not afraid to die. Someday death will come, and no matter how much we fret, rebel, and weep, it is still our fate. Down deep we know that we can accept even that.

Ethics touches true depth!

Deepening Understanding

Freedom is part of courage, and we will discuss it in Chapter 9 at length. But a quick cross-reference to it here is critical. Being ethical is always a decision. Animals may have feelings, capable of bonding and attachment, but we don't say they are ethical. Being ethical is typically human. And humans who tamper with their ethics endanger the integrity of their very humanity. The difference lies in the zone of freedom. For we choose our behavior in accordance with the criteria of what is ethical and what is not. A person may commit a heinous crime, but if that person lacks judgment, cannot reflect, cannot think, that person is given treatment instead of punishment.

Human freedom is rooted in the human fact of free will. And free will is scary. Why? Because we can choose anything we want. In the purity of our philosophical truth, the truth about freedom is that, like it or not, we are at least potentially and theoretically free to choose whether we are to *attach* ourselves to something, like our child, or whether we want to *distance* ourselves from, and *not care* what happens to, people at the other end of the world. We can also choose the reverse, like the countess in Tolstoy's novel who weeps in the theater about the fate of the actor on stage while her carriage footman is outside waiting for her in the snow freezing!

> The duty of change consultants is to free their clients from the handcuffs of evil so that they can unfold their true potential for the betterment of their organizations. It is the secret of inner strength and of the power to withstand adversity and come back triumphant after defeat—losing a sale, losing a job, a drop in a stock price, an invention going sour, the competition getting there first.

In the application of ethics to work, deepening means that you find answers and solutions not at the level where problems are created, which is the job and the business, but at the underlying level of human nature and the universal human fate, where philosophy tends to exist, and talk about life, death, guilt, and hope. How can you summon the inner peace, the subjective confidence, the inward faith, the rational belief that you will achieve freedom and community in the jungles that are today's organizations and marketplaces?

I have seen my clients pace the room and ask, not "What is in this for me?" or "What is the politically prudent thing to do?" but "What is the right and ethical thing to do?" Some put their struggles into religious form: "What here is the will of God?" Others maintain it at the level of "How can ethics help me find out what is right and wrong because I want to make sure I do what is right?" The chairman of one of America's most significant companies said to me, "It is our concern with values that has made this company great." Another said, "The day I find that we have violated our values, I am out of here, no matter what the economic consequences."

But I add a caveat: I am interested here in not only defending ethics for ethics sake, but I want always to be conscious of the business value that is derived from deepening philosophic activity in the nitty-gritty of business concerns. *And this is not to harness ethics in the service of commercialism. Far from it!* But it is to show in the end how philosophy, which includes ethics but is not limited to ethics, does make for better business, and not just as a self-serving addendum, but as a focal and core point. The connection between philosophy and better business is not automatic. It follows from the decision to use ethics, the resolve to make it happen.

Empathy

There are, as stated before, two elements of being ethical: empathy and principle. *Empathy* means that you have made a decision within the heart of your being to understand the thoughts and feelings of another human being. You are able to capture what it feels to be the other.

But empathy is not just knowledge—it is also desire. You *want* to know that, you *care* about how the person feels, it is *important* to you. Empathy is the willingness to forgive, to love, to feel connected, to bond. We like to think that feelings of connection are the norm and are natural and that persons who do not feel that way are sick. This may well be the case. But the philosophical reality is deeper than that. People make a choice. Caring is a choice, a decision, a commitment. You are doing the right thing. It feels good and you feel good about yourself. Pure. Clean. To listen to those feelings and to value them are your archaic and archetypal choices. When people choose not to care, it is not that they are simply numbed by birth or by early experiences. They also make a choice. They simply refuse to listen to their guilt of alienation.

We can ask whether or not empathy has business value. But if we said yes, then empathy would by that very act lose its meaning. To ground empathy on business results is not to understand the value of empathy in the first place. If there is business value to empathy, then that would be quite coincidental. And we would not know if we were truly empathic, for it could be confused with utilitarian pragmatism. But if this case of empathy were clearly negative for business, we would know the empathy is genuine.

To be a good business executive is to know that some things in human relations are more important than business. Is that good for business? Does it matter? Should it matter?

Principle

The second component of ethics is *principle,* which is also called *morality* or *integrity*—words that are perhaps more commonly associated with ethics.

Principle is derived from a very simple question: What motivates you? There are basically three forms of motivation: pain, pleasure, and conscience. The first two we share with the animals. The third is not part of the natural order. Principle chooses conscience.

Pain

We are motivated by the avoidance of pain. We have narcotics and painkillers, we have surgery and physiotherapy, much of which is geared to eliminate or at least alleviate pain. We avoid delicate emotional encounters to be protected from pain. We avoid anxiety-producing acts of courage because we do not wish to suffer pain. We allow ourselves to be degraded and suffer in silence because we do not wish the anguish of confrontation. This is not a case of acting on principle.

Pleasure

We are motivated by pleasure. We do things because they give us enjoyment, they make life easy, they are playful. There is nothing wrong with that, unless you say that this is all there is to being a good person. We like pictures of beaches and sun and palm trees and blue waters and pretty people because we think that is enchantment and delight and we should be able to spend our lives in just this fashion—swimming, snorkeling, surfing, drinking, and eating.

Avoiding pain and seeking pleasure are both worthy causes. But they are not the essence of principle in ethics. The animals avoid pain and seek pleasure as well.

Conscience

The third motivation is reason. Concepts like right, ought, good, honor, pride, and duty begin to make sense in this context. We may not agree on what is right. We may not even know how to defend a position about it. We may still be in search. In fact it is the struggle with these concepts that is more the mark of an ethical person than merely to do what is politically correct, consensual, or expected.

The reasonable aspect of our conscience is that we do know somewhere in our being that not all behaviors have the same moral tone. Some are patently right and others patently wrong. We seem to be able to consult an inner voice, a conscience, quite independent of social conformity and early upbringing. For our conscience can tell us, and often does, that the values by which we were raised, such as perhaps racism and sexism, are patently wrong. A person who is motivated by these kinds of so-called rational considerations, thoughtful investigations, pacing the floor at night not knowing what is the right thing to do and struggling to find an answer, *that is the moral person.*

We talk about a supreme principle of morality, such as the Golden Rule, of the greatest happiness principle, or justice and equality, or freedom, or camaraderie, or community, or individualism, and so forth. Being motivated by these rational considerations, these principles, these universal rules, that is moral behavior. That is different from avoiding pain and seeking pleasure.

And here there is no precedent among the animals. From plain consciousness to sophisticated self-consciousness, simple awareness to self-awareness, is a sudden and dramatic evolutionary leap, a leap that marks the beginning of the human species. Not that we want to malign the animals—far from it—but the point about ethical behavior being exclusively human should be strong and clear.

Acting on principle, being motivated by a principle, is a unique way of being. That is Socrates—historically speaking, the number one paragon of virtue. This differentiation is critical and results from an order of being far different from pleasure and pain. A person who is governed by reason gives a very different impression from one who is governed only by pleasure and pain. Also, the rewards are different from merely attaining pleasure and preventing pain. We now move upward in our value system to honor and self-esteem, and to fulfilling one's nature as a human being (see Figure 6.2). The result on the marketplace is greatly enhanced leadership credibility.

A consultant colleague writes:

"There is a lot of pain in the organization with which I consult. The CEO was expecting to continue to run his part of the newly acquired company but now he is out on the street. That is pain. Ninety nine percent of the people he was leading dearly wanted him as their leader. They are all in pain. Now if the company would have had effective leadership in the first place,

Motivations

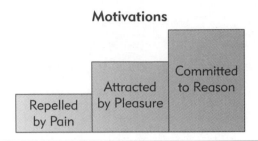

Figure 6.2. The Steps of Growth in Ethics

the acquisition would never have been allowed to occur. For me that would have been ethical motivation."

Tough Love

Business is tough, reality oriented, and often does not have use for the extreme sensitivity and softness that empathy implies. Love is always to be tempered with realism. *But we can ignore neither that part of love which is unrealistic nor that part of reality which is unloving.*

Tough love is then not empathy and forgiveness but it is principle. Children will not grow up, no one will grow up, until the person has come to terms with limits, with boundaries, with the full knowledge that there is a world outside and a society beyond that are infinitely more powerful than you are. And the collective wishes of others, not to speak of your biology, create a wall of finitude around you. And this is reality. To not recognize that is to grow up spoiled and overentitled, the result of which is that, when the real world appears, some people feel betrayed and cheated and can even become violent, for they are being deprived of what they have been taught are their rights.

These preliminary overview themes introduce ethics to the leadership consultant as a world view, a way of looking at reality, an attitude, a way of being intelligent. It is a hydrofoil skimming the tips of the waves. We now look more deeply.

CHAPTER 7

Empathy

EMPATHY INVARIABLY LEADS *also to talk about* community, *which is a big concern today and has always been. Ethics in business is also about* service, *calling on the part of you that wants to help other people. These are the broad applications of the leadership mind that will concern us now. Here you are visiting the healer's province. And familiarity with the language that one speaks in that land is the beginning of authentic leadership wisdom.*

The Essence of Empathy

What, after all is said and done, are the essential ingredients of empathy?

Understand better the subjective dimension. Empathy is to enter the realm of the inner self, and unless one is motivated to be there and explore and dialogue nothing much is going to happen.

Understand that subjectivity is not just you but is other people too. There is *subjectivity*, which is just you, and then there is *intersubjectivity*, which is more than one. The leap from subjectivity to intersubjectivity, from one to two, is as stirring as is the leap from animal to person, from consciousness to self-consciousness. This drama is abstractly restated in arithmetic as the fundamental shift in concepts from zero to one and then to two. These three numbers, each fundamentally different from the other two, are the axiomatic constituents of the entire edifice of mathematics (see Figure 7.1).

Realize that it is much healthier to live intersubjectively. This means it is better in family and in community not to live only subjectively, that is, alone. The latter is often alienation, described so well in Robert Putnam's (2001) thorough sociological study of contemporary America, *Bowling Alone*. Not facing this fact is sticking to a limited world view to avoid the anxiety of venturing. This is known as a psychoneurosis. Living on the edge is how one makes progress.

Have a desire to enter the soul of another. This is really the desire to connect with the soul of another. You know the *value* of this connection. But it can be a *greedy* connection, or it can be a *generous* connection, or a *curious* one, or a *committed* one. The latter is the most stimulating.

Commit yourself to another. The commitment means that you are dedicated to support the other person, in a state of intimacy, or intersubjectivity, family, community, love, or even a secure psychotherapeutic alliance.

Your role is then to ask for permission to enter another soul, know that your intention is the interests of that other soul rather than just you, and then, in the most generous way you know, you devote yourself to support that other person in doing what in his or her very depth he or she must do.

That is the intimacy so often and so beautifully recorded in the writings of the sensitive German poet Rainer Maria Rilke:

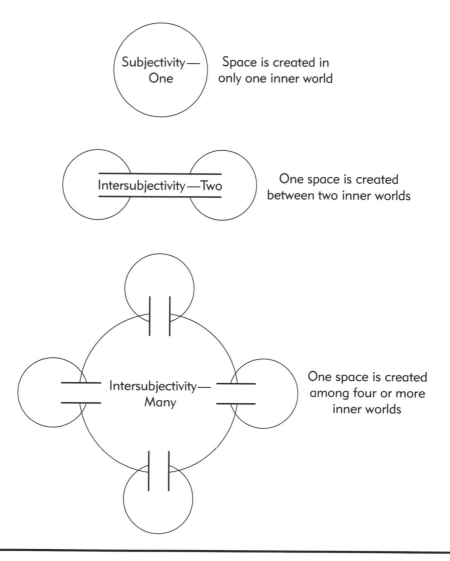

Figure 7.1. From Subjectivity to Intersubjectivity

"A good marriage is that in which each appoints the other guardian of his solitude" (1923).

"Love consists in this, that two solitudes protect and touch and greet each other" (1923).

"Perhaps everything that frightens us is, in its deepest essence, something helpless that wants our love" (1923).

Learn that souls mirror each other. They are witnesses. This means that a soul does not know what it is until and unless it is reflected in another soul. This is the difference between a feral child and a monk or nun. The former is wild because there never was another consciousness to teach the child what it means to be human. But monks or nuns had a normal childhood, let us assume, and, having been witnessed and discovered who they are, now want God's witness and talk only with God.

Recognize that intimacy is an ideal. And that empathy is a goal. But it is not always reached. We can say it must be established. But we must also be strong as steel to prepare for life and for fulfilling our obligations when love is missing, when empathy is conspicuous by its absence.

And there are many degrees of absence, from the temporary indifference of a spouse to assault by a criminal. Empathy is a mixture of intimacy and tough love. Infinite forgiveness and setting limits with ineluctable sanctions. What a tough polarity to master!

Understand that love is more than intimacy. It is to help a person grow. And growth requires opposition and confrontation. And they hurt. Growth hurts. We feel this especially with our children, as well as with students, patients, and customers. And with us, when we get the brunt of the growth treatment. The empathy therefore must extend to the growth itself as well. The leadership talk could be, for example, "I have empathy for the fact that it hurts" or "I am not unsympathetic to the fact that you are really upset and angry with me because of a confrontation that hurts me too and that both of us know is as painful as it is also necessary."

The Business of Relationships

How does all this apply to business? The best answer is that business is all about relationships. And that managing relationships competently is what makes business successful.

Many people look to their homes and families, many to their friends, as the intimacy relief from work. I have heard extreme statements such as, "I sell to my company time I take away from my family. That's my idea of business." No sense of results, only time spent. Conversely, people who seek intimacy at work will find themselves rebuffed and will be told that they are "high maintenance." Business is for performing a service, making product, and making money with it. No time for sentimentality. "If you want love, get a puppy!" is the oft-repeated refrain, attributed to Sunbeam's former CEO, "Chainsaw Al" Dunlap.

I think the formula for empathy in business is, first of all, to understand how important empathy is. It also is to recognize at the same time that many people are deprived of intimacy. They grow up with calloused souls. Their distance from others is a necessary adjustment; we know that. But when they finally allow themselves to feel the miracle of intimacy, their souls flood with joy. Feeling lighter, their spirits soar. Permission for intimacy is a relief from the stress of life. Can I allow myself to feel it? Can I believe that it is happening and happening to me? Will I be struck dumb again when I wake up? These are comments that people make who were cool to intimacy.

I think that big business should be prepared to comprehend people on the intimacy level and be able to connect with them in that spirit. To be ready. To be prepared. To be understanding. To be sensitive. But also, one should expect nothing. Giving without expectations of rewards is a splendid thing to do. It is good and it works well. It is the highest form of ethics. Nietzsche called it "radiant virtue."

Caveat: One should never confuse a work relationship with a personal relationship. That is why nepotism is a bad idea, to put it mildly. I think one should use one's competence with empathy to help people, to connect with people, to befriend people, to establish partnerships, to have constructive working relationships. But you must never forget that if there is an exchange of money then you are in the vortex of a business transaction. And these are contractual; at a minimum they are psychological contracts. People have business expectations and these business expectations must be met. Otherwise one person can abuse the other and in the end it will not feel good nor come out right. Multi-role relationships are difficult to sustain. Teacher and principal should not be in a personal relationship. Boss and subordinate should not. Student and teacher should not. It confuses the two and confuses the team.

Prevention and Enlightenment

Preventive care on intimacy problems in business is effective. Discussing these issues in advance will most of the time prevent problems. Recognizing the infinite importance of intimacy and its inappropriateness at work is a heartwarming as well as enlightening conversation for many employees and managers in today's organizations.

To repeat, the ability to conduct Intelligent Leadership Conversations (ILC) with the right people and at the right time on this subject—in the true who, what, where, when, why, how, whether, and which sequence, that is, Strategic Intervention Moments (SIM)—is a prerequisite to both activate and neutralize the intimacy question in the workplace.

In some areas of empathy there is not enough, and in other areas there is too much. To set the balance, to clear the air, to discuss the undiscussibles, those are the solutions to much of the energy drain in the workplace. Opening up these zones for discussion can, as in a nuclear explosion, release enormous quantities of energy and power that could well be put in the service of the organization. The cost impact is equivalent to massive downsizing. But there is neither write-off nor added cost for all the new energy "purchased." This is the power of ILC and SIM, changing the culture by innovating relationships. You are simply harvesting what is already there!

Figure 7.2 is an outline for the change consultant's role.

The consultant's role is to balance empathy: Too much or too little reduces the amount of energy available for constructive work. If the consultant helps to balance this, halting when there is too little or too much empathy, the energy released will add dimensionally to the productivity and the happiness of the team.

Ethics is about people. A major focus today is on how in a competitive, high-tech, fast-moving, and global reality we can build the important sense of community.

Community

We live in an age during which communities and the hoped-for sense of community are threatened and diminishing. Community based on a common space—"My grandparents built this house, my parents were born here, and

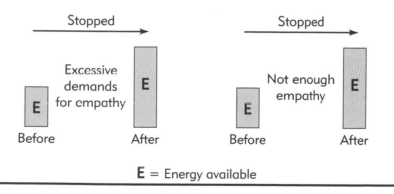

Figure 7.2. Balancing Empathy

so were my sisters and I, and we are still living here today"—is less and less common in an age of global mobility, surfing the net, and e-mail communication. We have instead communities of *interest,* of *meaning,* and of *practice.* We may be members of a community, but its membership changes. Permanent relationships and deep bonding are less likely when community becomes a network and we have membership in many networks.

But look at it this way: When there is no personal contact, 90 percent of what happens between people is lost. Do you want to lose that? The commitment is gone, the feelings are gone. We clearly move from three dimensions to only one. From obtaining information on your account from AT&T and AMEX, to establishing trust between you and your client, you and your boss, you and your employee, the rich sense of neighborliness, family, experiencing the full person, basking in the sun of inclusion, in a word, community, there is a colossal gap. We call it anomie or *alienation.* To be aware of this new phenomenon is part of ethics. To know how to live with it is also part of ethics. And to know how to do business within it is a priority. We have evil, the evil of alienation; we have empathy, the need for human closeness; and we have principle, to do business with integrity given this current cultural state of affairs. We are doing business in a period of history where we redefine the relationship between human purpose and economic purpose.

The voice to community is the most ancient call in the soul of human beings. We are gregarious, we live together, and we need one another's touch. We must feel part of something bigger, more important, older, and more lasting than we, in our fragility and insignificance, in fact are. When Jacob dies, he collects his twelve sons, gives a message to each, and does not literally die, but instead is *gathered to his people.* He returns to the whole from which he had temporarily withdrawn (*Genesis 49*).

Also, we cannot forget that as leadership becomes more pronounced, with increasing degrees of responsibility, it also becomes more lonely. And in some fashion, part of leadership is the choice of insularity and isolation that often is necessary when what Shakespeare calls "the storms of state" weigh heavily down upon our shoulders. The hackneyed Trumanesque expression, "The buck stops here" is not without its profound relevance to the question of community and leadership. People want a family feeling where they work. That is indeed commendable. And leaders who promote that have a good heart. Nevertheless, in business as in politics, you are a member of a community that depends for its existence on how your team is related to the needs of the stock market, and if you lose in the competitive game then you no longer exist as a community, or at best exist only as a decimated community, one with many casualties. So at all times you need to be prepared for the demise of the community that you so passionately desire.

What are we asking of a leader? That this zone of our experience, the continent called ethics, be richly attended by whoever claims leadership capacity. That this person be truly at home in this region, and that anyone in touch with this individual feels that the ethics facet of the Diamond is indeed well taken care of, competently, compassionately, and with commitment.

Are you one of those people? Do you have that reputation? What do you need to do to find out, and beyond that, what needs to happen for you to show through your words and actions that you have given your body and soul to become a person who is concerned non-stop with ethical matters in business?

Service

Ethics for business means *people skills*: What does it require for employees to rate the company high on employee satisfaction? What must occur for employees to say that this organization is a good place to work? How do you let a person go so that the employee nevertheless becomes a good-will ambassador after leaving? What kind of an environment should you be able to offer to prospective recruits so that the best will choose *your* organization? How do you give constructive criticism to people whose performance is slipping? How do you say difficult things about people's behavior and inappropriate language? How do you discuss eliminating whole divisions in your organization—known as "rationalizing"—in a way that feels like love? How do you handle salary requests and salary differences in a way people can accept?

One of the services that business owes to its employees is training in defeat management, not after it comes but before it strikes. And defeat is not only losing a job. Defeat is the many symbolic deaths that occur daily. Any rejection is a symbolic killing. Any "no" has the potential of pointing to the meaning of death.

Helping employees anticipate existential crises, perhaps by revisiting and redefining previous emotional catastrophes in a group setting, can quickly improve the work atmosphere, health, productivity, and loyalty of workers. All people have to learn, sooner or later, that it is impossible to navigate the rapids of life without leadership. And to discover that leadership is mature and healthful and we have the capacity to be leaders and are better off being challenged into leadership than remaining declawed cats indefinitely.

One must add that in human relations, on the empathy side, people want to feel

- Heard,
- Valued, and
- Included.

This adds up to *service*. The healer in you wants to help other people. The help feels good in its own right. Being of service is something you want to do for yourself, knowing thereby that you are a high-quality person.

So much for the soft side. On the tougher side, the principled side, what you offer employees that is of real value to them, to the mature ones you want to cultivate, is

- *Leadership* training, experience, coaching, growth, and, as a result,
- Their own increased *marketability*—both within your company and outside.

Ethics, in the context of leadership coaching, means to have the capacity to engage in discussion of relevant and meaningful topics at moments and opportunities of highest leverage. Ask people, "What do you need from me that you are not getting (Fig. 4.1, p. 65)?" and "What can I do to make it easy for you to answer with confidence?" You thereby give and receive a leverage point. Now is the time for an intelligent leadership conversation about ethics: *What are the ethical needs of the employees and the customers?*

The business value is the human contact that is established, the cooperation that you can expect from people who feel an enhanced sense of community, the good working conditions, and the resulting credibility of management and of the entire organization.

Why Should Anyone Be Ethical?

This is a tough question. We pick up here again the theme of conscience. Every CEO and manager needs to be able to carry out intelligent conversations on ethical issues. This includes the overarching one of why anyone should be ethical. I don't see how anyone can be a leader unless that person can make convincing points on ethical matters. Many answers are suggested in this chapter. There are superficial answers, such as it is the best policy or it brings pleasure and happiness. But there are more sophisticated answers, such as ethics makes a society work, and lack of ethics creates energy-draining conflicts and social and business complications. This is a pragmatic answer. A deep answer is, from the religious point of view, that this is how God constituted the world and it is our task to fall in line, or from the perspective of a more neutral answer, that there are objective standards of right and wrong that our conscience can discover. The bottom line is that to be ethical is to measure our actions by the dictates of our deepest conscience. And the rationale for this decision is not self-seeking but the unique sense of moral obligation—which is not duplicated in any other aspect of life. To understand this sense of obligation, called deontology in philosophy, is the subject of the second element of this chapter. If the motive is pragmatic, we have a different kind of person from one whose motive is simply to do what is right. We leave open for the time being the question of how one determines what is right. It is the attitude, the willingness to act on principle, that characterizes the moral person. Empathy, on the other hand, is deep feeling for the reality of others, it is to live in the soul of another and work for the empowerment of that soul. That is deeply emotional. It can be self-sacrificing. Good leadership is really to understand these two ways of being a good human being, a decent person.

If you have learned to move confidently within the inner world, you will find there the full panoply of empathy. Empathy is much like love. It is difficult to talk about one without the other. (More on deontology in the next chapter.)

Is that hard for managers and consultants to accomplish in the business world? Is that their proper role? To help people operate freely in the inner world so as to understand the deeper meaning of empathy, the kind of empathy they need in order to run a more powerful organization?

Does this focus on empathy apply also to groups? Is attention to the full spectrum of empathy justified in terms of investment and bottom-line considerations? Will the stock market really respond positively to your company's emphasis on empathy? Or is that some kind of rationalization for consultants needing jobs?

These are real issues.

The evidence—collected by the Emotional Intelligence community—clearly points in the direction that attention to empathy is well-correlated with satisfaction surveys and with organizational effectiveness. It doesn't take a rocket scientist to discover that happy people are also easier to work with than resentful and hostile complainers.

All I can say from the point of view of my own personal experience is that virtually all leadership coaching practice, both individual and in groups, sooner or later leads to rather personal topics, often very intimate and highly spiritual themes. And all that happens while I push the business implications, the business applications of philosophical deepening—and not the therapeutic ones. Many times leadership coaching conversations veer in the direction of the study of consciousness and its spiritual aspects, as well as in the direction of how to deal with intimacy, how to find love, and similarly touching and charged topics. People often want to see the question, "How are things in your business?" translated to "How are things in your marriage?" One high-powered, brilliant dot-com executive, who was a whiz at starting and selling companies, making a fortune, never found it interesting to talk about how to run his business, strategically or in terms of culture—he felt he knew this better than anyone—but he insisted instead on talking about his marriage. He had a greedy wife, he said, who wanted him only for his money: sex in exchange for a more generous prenuptial agreement.

Here's another story.

They're the words no one wants to hear from the boss: "We're going to let you go." They can feel like a knife in the chest. You may go numb. Panic. Feel anger flare through your body.

When teacher Tara Harmon recently heard the bad news from the principal at Buck Lake Elementary School in Tallahassee, Florida, she was so stunned she bolted from the office. "I didn't know what to say," said Harmon, the single mother of a fourteen-year-old girl. "I got out of there."

Afterward, she experienced what many people who are laid off go through: grief, anger, depression, self-recrimination, panic.

Counselors say losing a job is similar to getting over a death. (Rauch, 2001)

The Decision to Be Moral

It is not enough to accept that one should be ethical; one has to make a decision to be ethical and one's behavior should reflect that choice.

Leadership starts within, but it is expressed outside. You make a decision to be extroverted, to live in community. You make the added decision to stand up to evil. Now you are a good person. You sustain that decision, you know which of your social contexts support it, and you are on your way to be a reformer. You have indeed re-chosen yourself as a different person. This is both exhilarating and frightening. With this combination in your soul, you are now ready to embark on the life of a person committed to ethics.

Can you feel this? Do you sense the physical exhilaration of making this choice in an ongoing way? Is that how Martin Luther King, Jr., felt during his marches, expecting at any moment, as he led the crowd, that a bullet might pierce his forehead? And being both exhilarated and terrified by this combination of greatness and anxiety?

This is how it feels to be a leader, to make a decision for ethics. Perhaps the example seems exaggerated. But when you look at anything under a microscope, it indeed reveals its truth through exaggeration. This is what these chapters are all about: to invite you to feel what a move from *courage* to *ethics* is all about. As you emigrate from the continent of courage to the land of ethics, you carry the tradition of your place of birth. But your adventures are now elsewhere, in ethics. We shall move specifically to courage later.

> And when we now say to you that ethics is the decision to struggle against evil, and to do it in a community—or with a community, or through a community, somewhat similar to an organization—and that the commitments you need to make are to throw yourself into the life of empathy and then into the life of principle, then you have the formula for what is required to achieve greatness in ethics and manage the polarities that a commitment to ethics entails.
>
> You have arrived. You have clarified who you are. You are at peace with yourself. Your energy level rises. And you are on your way! Congratulations!

Your ability to live in this zone, which makes available to you the entire ethical side of your brain, that is to be able to use this tool, this foundation of who you are and for how you act. And to be at home here, ready at all times to activate this corner, that is part of the armamentarium of your leadership competencies.

The critical step is to realize that precisely because our pure inner freedom is free we are capable of the most sublime and most saintly good and the lowest and most bestial evil. The very existence of civilization—of decency, justice, fairness, respect, considerateness, commitment, help, caring—depends on one thing and one thing only. *It is the decision that we as human beings make to sustain ethical behavior in being, with our very lives if it must be.* It is to search for a moral order in society.

Science is not ethics. Nature is not ethics. Ethics is the human addition. There will be no morality by natural law. There will be no ethics by the laws of the jungle, or any other natural law. These are totally amoral. The kind of world that works is a moral world, a world that acknowledges ethical responsibility and moral courage. And that is a human world. A fully human world. A world that recognizes nobility of spirit, honor, truthfulness, honesty, promises kept, and the absence of betrayal, lies, and deception. And these are choices.

To address these timely issues, these matters so central to all that we call human, that is the role of business for establishing intelligent leadership conversations in ethics, and to redesign all non-ethical or unethical sentences into ethical sentences—with the expectation that behavior, attitude, and character follow.

Changes in attitude, behavior, and character will not follow automatically, but they can be made to follow through an additional, second-level, decision. This is the kind of implementation needed in all businesslike leadership situations.

It is important to make people aware of this philosophical state of affairs. There is no civilization unless we choose civilization. And that is leadership, ethical leadership, leadership in ethics. You cannot force people to be responsible, but you can challenge them to appreciate what it means *not* to be responsible.

What are you doing to deepen your understanding of the meaning of choice and responsibility? Are you talking about this to the right people in your business? Who are the employees in your business who are alienated from intelligent leadership conversations about ethical matters? What are your plans to bring talk about ethics to the sales process, to meetings of the board of directors, to how you handle a problem your client has with your product and service? To damage control? To marketing and advertising? To how you report your quarterly figures?

Empathy deals with emotions, principle with reason. These are two different ways of approaching the world. Both are important, both come up in leadership, and consultants need to discuss intelligently with their clients both orientations. To that we now turn.

CHAPTER 8

Principle and Duty
in Business

"I THINK WE ARE IRRESPONSIBLE, *even corrupt. It hurts me to say this. I think it's true. I didn't think it would come to this, and so early in our working together!" Mary Kay, the new vice president for human resources, has a hard time holding back tears.*

The management committee of a major venture capital company had discussions on investing in sustainability. Up to the arrival of a new human resources executive vice president, a woman with an impressive resume, the issue had never come up. Profitability was virtually the only criterion used. Reference to the environment occurred only if required by investor relations.

After the new VP's arrival, discussions became unpleasantly and uncharacteristically acrimonious. Mary Kay had brought to the meeting reams of what she called proof that investing in environmentally responsible ventures made good financial sense. Most of the others felt it was just a rationalization to bring extraneous values into investment theory. The committee wanted to focus only on financial targets. Surprisingly to the committee, the discussion moved away from finance and toward ethical responsibility. Mary Kay lost her cool. She blurted out, "Sustainability is not merely one among many of our investments. Our entire venture capital company is a wholly owned subsidiary of the environment. Without pleasing the environment, our owners, we are nothing. Don't you get it?"

Risk Deontology

Deontology is the study of *duty*. Not what, specifically, your duty is, but whether being ruled by duty makes sense in the first place, and, if so, how. How can you influence others? How do you find the place of duty in a stock-market governed milieu?

Mary Kay's management committee clearly did not get it—that questions of duty, obligation, and principle are proper questions to entertain in business. Following are real-life examples from business interviews of constructive and positive leadership conversations that make at least indirect reference to *motivation by principle* and are therefore ethics statements of the highest probity:

- "I really don't know what to do in this case. I have struggled hard and long thinking this situation through. I want to be sure that I make the right decision, but it is really hard to know what is the right thing to do."

- "It really hurts me to sign this letter of resignation. But there can be no doubt that it is the right and honorable thing to do. I just must learn to live with the pain of regret."

- "I will endanger my position in this company if I tell it like it is, but that is what I must do. It is also good practice at testing the world for decency. Perhaps if I stand up for decency I will also discover that this is a better world than my cynicism has led me to believe."

- "I read where in a third-world country powerful and high ranking generals have been arrested for corruption in connection with the very profitable drug trade. It takes courage for this nation's attorney general to take such a bold and unprecedented step. He may endanger his own and his family's life by this action, but he is clearly moving his nation forward in statesmanship. I admire this action and only wish I could have the same integrity myself in the face of real danger."

- "In some communities, judges risk assassination for sending high-ranking Mafioso or terrorists to prison. I hope I will never forget that when I have to make an ethical choice. I will measure myself by the very same high standards."

Conscience Is a Real Thing

One of the most neglected aspects of discussions of ethics is the idea of duty. We have forgotten it. It cannot be explained without loss in terms of behavioral science. Duty is a concept from philosophy and theology, from literature and the arts. To be motivated by duty is suspect in today's psychological and scientific atmosphere. And yet, in its own way, it is the responsibility of leadership coaching to revive the concept of duty, obligation, right and wrong—no matter how difficult these concepts might be. For there is a right and a wrong and we all know that there is, even though we differ and even though we are unclear and ambiguous about its exact meaning. The authentic consciousness sees in the distance that there is a right, but cannot make out clearly and unambiguously what exactly it looks like. It is in this cloudy atmosphere that the authentic leader finds the way—or, with risk and anxiety, chooses the way. And nothing is more powerful in human relations than to deal with right and wrong, justice and injustice, obligation and responsibility. That is the muscular hold which ethics has on the human psyche!

To be able to engage in intelligent conversations about principle requires an absolutely fundamental shift in how we think, in what we think about ourselves, and in what we consider to be true value. Suddenly *honor, pride, duty, self-respect, dignity, transparency,* and *truth* become important words. We see their value, we experience the hold that they have on us, we call that sensation of attraction our conscience, and we feel renewed, refreshed, upright, clean, simple, guilt-free. We are not motivated by pleasure nor by avoiding pain, but we are motivated by, we choose on the basis of, what we call right and just and fair and equitable. That is a new way of being. That is the ethical leader, without dogmatism, without arrogance, without being antidemocratic.

We say, "I can look myself in the mirror" and "I can look you squarely in the eye." We feel the human contact. Conscience is a real thing. We feel it. We don't know how we got it. And we have theories about conscience. Some say it is the voice of authenticity, our true nature. Others say it was instilled in early childhood and if misdirected it can damage us. We live with this ambiguity. But the conscience is there, even though it is a mystery, and the leader is the person who copes with that internal reality in an exemplary fashion that is a model to us all.

Violating our conscience obstructs this priceless human contact, for we are not all there, not fully present. And we have the strange feeling of guilt, often unanalyzed, but nagging at the soul nevertheless. To do what our conscience tells us is to be in true touch with another human being. To violate our conscience means we avert our eyes and thereby act out the fact that precious human contact—being one of several members in what we call a single "intersubjective field"—has been broken. That is the issue with adoption—managing the broken connection with the biological parent.

Reason

A philosophy of duty and of conscience, of guilt and of obligation, is often said to be a life governed by reason—by thinking, by logic, bringing the passion under the discipline of the duty of following what is right and calling it the true freedom. There is always the danger of rigidity and fanaticism here, just as there is danger of selfish irresponsibility if we go by our instincts alone. Leaders are the people who can choose the way through this quagmire and who can help others also find the path. This is the part of the journey of life where you are in a jungle and know that you must get out into the clearing, meeting again the open sky.

We have stepped up to a higher realm of existence, and that is the idea of rationality and of reason. Mankind used to think that human beings were governed by reason. Aristotle called a human being a rational animal, rationality being the defining and differentiating characteristic of human beings. Motivation by reason is not automatic; it is a choice to be rational.

The word *reason* directs us to the territory on the Atlas of the mind that, when it comes to ethics, thinks rather than feels. Reason means thinking rather than feeling in human relations, creating arguments and logical sequences rather than going by intuition when it comes to human beings.

You Have a Choice

What are some of the moral choices you have faced in your own life? A client asked me, "Can you work for two companies at one and the same time?" "What's behind this question?" I asked myself. The client went on, "I really owe all my commitment to my original company, and I feel unfaithful moon-lighting with the competition." This question, needless to say, has a strong ethical component. It is the paradox between opportunism and honesty, self-ishness and loyalty.

Another said, "My boss has been really cruel to my colleague. It turns out that it is to my advantage, because we are both salespeople and we compete for results. But it is patently unfair and makes me feel cheap. My boss has a temper. Should I tell him, if ever so diplomatically, that he is not treating my co-worker decently or fairly and that it bothers me? Or should I let it go and simply say business is business and if I now have unfair advantage it will just reverse itself at some other time?"

What these circumstances make clear is that when we choose how to respond to the paradoxes of life, we can choose as motive either passion or principle. And we can choose to lie to ourselves or tell the truth. And we can be reflective or instinctive. The lie would be: "I am unhappy in my job, espe-cially the pay, and I have a right to moonlight with the competition and look for something better. I need the extra income, for I do not get paid enough and I have a family to support." But you know in your heart of hearts that this answer is cowardly; it bypasses principle, no matter how hard you try to convince yourself that you have a case. You do not have the courage to admit that you choose to act unethically. You are face-to-face with principle as a key ethical dimension.

Being motivated by principle makes you into a very different kind of human being than if you were motivated by passion. The difference is a choice, a choice you make. Our alternatives are always four: (1) we chose A over B, (2) we choose B over A, (3) we choose to find a higher synthesis, or (4) we choose to be blind to the situation (we call it "denial"). Leaders under-stand this and are clear and articulate about the choices they make.

My point here is not to pontificate that you should choose on principle rather than passion. My point is that leaders be aware of this possibility and take responsibility for the decisions they make, own them, and acknowledge the wider implications of such a choice, namely, credibility. You do not look around for the effect you get, but you use an inner guidance system.

England's assistant prime minister gets hit point blank with an egg. The minister immediately reacts with an uppercut on the chin of the assailant. Later he apologizes. An immediate emotional reaction, a subsequent rational choice. But a choice is involved in both cases, just a different kind of a choice. How does a leader respond? With emotion or reason? Can you see that it is a choice?

You anticipate events like these and make an early choice about them. A leader has contingency plans for ethical dilemmas. Choosing in the moment is often decidedly not wise.

Atrocities have been committed in Africa, in Afghanistan, in the Middle East, in Kosovo, and in Bosnia—and right next door to where you live.

As a nation, do we choose to release our emotions in the face of this abuse, these atrocities? Do we attack the perpetrators and avenge the victims? Or do we choose to strategize a rational policy on how to react?

Do we calculate potential casualties? Do we assess the effects on the economy? Do we determine what precedent we will set, how national politics will react? Or do we ask what is the right thing to do for the suffering people?

These are choices: based on passion and outrage, based on business, based on world politics, or based on moral principle. We need to understand these distinctions, we need to make a choice among them, we need to take responsibility for how we choose, and we need to see clearly the empathy issues and the principle issues in the dimension of ethics in the leadership mind.

There is no ultimate right or wrong. This is how you choose. And there are the consequences. You are condemned to choose, and your fate is to be responsible for the consequences that ensue, for these consequences are events in the world and your fingerprints are all over them.

In one sense, there is no right or wrong. In another sense, this statement is ignominiously false! If all is based on choice, then there is no absolute right or wrong. And yet, we *can* choose immorally—as we believe that Saddam Hussein has done. We *are* responsible and we *do* have a conscience, and answers vary and differ, and yet we have powerful convictions. One thing to say here is that we have touched a toxic, radioactive paradox and polarity, one that is unsustainable—yet unavoidable! And we may have to leave it at that. . . ! If we can get to dialogue, that will, of course, help. This is the paradox facing people in a democracy, where tolerating differences is key and where, at the same time, vigorously moral convictions and uncompromising ethical stands are expected.

Psychology and Hidden Agendas

The problem with all this nobility of spirit is that, with the advent over one hundred years ago of Freud and his entourage, we have become heavily ingrained with the idea of the unconscious. It is the view that the ultimate governing factor of human existence is not something that we can meaningfully call reason, but that it is something that is more basic, more fundamental, more real than reason. Reason becomes the wall behind which feelings and primitive impulses hide. So the ground on which humanity stands is the irrational unconscious—concrete and basic thinking, primitive ideation, the kind one gets in mythology, like Medea killing her sons to avenge her husband Jason's infidelity, or Oedipus killing his father and marrying his mother in fulfillment of the prophecy—and not the product of centuries of rational calculations and analyses. This indeed is primal stuff!

But we can also choose to reverse that.

In truth, our choice is neither rational nor irrational. It is *pre-rational.* We choose whether to be rational or irrational; we choose whether to promote our rational faculty and live according to its dictates, or whether to choose to abandon ourselves to our irrational unconscious, or not even make the effort to be aware of it.

In the latter case our ground is reason, and reason then discovers the unconscious. It does not matter what our final metaphysics looks like. What does matter is that we can choose to build a human enterprise based on rational choices, choices rooted in a fundamental principle, such as equality. This means that I do not make an exception of myself when it comes to a universal rule that we need to establish in order to have a working society and transparent relationship bonds among people.

"Archetypal Choices"

What is required of us at this moment is to understand what it is like to make the archetypal choice to base our life on reason and then act on it by searching for a universal principle of morality, such as the Golden Rule, or by the processes of democratic institutions, and then abiding by it. It is a central factor in how the mind of a leader functions, or can function, or should function.

The crux is to take full responsibility for the direction of our choices. And the anxiety—and the guilt—is in the strange feeling of being one's own foundation. If you feel strongly about religion, that God is your ground and that God will take care of you, you nevertheless always find, on introspective examination, congeries of choices and free decisions at the root of everything you say, do, feel, and think. You *choose* to believe in God. You *choose* to surrender your soul to the experiences you have surrounding religion. Billy Graham at the end of his sermons always challenged his huge audiences to *come forward and make a decision for Christ.*

Such a shift, from non-reason to reason, has great impact on credibility, on personality, on trust, on predictability, on respect, and on the willingness to be followed. It often lacks passion, for passion may be a substitute for thought. Thought has its own form of power: persuasion.

Take a look at Figure 8.1. Are you comfortably ensconced at level A? Do you own the decisions that you are making in that zone? Do you manage the anxiety and the guilt? Do you choose to define these primordial feelings (anxiety and guilt) as cognitive states and as the normal concomitants of success? Can you describe the two different kinds of personality and life that follow from either choice? Can you alternate? How do you weave this polarity into your leadership presence?

Duty Matters

Ethics in life and ethics in business may be your most important concerns. All else follows. That is where every businessperson finds definitive dignity and ultimate self-respect. Change begins right here at this nerve center of everything that is real. The change consultant needs to be right at this juncture for both the CEO and the lowliest employee.

In life, duty matters. And duty is based on thinking more than on feeling. Ethics is not just doing what feels good nor is it enshrined in the banal homily

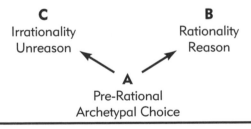

Figure 8.1. Archetypal Choices

that "honesty is the best policy." Ethics is rooted in the foundation of this universe, namely, the basic act of freedom, from cosmic to individual.

And to express all that in the way you conduct your business—realizing that the economy is the fulcrum of our lives as a society and as persons—with the support of a trained OD cadre—is really all there is to say about the change and the innovation that today's prophets proclaim with such strident vehemence.

What Is the Face of an Ethical Workplace?

What pays off in business—ruthlessness or rectitude, conniving or compassion, indifference or inclusiveness? How many times have you felt that pursuing the path of ethics, far from being effective in financial terms, does no more than make you look like a dunce? What about Robert Ross, fugitive from the IRS, living "the good life" on the lam? "Hell, these last twenty years have been the happiest of my life. This is paradise here," he says from Belize (Fritsch, 2001).

Does the question really matter? Is it not true that in the end being ethical is more important than being rich? How does that ethical truism show itself in your business? How do you synthesize business and ethics?

The general implication of ethics for business is that you cannot do good business in a non-ethical atmosphere, and the more ethical the atmosphere is with which you surround yourself the easier and more successful will it be to conduct your business. In simplest terms, an ethical society is a society that works. And a society that works makes it smooth for business. An ethical society is one with laws and with equity. It is where people keep their promises. Where they know what is expected. Where transactions are transparent. Where human beings are connected, can talk to each other, be understood, and feel in touch. That is a society that works. Energy is spent on constructive building, not on defensive maneuvers that distract from the goals and alienate people from each other who instead should cooperate.

Here are six themes to consider when assessing the impact of ethics and morality, integrity and principle, on the successful conduct of a business.

1. Maturity

A person who naturally has a high regard for ethics in all aspects of life, private and public, is generally a good person to have around: trustworthy, reliable, safe, predictable, someone not to be feared but to be loved, not to be resented but welcomed.

2. Emotional Restraint

Ethical and rational people take care of their own feelings. One of the meanings of maturity is that people are aware that whenever you put groups of human beings together and expect them to work together, under often stressful conditions, unpleasant emotions will naturally surface. The common tendency regrettably is to blame others and to take it out on the innocent. To take care of your own feelings means to add a rational superstructure that then deals with your emotions professionally and objectively. But *you* do it. *You* initiate it. And you do it to yourself and for yourself, and it leads to cleaner relationships in the business environment. You are that superstructure. That's where the merit lies.

3. Rational Democracy

Rational democracy refers to a civic and governmental structure of reason, justice, fairness, equity. Political science theories are like that, such as the social contract theory. Rather than acting out emotions, good governance is based on fairness, on the conviction that difficult decisions, career moves, pain, and sacrifice are all imposed not with partiality or favoritism, not dishonestly or opportunistically, but with consummate fairness and justice. Then there are no complaints. Then there are good feelings.

But this is a highly rational and ethical activity, that is, principled, detached from the outbursts of emotions. No one feels neglected or short-changed. No one feels rejected. Everyone is included. And the stark reality is distributed among all with equity. When people feel that society works, the personality works, relationships work, and even the endocrine, immune, and psychoneurological systems of the body are in better functioning shape. This is how ethics, reason, and business are connected, invariably.

4. Motivation

There is a correlation between ethical motivation and maturity. It is important to ascertain what the motives are for people's ethical behavior. For the level of elevation of the motive is correlated with the general quality and grown-up behavior of the person. It is also an excellent measure of overall health, and, as a result, of leadership capacity and performance. Here is a scale of ethical motivation:

Why do people "not steal"?

a. The police may catch them.

b. They may go to jail.

c. They may lose face. It is an embarrassment to be caught.

d. They do it out of respect for others, to help institute a more civilized society, to generate trust among human beings as the most prudent way to relate.

e. The motive follows from accepting a higher principle of morality, such as "pursue, especially in legislation, the greatest good for the greatest number," which is utilitarianism, or "treat your neighbor as you yourself would like to be treated," which is the Golden Rule.

As people move from "a" to "e" on this scale they also tend to be more mature in other respects: more intelligent, kinder, more successful, more respected, more trusted, more accepted as leaders. People will value them because they are *fair*.

Ethics is like a holograph. Honesty is the visible surface of a larger professionalism. It leads to confidence and thus to good business.

5. Ethical Public Relations

When talking of the importance of ethics for business, we cannot overlook the critical role of public relations (PR), the public image, especially of politicians and corporations. The concept of PR requires analysis, for it always raises the question of honesty. Public relations is tailored to the audience, based on polls, stated in sound bytes, and therefore invariably superficial.

Of particular importance in our culture is the unqualified incorruptibility of ministers and doctors. That is why when ethical lapses occur, as they have recently in the priesthood, it is so profoundly upsetting to the population.

Of course, ethical principles apply also to a high degree to teachers, brokers, lawyers, and bankers. And then of course to business in general. A corrupt ethical image is certainly the downfall of reputable businesses.

6. Laws

The key to doing business in developing countries and in much of today's Eastern Europe is the need for laws. And laws are principles of human interaction. The wisdom of a law lies in its application. The law needs to be applied evenly and equally and consistently. Then you can do business. Otherwise you are in a maelstrom. You need reason at work, ethics in business as a commercial necessity. That is the value of the law.

> The basis of it all is this: Ethics is good business, but it is only good business if the motive is principle and not opportunism, that is, regardless of whether it is or leads to good business. This is paradoxical. But that only proves it is true to life.

◆ Activity

The point of these chapters on ethics has been to make people conscious of the importance of that subject and to call attention to the experiences that, in organizations and in the inner self alike, give rise to the magnetic power of ethical norms. The big themes in these chapters were evil, empathy, principle, community, duty, and choice.

You can monitor what is happening regarding ethics in your organization by using this fifteen-item questionnaire for yourself and for a representative sample of your employees and customer populations.

The scoring scheme is based on the following five-point scale:

(1) I strongly disagree (1 point)

(2) I disagree (2 points)

(3) I neither agree nor disagree (3 points)

(4) I agree (4 points)

(5) I strongly agree (5 points)

As you read each item below, assign to it the appropriate number from the scale based on your response.

_____ 1. There have been no significant ethical lapses in our company.

_____ 2. Our top executives frequently refer to the importance of values in making this company great.

_____ 3. This emphasis on values in our company is particularly evident during hard times.

_____ 4. Our company has the reputation on the market that customers can trust our promises.

_____ 5. Most of our people feel that our employees are being treated fairly.

_____ 6. When discussing our company with outsiders, the expressions "the people in this company are decent" and "you can count on them" come readily into the conversation.

_____ 7. We are confident that the people of this company, when asked, "Why does it make sense for you to be ethical?" are able to give meaningful answers.

_____ 8. We are the defendants in fewer lawsuits than the competition.

_____ 9. We initiate fewer legal actions than the competition.

_____ 10. We are proud of how conscientiously our company adheres to the basic ethical laws on diversity, sexual harassment, the environment, and disclosure.

_____ 11 Our company has an effective ethics office.

_____ 12. Our company has a hot line where people can speak freely and in confidence about their concerns. They receive sound advice.

_____ 13. In our company, management "walks its talk." Our culture is such that executives model what they preach.

_____ 14. Our company's ethical performance, like that of Johnson & Johnson during the famous Tylenol crisis, is recognized by the media.

_____ 15. Our company's best employees stay here because they see that this is a good place to work.

Interpretation

      61 and above: very good

      46 to 60: acceptable

      31 to 45: start worrying

      30 and below: company needs help!

Considering some of the answers you received to the above questionnaire, what strategies and actions are appropriate in order to develop more ethical awareness in your company?

What is the relationship in your company between ethical awareness and economic measures?

Give an example of an ethical decision your company made that cost money—a case where ignoring ethics would have added results to the bottom line.

In order to be ethical we need *courage*. To that we now turn.

COURAGE

These are times in which genius would wish to live. It is not in the still calm of life, or in the repose of a pacific station, that great challenges are formed. . . . Great necessities call out great virtues.

ABIGAIL ADAMS

For the whole earth is the sepulchre of famous men and their story is not graven only on stone over their native earth but lives on far away without visible symbol woven into the stuff of other men's lives.

PERICLES

One man with courage makes a majority.

BLACK HAWK

I can't overemphasize the need for accountability. Without it, growth doesn't take place. Accountability provides the structure for growth and development. . . . Recognize that the negative connotations of accountability—that it's the whip used by sadistic managers to torture employees—are false. In fact, when managers don't hold their people accountable, they're abandoning them, and nothing could be more cruel than that action. In every organization, accountability provides an essential function: shaping individuals as they grow, develop, and form as responsible adults.

MORRIS R. SHECHTMAN

One is not born a woman, one becomes one.

SIMONE DE BEAUVOIR

Life shrinks or expands in proportion to one's courage.

ANAIS NIN

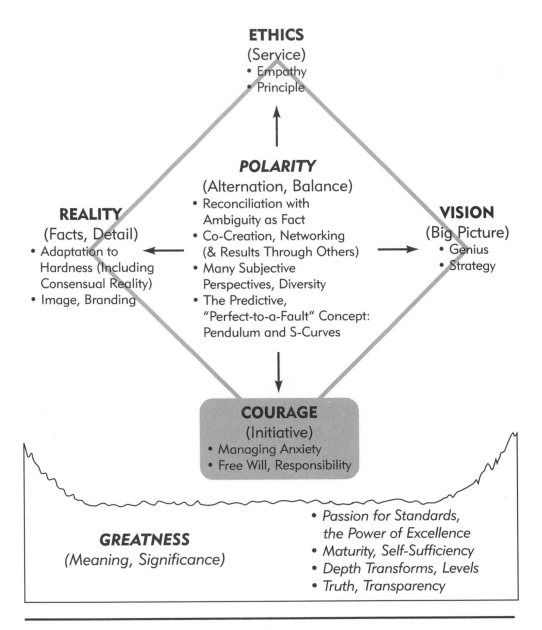

Figure 9.1. The Leadership Diamond®: Courage

CHAPTER 9

What Is Courage?

DEFINITION: Initiative, Self-Starter

ELEMENTS: Anxiety, Free Will

O N THE JOURNEY OF OUR LIFE *we have now reached the warrior. We draw heavily on the inner world: free will, freedom, guilt, anxiety, personal responsibility, and the like. And we learn how to speak the language of courage.*

In our heroic journey, courage is the warrior, the action zone of the total leadership personality. After you have it all figured out, the time has come to call on the warrior to start the action, to make the commitment for implementation of strategy. You are careful not to overdo courage at the expense of another helper. It may silence the seer. But not enough courage takes away support from the seer when it comes to action.

Courage is the capacity be to a self starter, to take the initiative, to take charge, to know that everything starts with you, to be prepared to take the plunge. These are not really capacities; they are choices of who you are and what you do. The opposite is spinelessness, cowardice, cold feet, acting out of fear, lack of boldness, lack of daring, unwillingness to live on the edge, going through life with your tail between your legs. That attitude is the enemy. That is the Shadow Diamond, what we guard against.

In the following discussions on courage our goal is to extol and give a hearing to the experiences of choice, free will, personal responsibility, managing guilt and anxiety, and knowing what it means to take bold steps into uncharted territories. It is to be expected that a trip through the geography of courage will change your life and the way that you do business and armor you to face change as a victor and not a loser.

The Structure of Courage

> Consultants gain credibility with leaders and become change
> agents if they learn to talk better, more profoundly, and more
> persuasively than the competition about the deep structure of
> courage.

In order to understand courage, you must become familiar with its two subtypes: anxiety and free will. That is how change is accomplished. The shadow side of anxiety is to fear fear, to seek security above all else, to lack confidence that you can handle frightening circumstances. And the shadow of free will or freedom is encapsulated in Erich Fromm's (1994) classic book, *Escape from Freedom,* which was first published early during WW II. That is the conviction that you have no power but are totally at the mercy of forces outside of yourself. This makes you forever subservient, a vassal, a person without dignity or pride.

Table 9.1 presents a summary of courage, anxiety, and free will.

The big questions in courage are how to define and understand responsibility and accountability, how to challenge people to consider the needs of the

Table 9.1. Courage

Deep Structure with Subsets	What It Is/Definition/ Description	The Shadow Against Which We Fight
Courage	Being a self-starter, taking the initiative, ready to live on the edge; action—when the inner world intersects with the outer world; "throwing" yourself into your body and your social role; herein resides your crucial sense of responsibility	Paralyzing obsession with security; extreme fear of daring; depression and inaction—when the inner world doesn't venture into the outer world
Anxiety	The shaking of the foundations; the dizzying but necessary medium for growth; the crazy-making transition interval from dead past to living future	Repression of feelings and of self-affirmation, the fear of giving voice to who you are; denying the tragic sense of life
Free will	Empty and ungrounded spontaneity, choosing hope over depression, morality over opportunism, vigor over ennui, civilization over barbarism	Escape from freedom and from responsibility; passing-the-buck mentality; remaining a dependent child forever; never going past innocence

whole, and how to keep promises. There can be no civilized interaction nor can there be business in the first place if these ingredients are lacking. Numerous surveys of managers and executives on their essential needs boil down, it seems, always, to the same, "I want people who hold themselves accountable, keep their promises, and consider in their decisions the needs of the whole organization. You give me people like that, and we are bullet-proof, having no competition." As the chorus in a folk song, this refrain never changes.

Responsibility occurs when free will, clothed with the mantle of anxiety (both are inner phenomena) crosses the line and ventures into the outer world, the realm where business is conducted. That is a special feeling, the sense of embodiment—being a body, but not just *any* body, but *your* body—the sensation of being sucked toward the edge, where the soul is seized, gripped amid a lion's jaws, with the galvanizing mystery of risk.

This may be excessive language, but it is about the anxiety that lurks underground when you allow yourself to deepen your self-discovery.

Radical Freedom

We begin our discussion of freedom with an insight.

Descartes, by doubting everything, ended with certainty. He argued that if he cast aside any belief that he could possibly doubt, whatever was left would be the undoubtable truth. He came up with his famous "I think, therefore I am," which then formed the basis of what is commonly known as "modern" philosophy. He built a world on this foundation, complete with God at the center. It gave a subjective turn to subsequent thinking. Actually, he reconstructed common sense. So that we don't see a different world after philosophic analysis. What we do have is the same world, but now demonstrated logically.

In contemporary philosophy, this negative to positive transition is stated not in conceptual terms but in emotional terms. The negative is anxiety, and the positive product is courage, or what comes out of courage, after it. Anxiety proves the need for courage, and courage enables us to transform pain into meaning. The human enterprise begins with freedom and free will. But we do it. We act. We choose. This is the final payoff that applies to knowing about courage in leadership.

It is as difficult as it is important to understand the role of free will and responsibility in life. And the position is radical. The United States is founded on two fundamental documents: the Declaration of Independence and the Constitution. The Declaration of Independence is the theme of the independent, isolated, unique individual: "All men are endowed by their creator with certain unalienable rights." The Constitution is the theme of the system, the family, the culture, society, and community: "In order to form a more perfect union."

Similarly, the two great intellectual movements of the 20th Century were systems thinking and existentialism. Systems thinking makes community the central paradigm for understanding human beings in their world, and existentialism makes the isolated individual the final explanatory principle of existence.

In business, the conflicts are seen in terms of the individual and the team, that is, the person and the company. For today's workers, the insoluble conflicts are change and stability, short-term versus long-term, family versus career, and so forth. The truth, of course, is on both sides. Choosing sides is unfair. Integration is impossible. We learn to live with paradox. Therein lies maturity and adulthood. And the success we experience as individuals and in our organizations depends on how well we manage the stress of these contradictions.

Courage is the existential pole, the side of free will and responsibility. And the differentiating criterion is anxiety. If I surrender to the culture, the culture will take care of me, I feel secure, and my anxiety is low. But if I stand out as an individual, then I must take care of myself, I feel insecure, and my anxiety is high—but I am my own person!

Let us see if we can experience together as it were the power of freedom, the nobility of uniqueness, and the dignity of independence. There are *culture* audits. Let us here, however, embark instead on a *personal responsibility* audit. There is whole-scale *system* change. Let us talk about whole-scale *individual* change. The following sections fulfill the role of a *personal* responsibility audit and a whole-scale *individual* change program in the context, however, of organizations. For in business today it is the organization that matters, that receives the attention, and where we search for change and results.

Extreme Accountability

One thing that has struck me in consulting is that people of high responsibility, those who clearly feel that the buck stops with them, tend to be people of courage. Each finds his or her own way of managing the anxiety of facing disagreeable situations. But on average they do face them. One leader faces a town hall meeting of angry employees. The options so generously bestowed only a year ago have now turned out to be worthless. The boss is called on to defend controversial actions, like spending too much on perks for the top brass. Others face irate stockholders. Someone can threaten them for not firing an employee they have decided must be let go. To most people, these are scary situations. Being a leader means finding ways to swallow the anxiety and act calmly and correctly in the face of situations that would give rubber knees to other people. Many leaders handle this well, but some avoid these confrontations at all costs.

> I have never met a successful executive who was not also totally sold on the idea of freedom, freedom inside and freedom to be used on the outside. "The responsibility is mine." "The initiative is mine." These axioms, uttered with pride, are etched on their brains and coursing through their veins. "I am wired that way," several of them said.

But how do they reinforce this experience? And how do they pass it on? There is nothing else to do in leadership than to promote freedom, its pains and its joys.

For leadership and organization development coaches and consultants, inviting their clients to intelligent leadership conversations about courage becomes then the high priority. No change occurs unless leaders take bold steps. Kierkegaard said it well, "To dare is to lose one's footing momentarily. To not dare is to lose oneself."

Leaders, when selecting consultants and coaches, will ask themselves about risk. Some want people in their organizations to be encouraged to risk. It is an aggressive personality trait much valued in business circles. But sometimes only lip service is given to it. Consultants need to teach the skill to choose risking. To say it's not safe to risk in a company is still a self-contradictory statement.

◆ Activity 1

Think of how anxiety and free will are connected when someone is faced with these facts of organizational life:

- You and your partner have established a thriving business. You no longer get along. You have a week in which you can still decide whether to buy out your partner or accept the offer for your partner to buy you out. Your decision will affect dramatically your and your family's future: in debt but owning a good business or without the business but with funds. Which will it be?

- Your company is bringing out a new hand-held computer with many times the features of the current best seller. Research shows the market for hand-held computers is drying up. The up-front investment is one-half billion dollars. If you win, your company will recover its number one position. If you lose, you go into Chapter 11. Which way will you decide?

What keeps *you* awake at night, anxious and worrying? What *is* this act of courage that *your* business demands of you?

1. Describe the objective facts of your situation.

2. What are your feelings, your emotions?

3. Can you realistically project into the future and actually "taste" the various consequences of your decision now? Describe at least three of these alternative scenarios and what they feel like? Can you live with each of them?

4. Can you see the fork in the road ahead? Can you tell the difference between avoiding the anxiety of the decision and riding on that anxiety as if it were a wave and you a surfer?

5. Have you "learned your lesson"? Will you avoid responsibilities in the future that place you into a corner where you have to make decisions for which you are damned if you do and damned if you don't?

6. What kind of conversation, what type of dialogue, if any, would help you move past the anxiety of making choices?

7. How might your struggle with these questions help you become a better leader?

The Fourth "R"

I was teaching in Peter Block's former School for Managing and Leading Change. One of the teams in attendance was the local fire department, the chief and his direct reports. Their project was to teach courage in junior high school. They showed the class a film they had made, integrating the teachings into their work. The film showed the chief at a junior high school. And did he get attention wearing his uniform and his hard hat, accompanied by his fire truck, sirens, and a collection of impressive firefighting paraphernalia dangling from his thick belt! What did he talk about? He told the youngsters that they have inside a gyroscope, a directional guidance system, that will always steer them in the right path—no drugs, responsible study habits, and so on. And there would be times when they had no friends, perhaps not even at home, and would feel totally alone.

They are not alone, he assured them. There is a voice inside that says, "I value you and I love you." An inner voice that comes to your rescue when you feel lost. It tells you that you are important. It tells you that you are meant to be in this world. Someday you will remember that voice of inner strength. You will call it up and you will be reassured by it. It will give you confidence, faith, and hope. He said he himself had many times in his life found the need to call on this inner voice to give him strength and stability. He learned about it in his youth from a minister, a very religious man. But he said it worked also for people of different religions. He had promised his minister that if it worked for him he would pass it on. Well, he is giving the same gift to the children today that he received when he was their age. He kept his promise. I hope you will pass it on as well to those who need it.

What an impression he made! That is teaching leadership philosophy in a way that makes it stick.

Regrettably, in business we tend to reserve this topic of inner courage for the outer world alone. But freedom of the will is a resource of the inner world. We have fallen into the materialistic fallacy: We believe the outer world is more real and important than the inner. For example, one of the major issues that business has been asked to address is the problem of water and air quality. U.S. businesses, by law, are required to invest in keeping a clean environment, something that cuts heavily into profits and into global competitiveness.

This problem exists in the outer world. But only a shift in motivation, changing the will in the inner world, can bring about any concerted effort to change this menacing outer reality with which business is charged.

> Outer action requires using inner resources.
>
> *The individual's inner free responsibility for the outer perfor-*
> *mance of the whole—not as a mere value but as an irreversible*
> *fact—is perhaps the single most sensitive bit of knowledge that*
> *exists for the future of mankind.*
>
> Not teaching this in the schools is a dangerous omission.
> Adding it to the three R's—comprehensive responsibility for the
> whole being the fourth—is education's inevitable new wave.

◆ Activity 2

Take a quick survey. Create a five-point scale. Measure people with respect to your perception of their commitment to the welfare of a larger whole, where the latter can be their family, their team, their company, their organization, the city, the nation, a charity . . . or the world.

Note how this mindset has affected the "life-world" that they have created for themselves. And also look at what they might have lost as a result.

What messages does this thought experiment have in it for you and your business?

◆ Activity 3

You have hurt someone's feelings. How do you respond?

1. You don't even notice it.

2. You notice it and feel bad but say nothing.

3. You overcome both your insensitivity and/or ignorance and your anxiety to raise the issue—and you acknowledge your mistake or misjudgment and you apologize for it. Perhaps you accompany your words with a small gift, such as an appropriate thoughtful book, something that doesn't carry with it a hidden agenda.

This last response consists of small acts of courage. Now, consider these questions:

- What are the business implications of your behavior in the areas of morale, credibility, removing stress, motivation, loyalty, and customer relations?

- Can you see the value of turning mere factual conversations into courage dialogues? Instead of saying, "I am depressed," say, "I choose not to fight my depression." Instead of saying "I have had bad luck," say, "I have not yet chosen to compensate for my bad luck." Instead of "My boss will not give me a bonus," say "I have not yet chosen to figure out how to sell my boss on the idea of giving me a bonus." The trick is to bring everything back to an understanding of the personal power and personal responsibility that free will gives you in every leadership situation.

When we talk about *courage* we talk about the need to stand our ground with another human being, the willingness to risk, and to live with the feeling of vulnerability and uncertainty. Moreover, we deal specifically with the sense of free will at the seat of the soul and the host of negative feelings, threats, especially anxiety, that surround that tender and yet powerful free will at the core of our being.

CHAPTER 10

Freedom

The Structure of the Experience

The God who gave us life, gave us liberty at the same time.
THOMAS JEFFERSON

W E DISTINGUISHED EARLIER BETWEEN TWO WORLDS *of leadership. If we exclude attention to the inner world, then all our talk about courage and anxiety and free will comes to naught. Free will exists in the inner world, and it is our life's task to make it operational in outer space. Science tells us that in the outer world, free will makes no sense. Everything is causative. Fine. So be it. But it does make sense in the inner world. Free will is an insight, a discovery in the inner self, the intimate ego.*

Courage, anxiety, free will—and all their many cognates—express states of mind in which inner freedom tries to step out into the world and become efficacious literally on the other side of being. This is the fundamental experience of maturity, of realizing that unless you live on the edge you are not really a leader.

How Does It Feel to Be Free?

"You are responsible, you are accountable, it is up to you, it is in your hands, we met the enemy and it is us, it's no one's fault but our own, we should have known better, we had it coming. . . ." You hear this talk today.

When I was younger, psychology dominated the language. The language of choice was not yet in the popular culture. It was rather the language of escaping responsibility. It was always "your mother, your father, your family, how you were wired, how you were brought up, what your teachers taught you, the society at large, what everybody did." And on and on. It was never up to me, it was never my doing, it was always something in my childhood that conditioned me and caused my behavior.

Today, you never leave an airplane without the pilot or purser thanking you for choosing that airline. "We know you have a choice," they say, "and we appreciate your choosing us." The language has changed.

Freedom and choice, responsibility and accountability have entered our common vocabulary. That is good. The question is, do people in business and in the professions understand experientially what these words mean, to what in human experience they refer? Can they talk intelligently, that is, informatively and persuasively, about these inner territories of the soul? Are they aware of the correlations between understanding freedom and performance on the job? Being results-oriented—"We will correct the absentee problem in this plant"—is to take personal and free responsibility for achieving those results.

To be free, you must know how to claim your freedom. When are you free? What do you do with this state? To think you are free because you use the word "freedom" does not mean to comprehend that freedom is more important than life itself.

The fulcrum of leadership is freedom. Leadership begins with your unshakeable conviction—and feeling—that you are in charge of your life, that you are responsible for your actions, that you are accountable for the consequences of your deeds, intended or not. This shows in how you walk, talk, and present yourself. It shows in how you look others in the eye, how you stand up to stress, and how you are gentle when you reproach someone. You smile when others despair. You are relaxed when others panic. You always do something, plan something, envision something. You do not wait for chance, and you do not hold off for fate to take over. And you are prepared—to win but also to lose.

As you live you also choose. And as you choose you create around you a world that moves when you move and is still when you are still. It is as if the people and things surrounding you are attached to you—and to each other—by rods. And as you shift, they shift with you. The world responds to you. If you are Napoleon or Caesar, a top executive or political leader, your slightest move will have a major impact, and you are aware of that. You have mass and weight, and the world reacts to that. To a lesser degree and in secret ways, it is always like that—for you and for us all. This is good and this is bad, for it shows that your impact is greater than you may know and wish, and that your limits, likewise, are more confining than you had realized and you would want.

This is how it feels to be free. That is the experience of freedom. It is exactly the same as the experience of responsibility. And accountability is simply the public version of it. The world expects it. Consequences, punishments, rewards. Those are the operative words. Living in that zone of the mind and integrating the reality of that move into the way you do business is how your new leadership powers will arise.

Images of Freedom

We are a consciousness. We are free. There are images that can help us understand what it means to be free.

Words

Cognates of freedom are important. A short list follows:

- Will

- Free will

- Owning, owning the consequences of a free action

- Responsibility

- Accountability

- Choosing accountability

- Being grounded

- Being centered

- Rooted

- Serene

- Imperturbable

- Bulletproof

- Hardy

- Sturdy

- Independent

- Being a self-starter

- Autonomous

- Self-authenticating

This may be a lot of words, but they create an image, an awareness, that locates the zone of our free will. They are all good words and they are power words. Use them freely. Understand what they mean. Feel the passion they generate. Pass them on. Offer them as gifts. Be humble.

Freedom as an Organ

The freedom in you is like a bodily organ, like a stomach or a liver. It is not enough for you to think this. You need to *feel* it, it needs to become biological, part of your physiology, the pedestal on which your body stands. It needs to become integrated into the system of which you are a part.

Talk like this, think like this, feel like this, have this attitude, exhibit this behavior, teach this, connect this with your business, be like this with your customers, and you will be empowered—the world around you will welcome your impact! This is the power of freedom.

Crashing Freedom

The only Nobel Prize winner ever to turn down the honor was the French philosopher of freedom, Jean-Paul Sartre. In his play *The Flies* he puts the experience of freedom this way:

> I am free. . . . Freedom has crashed down on me like a thunderbolt. . . . I am free. Beyond anguish beyond remorse. Free. . . . Suddenly, out of the blue, freedom crashes down on me and swept me off my feet. . . . I knew myself alone, utterly alone in the midst of this well-meaning little universe of yours. I was like a man who's lost his shadow. And there was nothing left in heaven, no right or wrong, nor anyone to give me orders. (Sartre, 1992)

What do you think of Sartre's testimony? What does it do to you and for you? Is it beneficial or can it be harmful? Does it give you hope, self-assurance, and power, or does it weaken you and perhaps even seem irrelevant? I think it can turn your life around, to be in charge and to teach others—"help others learn" is better—how to also be in charge themselves.

We Not Only Choose, We Also Choose to Choose

Where are you in this part of your journey of life, the part that discovers the enormity of your freedom, its blessings and its agonies?

Deep choices are not made logically, in a calculating way, but by the unconscious, the intuitive faculty. Nor can they be rushed to "closure." If you are not ready to make a decision, then you just won't make a decision, no matter how hard you try to make it. And if you do actually find the power to make one against your instincts, you will have made a serious error, similar to having a psychotic break. You have engaged in an "unnatural" act. Deep choices require dialogue. For as we think and talk and journal about choosing, the reality that surrounds us and in the context of which we must choose also changes.

Deep choices require the willingness to risk, which means to tolerate the anxiety and commit to the tenacity of improvising, of having the faith that we can make the decision succeed. We never have all the facts. And anyway the facts change, right as we choose. Making a decision is more a matter of displaying faith in ourselves.

We always need to ask, "What can we learn from history to apply to our own life and our own business?"

We look at big decisions, like the Gulf War or a trillion-dollar tax cut, in order to understand better our own. As we see from war and taxes, to make a decision is to choose to continue to choose as we have. And that is where persistence in the experience of freedom and free will make all the difference. I go to war; I must see it through. Going to war is easy. Seeing it through is the baptism of fire. Buying a company is easy. Making the acquisition work tests your true leadership mettle. Making a sale for a decade of IT storage services is hard enough, but delivering the services over that period of time in a referenceable way is where true leadership authenticity shows. The soul first chooses and then it chooses to continue to choose in the same manner. Here is where a strong philosophy of freedom is of the essence.

Unconscious Freedom

After all this praise for free will, we must also be open to the fact that free will is an illusion. Not because of logical contradictions between scientific causation and intuitive spontaneity, but because of the insight and intuition that follow from direct experience. We cannot contradict the idea of the primacy of free will, the pure spontaneity, the pure self-start, the sense of absolute initiative, that "I did it!" None of that can be denied.

However, look back on important and difficult decisions you may have confronted:

- Where to go to college
- What major to select
- To change jobs or not
- To make a major investment
- To buy a home
- To leave a home
- To change careers
- To take legal action
- To respond to legal action
- To fire someone
- To initiate a merger or make an acquisition
- To set up or dissolve a partnership
- To accuse someone of embezzlement

- To confront an unreasonable customer and risk losing the account

- To confront an unreasonable boss and risk losing your job

How did you make the decision? In a manner of speaking, it made itself, it made you make it, the unconscious pushed you into a certain direction. When you struggle with the choice, it is not about what to do but about what you really plan to do but don't know it yet. The indecision is really waiting for the unconscious to speak, and what's more, to gently but inevitably allow it to "make" your move. Is not that how it feels to make a major decision?

In the end, the choice you have made seems inevitable. It will occur, even though you think it is wrong. Nevertheless, it still feels free, for you know you could always have acted otherwise.

That is why we say that with your choices you define yourself. As you choose, one of two things happens: Either you create who you are or you reveal your true nature by your choice. In other words, the question of who you are is answered by the choices you make or, conversely, you choose as you are.

Go back to the previous list of difficult choices: Do you define who you are by deciding what job offer to accept, such as line or staff, sales or HR? Or is that choice the result of a prior decision? Does it matter? What is important is that you converse about free will, that you feel it, and that you see what it does to you and your effectiveness with responsibility and accountability.

The free-will trick is not that you make a decision, but that you have to choose how to respond to the decision you made, as it is in the process of unfolding itself. Suppose, for example, that you fired an executive, or you made an acquisition, or you discontinued a product—as Apple stopped its expensive and much advertised "CUBE." All of these are very difficult decisions, decisions with repercussions, decisions that must be sustained with persistent additional choices and anxious choices. And if you guess wrong in how you choose, you will be held accountable.

Understanding this structure of freedom, talking about it clearly, exhibiting it in personal and professional life, and modeling and teaching it, these are the responsibilities of those who lead and change our organizations.

And you still think freedom is a blessing? And you wonder why anxiety runs through it like a cancer? A leader is a hero in this territory.

Anxiety and the Sense of Self

Access to this core of being, the free-will zone, requires us to traverse a fire wall of serious negatives. In terms of space travel, it means that *getting into and out of the zone of freedom requires passing through a black hole,* a meteor shower, a radioactive belt. The journey will not weaken you but strengthen you. (Who knows, perhaps our theories of the universe are but projections of the inner nature of our soul!)

In other words, our inner freedom, our free will, our core nature, is surrounded with anxiety, guilt, depression, pain, ennui, exhaustion, hopelessness, illness, frustration, betrayal, loss, abandonment, separation, insanity, ridicule, shame, betrayal, and death. (Forgive the litany of words, but they all matter. They all describe. They are all part of what we live with.) It adds up to what we call the Shadow Diamond: enabling learned helplessness and co-dependency.

Courage is then the interplay between *free will* and *anxiety.* And free will is identical to *responsibility.*

Courage is the foundation—the *deep structure* of human existence. The courage to lead the life that you believe you must lead, that you—with full awareness of the consequences and of your responsibility for them—choose to build, is the beginning and the end of all wisdom. To the extent that you have come to terms with this facet of what it means to be human, with this deep structure of what it means to exist as a human being in the world—no exceptions—to that extent you also have earned and you deserve the titles of maturity, adulthood, authenticity, leadership, and eventually even of statesmanship.

Albert Camus said it well, "What does not kill me, strengthens me."

At Home

To have courage is to do against grave danger what one knows to be right. This danger threatens "the shaking of the foundations." To be at home in that zone, to feel comfortable in that black hole of the soul, is also to live at the foundation of what it is to be a leader. The good news is that you can get there by yourself. It is not easy, but in the last analysis it is your choice. And not just a choice of how you think but also a choice of how you strategize your environmental manipulation: You know what kind of environment depresses you and what kind of environment energizes you and what the optimum combination is of the two. And then you choose to set up precisely the right kind of environment, for which you hold yourself both responsible and accountable.

You do not get rid of your anxiety; you become contented in it, as you would swimming in cool waters, or being buoyed by the excitement of being onstage, or piloting an airplane, and even sky diving!

The sense of self involves comfort with anxiety and resoluteness in being your body. Leadership athletes create for themselves anxiety-producing situations, such as rock climbing, and conditions of embodiment, such as all types of vigorous competitive sports.

Your Business Needs Your Freedom

What has this got to do with business? Responsibility starts when we understand the consequences of making a free decision. When bringing free will to business, it translates into responsibility and accountability and therefore the three key ensuing themes are

- Increasing personal *responsibility,*

- Holding people *accountable,* and

- Making it clear to people that there are *consequences.*

This is how discipline and dignity are introduced into business environments.

Do you have a sales talk to give? Do you have a presentation to the management committee about negotiating a major contract? What if you were to raise, rather than repress, issues of anxiety, free will, and responsibility—and not with slick slogans but with credible depth—at the right moment? The sales process—from selling cars to political alliances—requires anxiety management. Could that not create a bond between you and your customer? Could that not enhance your believability as a source of business value? Could you not be perceived as a businessperson who is dependable? You can make that happen—translate anxiety into trust, fear into comfort. Talk about courage, the anxiety, and the free will that bonds all of you in the board room. Trust the power of intelligent leadership conversations at strategic intervention moments.

For example, you address your prospective client with a sophisticated presentation. You add, "There is anxiety in this room. It is understandable. Whenever big decisions are made we should expect anxiety. Anxiety is the fuel. These are difficult decisions for you."

You ask difficult questions:

- Are we helping you to make a decision?

- Are we making it more difficult for you?

- What are some of the unspoken topics we need to discuss?

- Are we deciding here on rational grounds alone?

- What about feelings of trust?

- What about your own anxiety?

- Do you want to mention it?

- What can we do to allay your anxieties?

- What anxieties do you have about signing with us?

- Do we and do you understand people? What do you think?

- Do you have a role in helping us manage our own anxieties so that we can communicate better and serve you better?

Is there a place for this kind of a subject matter? Even if touched on but briefly? What would be the effect?

While you prepare for your sales presentation, you ask yourself where your prospective clients' anxieties lie, what acts of courage are required of them, what their obstacles are to being courageous, what the consequences will be for not taking courageous action, and what the consequences will be for taking courageous action. You ask yourself how much people are engaged in the purchasing process, how cautious they are, and so forth.

The proposal here is not to answer these questions but to let people know you understand. You cannot take over the anxiety of others, but you can let them know you have the same experience, that you value it, that it is normal, and that interjecting anxiety, locating it in a place in the body if at all possible, gives you the chance to work with it, feel it as a physical reality, and transform its use from worry to energy, from trying to get rid of it to riding it instead. It is the true martial arts technique of using the power of the negative and making it your own for your positive use. This is a physical meditation practice. It is the drug-free management of pain.

What Is the Upside of Freedom?

That's a truly tough question. Especially for philosophers who never stop talking about anxiety, its revealing powers, and its exalted virtues. For the answer to this question is but an experience, a discovery, a feeling, a sensation. The upside of freedom is that it makes you into a *you*. It is the very essence of what makes you real. The Velveteen Rabbit, like Pinocchio, had but one dream: to be real. Well, in *your* leadership story it is dwelling in your freedom and adorned with anxiety that makes you real. Being you is a physical sensation of courage, freedom, and anxiety. Consulting firms advertising e-business support give you essentially this message: Your decision for e-business is fraught with anxiety. You are shamed by the ads for not knowing your business, but IBM, EDS, and the rest—for a price of course—are quick and ready to come to the rescue! The words and pictures in their ads say, "Our firm can help you manage this anxiety." To the anxious executive, aching to make a decision, and not wishing to be embarrassed, this is just the right soothing message to contact his or her unconscious, where the risky financial decisions are made.

There is no upside to freedom, not in the ordinary sense of pleasure, fun, and benefits. Freedom introduces you to the non-natural order, the realm of reality beyond what science can describe. The capacity to decide introduces you to the realm of inwardness and subjectivity. The power to choose explains to you the meaning of being a subject rather than an object, a self rather than a thing. Freedom explains to you the nature of ethics, ethical choices, and moral courage. Freedom explains pride and dignity, honor and glory. The self-esteem of being responsible, keeping your promises, doing your duty, and choosing accountability—in short, building civilized behavior among people—would be bereft of any meaning without its foundation in free will. Being in charge of who we are is the essence of being human, and denying that freedom is the essence of regression to animal nature and animal behavior. To feel this, to live this, to experience its weight, and to communicate it readily—those are the inner sensations of the authentic leader.

The great danger in being free is the temptation to use the organization not as a practice field for freedom but as *the excuse for the escape from freedom—the denial of free will, choosing not be a chooser!*

Will you cultivate the free part of you? Is your inner power inspiring? Is your energy contagious? Does claiming your freedom bring results in your organization?

In Sum

This chapter has focused on the experience of free will. We will develop later the concepts of body and will and the like. It is difficult, no, impossible, to discuss any one of these crucial leadership themes in isolation. Life is one, the mind and body are one, energy and will are one, consciousness and inner space-time are one. Separation, and fragmentation, like specialization, are necessary because that is how we communicate.

A good executive sees a complex company with its history and its future, its innumerable stakeholders, and the opinions of the public, as a single event, which in the boardroom and the management committees and before analysts and customers needs to be stretched out, parceled into pieces, supported by data provided by the controller and others. The company may be your own, or one you contemplate purchasing, or your prospective customer. The unitary, integrated, systemic view is always there.

But when you live in the real world and have to communicate, you become sequential. And that distorts.

So it is with the comments here. Even though each chapter has a focal point, they radiate like the sun and touch all else that is around them.

◆ Activity
Choice Points

Each person has made important decisions in life. We often do not reflect enough on what they were like and what they meant.

- What were your significant decision points, turning points?

- How hard was it for you to go through these turning points in your life?

- What anxieties did you feel?

- Are you satisfied with how you made the choices?

- What have been the consequences?

- How could you have been better prepared?

- What did you learn from how you managed your turning points?

- What can you pass on?

- How will these reflections help in your current leadership?

- How will these thoughts and insights about yourself improve your coaching and training work?

CHAPTER 11

The Resistance to Courage

IT IS AMAZING *how much of life and how many of our institutions and belief systems are carefully constructed to serve but one overwhelming purpose: to protect ourselves from our freedom, to escape our freedom, to deny our free will.*

What I learned from psychiatrists is the utility of the concept of the resistance. It's part of the unconscious. The things we do without acknowledging that we do them. The strategies we use to sabotage our own professed goals. And when we use such concepts as tools, you can make real progress in raising your life to new levels of effectiveness, excitement, and fulfillment. This is how you turn the light on the shadow.

But it's also a tricky situation. If you disagree with something fundamentally, it's not called a difference of opinion, but a resistance to the truth. If you feel that love and harmony are the meaning of life, then you are told that is a reaction-formation against the deeper needs for wealth and power. If you are friendly, you are told it is because you are too weak and cowardly to stand up for your own rights. Whereas this undermining of your normal way of thinking may be quite inconsiderate and even unethical, it does have the muscle to shake you to your foundations and open you up to different and new ways of thinking, of perceiving, and of feeling. And these may indeed be constructive and transformative. And lead to a better life for you.

Two Meanings of Responsibility

Many people who are into learning more about leadership nevertheless offer a resistance to this effort that can make coaching a rugged experience. We need to develop a sensitivity to the gross difference in perception, mindset, and world views among people. An interesting example occurred when I was discussing the topic of responsibility. The immediate meaning to my client of the word *responsibility* was the delineation of assignments and duties:

- "You guard this building";
- "You visit this client twice a month";
- "You operate this lathe on the night shift";
- "You are expected to be prepared to take the examination on Chapters 6 through 10 next Thursday";
- "You have full profit and loss responsibility for Region A";
- "These six companies here are your accounts. You have been assigned to them."

Those are the structures—measurable performances—for which you are held responsible. This is one meaning of responsibility.

But there is an entirely different meaning of the same word. And that is the subjective sense of freedom and free will—and the responsibility that results from this free agency that you are. I feel internally that I am free; I can make choices, lots of choices. I experience *subjectively* that I can make decisions. And since how I elect has consequences, I feel that also as a responsibility. Objective responsibility is what you do. Subjective responsibility is who you are.

In our ordinary discourse, the distinction between objective and subjective responsibility does not exist, or, at best, is clouded. All responsibility is thought to be objective. All responsibility is a job description. All responsibility is structure and process. All responsibility is the parameters within which you will be rewarded or punished according to the results that you deliver. These are all organizational facts, engineering concepts, technical constructs, external realities.

What is missing in this consciousness and conversation is an entirely different meaning of responsibility. It is the sense of free will, the emotional burden, the inner struggles, the interior strengths. Both meanings need to be clear, not only one.

Why is the inner side factored out? Most likely for two reasons: because we do not know how to deal with it, and because we have been indoctrinated to think the region of the subjective is inferior, less real, less significant, than the region of the objective. But that is a decision, not a provable fact.

This is how we differentiate between *spirituality* and *materialism.* The former accepts the primacy of inner space, whereas the latter sees outer space as the only region of the concrete and the real. Both are true. But your life becomes inverted as you move from one to the other. We have here a true polarity and paradox. The root cause of your belief system, as suggested earlier, is this *archetypal decision,* the choice underlying all of your theories about what this world truly is and was meant to be. Life itself invites you to take charge of making that decision and to become strong as a result of accepting the consequences.

You are not just happy or unhappy, but up to a point—a major point—you choose whether to be happy or unhappy. You have more control than you think. You choose to be helpless, just as you choose to be able to help yourself. You choose to give up or you choose to continue. The more deeply into your soul you are able to trace these choices, the more of a leader you are. And the more you stay on the surface, the less you are in control of your life. This is the meaning of contacting the archetypal choices that inform your existence and the way you view the world. Your physical health is part of this. A person who can claim the depth of his or her freedom is also a person with the best possible physical health. Look at the waiting room of many a county hospital. You can tell those who are unavoidably ill from those who have given up on life and have therefore become ill. Hope is still the best medicine, and you can choose a philosophy of life that helps you in hope. It need not be a chimera. You can choose realism for hope, and not fantasy. Fantasy does not give hope, for it has no ground. Finding your own way to hope without illusion, is that not the secret of a successful life? Is that not what consultants and leaders and coaches want to help make real?

Any choice is okay, if you make such a choice consciously. But it is a trap if you accept your choice as a given, as the truth—without further careful examination. Socrates is often quoted as saying that the unexamined life is not worth living. How do you feel about this view?

Remedies

These insights into responsibility, freedom, and courage are *attitudes* and they are the roots of *action* and the soil of *results*. *Structure* does not yield results. *Will* does. *Form* does not yield results, *resoluteness* does. They are the true secret of *implementation,* the action link. Structure without free choice is empty. Nothing happens when you have only the form, order, plans. You need to fill the shell with human freedom of choice. We refocus the mind from the way you are *organized* to the way in which you make and live with *decisions,* with what happens at the core of your ego, the center of your soul, when you are called on to rev up your *energy* and good cheer, your *stamina* and your resoluteness. We must be ready to live in the zone of subjective reality in order to marshal the power to succeed in the world of objective reality.

If this point does not seem clear to you or important, then in some basic fashion we are not communicating. We must join hands to try to understand how each of us feels and how we each think. This can be done by repeating, restating, each other's respective explanations and descriptions of the world as we individually and separately see it. This is diversity at its best—and at its most difficult.

What now is the quintessence of all this, this overview of leadership? The relevant applications for you in the workplace and for your life in general? The old way of leading, perhaps that of a Teddy Roosevelt or a George Washington, was to rouse the troops to enthusiasm. Today's way of leading is to be prepared for *Intelligent Leadership Conversations (ILC)*—with equals. Rather than to arouse the troops and *solve the problem* of meaning in life for them, we, among ourselves as authentic persons, *live with and adapt to the question.* The latter gives rise to much nobler virtues than the former. *It is the difference between command by fear and credibility by respect.* It attracts and retains the kinds of quality people needed to run the new types of businesses that the new economics require. This may sound simple and romantic, neither of which is the case. But we are touching here on the foundation for the tough maturity that happens when wisdom is injected into leadership to grow all the way up into statesmanship.

The key to leadership is to make the choice to go through blackness, both in understanding free will and in implementing free will—and knowing the resistances surrounding our core freedom. Managing the resistance is managing anxiety: the anxiety of facing death, the despair of resolving conflicts, and the courage of being your own person. The anxiety of making a difficult sales call, having an honest talk with the boss, meeting the analysts after the quarterly reports, being threatened by an angry investor, being unable to fix a client's problem. All of these are bad words and they are words of weakness. Leadership is to turn the negative into a positive, to the power that resides secretly in the negative, and make that work not only for ourselves but even more so for our organization.

This is why the best leaders understand the anxiety of free will. This is why managers and executives, organization change practitioners and consultants are able to help their teams and clients to have intelligent leadership conversations about the many rooms in the mansion of freedom and free will.

"We are going to have to raise your sales quota. And let me tell you why we are asking this of you. The securities analysts are telling the press that margins are higher for our main competitor, and that will immediately lower our stock price. Our ability to give stock options to our employees depends on continuing to raise the stock price. The connection between cause and effect is not immediate, but it is no less real. As you pump up your energy and your enthusiasm and hone your imagination for more sales, you also know that not only will you make commissions but your options will as a result grow in value." This is a leadership conversation. "Tell me ways in which I can support you so that you will sleep better at night." This is a leadership conversation. "It's a hard thing for me to say, but I am not your mother. But I care about you and I will not ignore you or abandon you but help you through this rough time." This also is a leadership conversation.

◆ Activity

How about sharing some of these reflections on courage, anxiety, freedom, and resistance with your prospective customers? These are all matters to consider: having Intelligent Leadership Conversations and looking for the appropriate Strategic Leadership Moment and setting up opportunities for both. Your preparation includes assessing the personalities of the prospects. Here the corners of the Diamond will serve you well.

- Think of a scenario you went through recently or on which you are about to embark: How could you serve your customer better if you were to engage at a strategic moment in an Intelligent Leadership Conversation, in a business context and on a business topic, with that individual's organization?

- Would the focus be on the product? On the service? On the relationship? On side benefits? On the future? On values only peripheral to the business interaction?

Conversations, timing, appropriateness, leveraging, teaching others, spontaneity, product design, salesmanship, and delivery—these are your key intersections for making good business out of a deep philosophy of personal freedom.

Courage is scary. To see it in action is always impressive. The story in the next chapter is a case in point.

CHAPTER 12

A Bad Decision?

A Case Study in Leadership Coaching

FOLLOWING IS THE STORY *of a successful and high level executive who left his lucrative and safe job to enter a seductively promising new venture, and he failed. The story is especially for all people who have been downsized or lost their fortunes in failed entrepreneurial ventures. The prose may be a bit esoteric, but I believe it has the possibility of being profound. And I am not convinced that the message can be given in much simpler language, or even in a different style, without canceling out the very insights that should make it worth reading.*

The Situation

I had an excellent position with a well-established Fortune 100 company— great salary, security, stock options—and I was judged to be one of the best ever to occupy this high-level position. I had four problems: I was not challenged enough, I felt like an outsider, there was no prospect for serious wealth, and no meaningful promotion possibilities were in sight. Head-hunters had been after me for a long time with tempting propositions. After detailed research and careful consideration I decided to accept an offer that was a promotion, but in a smaller and new company. The greatest attractions were that I was in charge, that the atmosphere was exciting and challenging, and that the opportunity for real wealth creation was significant indeed.

Now, exactly one year later, everything has collapsed. I still feel that objectively I made the right decision. What happened to the markets on which we depended was not only difficult to predict but was, on objective criteria, extremely unlikely to ever have occurred. Nevertheless, my reputation has been tarnished. We may be bankrupt next week. And there are legal entanglements. Matters couldn't be worse. I have very heavy family obligations and my wife is devastated.

I am a religious man. That has saved me. I read daily Hebrews, Chapter 13, Verses 5 and 6: "My son, do not make light of the Lord's discipline, and do not lose heart when he rebukes you, because the Lord disciplines those he loves and punishes everyone he accepts as a son."

The Analysis and Response

Imagine that you are the person who told me that story. How would we begin a process of leadership coaching support?

We would need to talk about *loss, real* loss, and how to deal with it. And the question is not just to *feel* better, but to *do* better. You do not want tranquilizers so as to worry less, but rather the courage to worry more, to be more anxious, to be more energized, so as to get *more action, more results, more change.*

The idea is not to be satisfied with less but rather to receive more, not to withdraw but to pitch in. An airplane stays aloft only with forward thrusting speed. Slow down, look back, and it crashes.

A Tough Situation!

There are no easy answers. There are no "how-to" solutions. The change required is *deep* change. For you have reached the "stuck point" of life, where old and tested methods to solve problems have arrived at their end point. They simply do not work any longer. You now proceed to *transformation,* reaching a new level of action and results, which is the precise opposite of the depression that many people sink into when they get frustrated. And depression leads you to blame others for situations that you yourself need to resolve.

You wouldn't be reading this if you were not well along the way to transformation yourself. And your transformation is not spiritual and psychological alone; it needs to manifest itself in a new way of doing business and in a new level of business results.

Tools for Moving Forward

How do you face what's real—both inside you and out? The truth is that your possibilities are endless.

New business idea. Take what you have learned—about finance, running a growth business, managing people, keeping up morale under stress, your own emotional strengths and weaknesses, and what you don't know—and package it into the new "I, Inc.," which you will take to market. Your new business idea carries in it the seed for the wealth that you seek.

This new product is your value-added leadership package. Translate it into your customers' needs—old and new customers. Educate your markets and search out new ones. What you offer the market—as either independent entrepreneur or corporate employee—now comes with value added: the leadership increment. What does this wisdom mean to your customers—and from their point of view? How will they pay for the wisdom added to your competence area, that is, financial services? You need to plan for margins and growth. Then you have the best of all possible worlds: making others powerful through your own philosophy of life. What could be more exciting?

Deepen the negative. To get to your new business idea, that is, financial competence plus leadership authenticity, both of which you can teach, requires deepening. What we have done is to deepen your experience of disaster, defeat, by finding layers in the unconscious. You have lost money, but you have found that it strengthens your religion, you have learned how to rely on your family and your community, you have been challenged to rise to the occasion and to respond with courage and character. Your frustration becomes a nuclear learning occasion for your children, for it is a fresh opportunity for you to demonstrate your love for them. These are real values, not surrogates that you dust off for emergencies!

Universalize the learning. You universalize. You are now experiencing first-hand the character of the Post New Economy: ample in opportunities but also thickly crowded with threats. Your current situation unveils the basic fragility of the human condition. Rather than at all costs to escape the awareness of your frailty—denying, attacking, raging, sobbing, begging, escaping into insanity, attempting suicide—*you choose now more than ever to become a leader.*

This is the ultimate and complete act of authenticity. This is the creation of a human being, an inward powerhouse, not a mere outward shell of a body. It is a transformation, a change in who you are. It is a choice of reason and strategy, but also of sobriety and sustenance, of endurance and presence of mind, of keeping calm and healthy, of not allowing your skull to cave in on you.

Embrace humility. You become humble. You are pushed down onto your knees, learning once and for all the naive pitfalls of arrogance. This can make us all into superior human beings. You have a head start!

Hear the message. You get the message. It is to realize that life is not about making profits—the ambition for wealth notwithstanding—but about building character. Profits do not build character, but character builds profits. In fact, what in truth builds character is the *lack* of profits. You had both; now you strive one more time.

Become a teacher. You learn that you are not a maker of profits but a teacher for makers of profits. That is the kernel of your new business idea. And what you teach is that you make profits only after you have first learned how to rescue yourself from *not* making profits. And if you happen to be in the financial services industry, then you have maximum opportunities to teach people how to deal with financial failures—first, emotionally, and then strategically.

A smart accountant can help you minimize your taxes. But that is only a half-smart accountant. A fully smart accountant helps you to realize that what you think you earn, actually you do not. You earn only that which remains after taxes. In a larger sense, you earn only that which remains after bare essentials, the so-called disposable income. And the viability of that depends on inflation being under control. This is a state of mind and a critical decision for sanity and peace of soul. To think that what has been taxed was ever yours is an illusion. If these attitudes are pervasive in your life, and not just when the chips are down, you will discover that catastrophes are much less likely to occur.

Learn. The last thought to bring up for support in downsizing and bankruptcy situations is the preeminence of teaching and learning. The meaning of life is to *learn.* You learn how to *make* money, how you *lose* it, and how you *respond with leadership* to losing it. You maintain at all times your dignity. However, the meaning of life is to learn only because the deeper meaning of life is to teach—or, stated less arrogantly, to help others learn. This is the generosity of spirit that marks the healthy person. You make this sequence the heart of your teaching, the core of your curriculum.

But you are a teacher only metaphorically. Externally you are a businessperson. You teach through your business. You teach others how to make money. You teach others how they can lose it. You teach others how to strengthen the soul against loss. And you teach others how they can in turn teach others how to strengthen their souls against loss. Having done that, you make a business out of this kind of teaching. But you do not make it a direct business. You teach subtly, surreptitiously. You translate your lessons into the businesses of your clients, the products and services of your customers, the needs, hopes, and aspirations of the end user. You speak in their language not yours, you use their tools not yours.

Your business, like all else in leadership, is the sum of two right-angle vectors: competence and authenticity. Traditional business offerings derive from your competence. But what can make you now into a market leader is that you know how to add authenticity to your product as well, so that your customers receive added value. Therein lies your differentiation, your competitive advantage, and your growth and your margins. That is your new business idea, one that you could not have either invented or learned without this temporary defeat on the journey of your life.

Using these tools will change your personality. They will add dimensions of maturity to your character. Your inner mindset builds your world, step by step, day by day, small act by small act, to harmonize with your basic conscious and unconscious values. This spells out for you new levels of credibility.

All of this is for you to teach, to give to your stakeholders, to the people who make decisions about you that matter to you. It is not for you. It is for them!

Choosing Who You Are

It may not be easy to see the connection between what sounds philosophically abstract and the daily business crises that demand your decisions and that require non-stop that you perform at your best. But, as all "reverse engineering" makes clear, change starts with a decision. Results out in the world have their origins in a powerful choice made at the center of your inner self. The former would be dead without the latter being alive. Achieving business results starts with opening your mind to the operations of the mind.

Your Archetypal Choice

Some choices are conscious and others unconscious. Some we feel, others we potentially can feel. As you act under stress or passion, you may not feel that you are choosing. But as you reflect later, perhaps years later, on what you did, you will see it as a choice you made and did not need to have made. The logic when it happened is different from the logic at the time you reflected on it. A good example is how President Clinton must have felt about his relationship with Monica Lewinsky when it occurred, as opposed to later, when it came to impeachment. This tool was introduced in Chapter 8 (Figure 8.1).

Responsibility for Who You Are

The Theory of Archetypal Choices helps you take a much greater level of responsibility for who you are. Who you are is not something that happens automatically. It may not be the result of a deliberate choice, although that is precisely what you expect from an authentic person. Who you are does follow from an unconscious choice, in that you can bring the choice to consciousness, articulate it, and even change it. This is the power of reflection. It is this possibility for change—the underlying goal of a liberal education, to provide people with choices—which gives you the resounding "Aha!" that you are responsible for your sense of self and its world that you created. "Created" is excessive. The correct statement would be "helped co-create." But what you have helped co-create you can again help "un-co-create." And that is your choice, and it is your choice *now.*

Archetypal choices are the foundation of your self-image, your philosophy of life, your expectations, your fears, your values, your belief systems. You may have been persuaded or indoctrinated in them in early childhood. That is what socializing children is all about. But part of the indoctrination, if successful, is to insert the seed of free will in the soul of the child. This is the key to maturity, to success in life, but possibly also to all the agonies that accompany our time on earth.

Is There Meaning, or Not?

Life now calls on you to make an archetypal decision: Is there meaning in the collapse of your financial situation, true meaning, meaning that you can trust, meaning that in some deeper sense has to do with winning? Or did you make a bad decision, did you encounter bad luck, and are you just plain defeated, that is, the bubble of your dreams has burst? The answer to your question determines whether we can go on in this leadership "conversation." Whatever you say in response must feel genuine. If you choose meaning, it can't be of the order of a rationalization, accommodating your feelings to what in truth is your failure. If you take the negative option, that indeed you have failed, then you may have been seduced by evil—angrily undermining your potential for a real solution. Thus, choosing archetypally is no minor matter.

There is one consolation, and that is William James' idea, from his influential essay "The Will to Believe," that when you are not certain, and can never know, it is rational to take the practical point of view. You can force the issue. There is no final answer to the question "Is there a purpose in your financial collapse or is there not?" You can simply *choose to make* purpose, learning, and a victory out of it. And that *is* an archetypal choice. That *does* change your world. That *does* have sound consequences. And it *is* true, for your passionate choosing *makes* it so.

Changing Who You Are

Once you have made this decision, or are prepared to work in this direction, then we can start our conversation seriously. For at that moment you can find answers and solutions and begin your new life.

In your failures you have had an experience—a religious experience, an aesthetic experience, a terrifying experience, a mystery of an experience, to be sure—of what is really the authentic character of *reality*. Of reality as the truly "Other," that which is not you, that which is completely different from you. You have seen reality as that which totally opposes you, contradicts you, stands in your way, does not even know that you exist. Up to now, this knowledge was conceptual, safe theory. Now it is real. It is like death, not the thought but the fact, the experience, the reality. It is like losing your reputation, like being found out; it is like meeting the enemy, who is winning. Your experience of defeat, which, as in religion, adds new dimensions to the thought, makes the "word become flesh," "incarnates" the idea.

Many people do not adequately integrate into their awareness the hardness of the Other, the granite makeup of "reality." A trace of illusion—that it isn't so—almost always remains.

Your task? Allow this insight to change your world, as it should and as it must. Listen to the pain. Let it tell you what it will. Change your values, your perspective, your expectations, your relationships.

Your Business Idea

This new situation now becomes your new business idea. That is the key, the turning point, the jewel. Internalizing its impact and knowing how to respond is your ultimate existential assignment. It comes to you in the form of a certain story, in certain colors and shapes, certain metaphors and figures. Marketing this idea complex to others, in their language, in terms of their stories, using their metaphors, adapted to their needs, that is what you now offer to the world.

To make this translation, and to make it well—with genius, imagination, and very hard work—is the new avenue for the journey of your life. Only you can flesh it out. The rest of us can but imagine how you might do it. But we can do it for ourselves.

Religious Metaphors?

You might ask, are religious metaphors only for the religious? For many people, religion is the only philosophy they will ever have. We all need depth. For many, depth is found in religious terminology and a religious worldview. That is a matter of individual preference, and of culture. In a democracy, we respect freedom of thought. This means freedom of metaphor. Philosophy is more general, but religion is more practical. Philosophy can be abstract, religion can be concrete. The former is conceptual, the latter, passionate. You are a religious man. Not everyone is. You should find religious metaphors appealing and find that they help communication and understanding.

Your Life Assignment

Work out now in detail, given your specific circumstances, how you will carry out this self-imposed leadership mandate—to choose who you are. The sooner this task is completed in the inside (to the extent it ever can be!) the sooner will you see business results on the outside.

◆ Activity

Bad Luck?

Here you have read the story of a good man, defeated by circumstances, living the consequences of a prima facie sound decision that nevertheless went sour.

- Do you recall in your past business experience a perfectly honorable and reasonable decision that you took in good faith and which nevertheless backfired terribly?

- What leadership lessons do you draw from this case and from your own experience?

- Could words like pride, hubris, arrogance, and greed play a role?

- How would you redefine what it means to be you and, in general, what it means to be a person, in order to integrate your experience of defeat into the meaning of your life, and of all life?

- Is there a monetary value for your company associated with your change of personal philosophy?

- Does defeat mean that in our leadership roles we are expected to be much more humble than traditional competitive business ambition would allow?

- Does this mean we should tone down our enthusiasm for change and innovation, that there is also a need for stability and tradition?

CHAPTER 13

Courage As My-Body

WHY A SECTION ON MY-BODY? *Because my-body is the most concrete event in the universe and it is where the inner and the outer worlds meet. They are the vestibules of each other's houses. That is where the will resides—concretely. That is where the existing you resides. That is the core of all existence, the ultimate embodied subject. And leadership is no more and no less than to achieve access to that rich cornucopia of what your life truly is. From that center you gain your strength and grasp your meaning. There you find your dignity, your power, but also here you can sow the seeds of defeat. Understanding what goes on when the inner universe and the outer universe converge in the unique experience that it is to be a body and a mind—your bodymind— is to finally have heard the answer to the Delphic Oracle's gnothi seauton, "know thyself!"*

We now explore in greater depth the description of *my-body* that was introduced in Chapter 2.

This is a complex and perhaps difficult section. Some thoughts in it are new and may therefore be difficult to assimilate. One of these mystery themes is to gain a better understanding of the human body. We are here not talking about the body as a physiologist might see it, or a photographer, but as I myself see from within my own subjectivity. The subject matter is the body as we ourselves experience it, our own body.

What do I feel, sense, see, perceive, think when I say something like that? The subjective feeling of being or having a body is elusive, and yet we all have that experience. There is a view in philosophy that describes my body, the body I experience as mine (something that is true of every human being), as the interface, the connecting integument, the bridge between the two worlds of which we spoke early in this book: the realm of inner space and time versus the realm of outer space and time. These two real worlds actually intersect in my body— not yours, not his, not hers, but mine. I feel it, I know it, and so do you!

What is the value of this kind of talk, and what does it have to do with coaching leaders and, for that matter, with business in general? These are important questions and they deserve close attention. If you look at your body as the intersection of the inner and the outer worlds, with both of which you are acquainted, then you recognize that you have just now described the very essence of what it means to be a living, throbbing, yearning, suffering, and hoping individual. The concept of the body as mine, my body—technically as the body-qua-mine—helps us gain a sense of uniqueness, identity, special-ness, and with it freedom and responsibility, achievement and defeat. And right there at the heart of business is the entrepreneurial mind, the freedom fighter, the builder, the bastion of any economy.

There is in business much love of sports and use of sports analogies. They are all judicious and relevant—their focus on the living body well-taken. All the power that is inherent in being human arises when we see ourselves as bodyminds. The meaning of freedom and responsibility, the meaning of greatness, of courage, of determination, of commitment, all of these powerful experiences—emotions or realities—become flesh, incarnated, embodied, when we learn to think of ourselves as the one place in the universe where the spiritual and the material, the mental and the physical, actually merge, become one, intersect, interface.

And that is where you are. That is where life is conducted. Therefore, concepts alone are empty and practical applications alone, superficial. It is only in the richness of the total blending, melding, interconnection, that the full-bodied and fully conscious life of the individual person, with all its glories and its pains, becomes real.

So that when we talk about applications, here is where we must be. You, the individual, the self as instrument, the power of self, the seat of the soul, emerge, affirm yourself, confess your freedom and responsibility, and you can be sure that we will get results. For the first time we have real results and we know how to get them. Indeed you are the application. Once this is understood, and repeated daily and multiplied among the multitudes, we have the community, the organization, to support the kind of ethical world that we want and need.

You Are Your Courage

Go back to the matrix at the beginning of the courage section (Table 9.1) on page 159.

"'Throwing' yourself into your body and social role" nails courage down. The bottom line of courage is to throw yourself into the situation in which you find yourself and work out your destiny from within there. For that is not only your ultimate act of courage, but it is also your definitive truth.

Thinkers have referred to that focus as your *situation,* your *uniqueness,* your *individuation.* But it is also your *body,* the body that you live, your lived body. That has been called the *bodymind*. But the final expression of your real-life situation, the defining act of courage, is the recognition that your situation is not just your mind nor is it your body. It is also the society in which you exist, for that is the context in which you live. The total clustered configuration of who you are is then best called your *social bodymind*.

You are a mind that exists in a body, which in turn exists in nature and in a social context. Courage is deliberately to throw yourself into that state and live from within there, for that is the most real way you can be. This is the antithesis of escaping from reality. This is engagement, commitment, being fully alive.

This is the entrepreneur, the person who takes pride to build a business with her own hands. It is the artisan who shapes raw materials and an idea into something of value. It is the builder, the master builder, who literally *is* his creation.

These may be odd and tough points. But those who master them have also mastered leadership. The entrepreneur, the artisan, the master builder symbolize the fully alive person, a 360-degree, 24/7 dynamo. They also carry the message of focusing less on what you do and more on who you are. The former is fragmented, whereas the latter is whole. And you are who you choose to be, not who you were made to be. That is the glory of being human.

And for successful leaders, that is also their business. The role of the consultant often is to shoehorn the executive into finding true joy in building the business, in doing the work that needs to be done—if that is the choice. Work is not inherently good or bad, fun or burdensome: Up to a point, you make it that way. And up to another point, you can choose to change it. And this joy is not dependent on good times. There is more opportunity for joyful creativity in bad times. The secret lies in your resoluteness, the extent to which you are prepared to mobilize the power of your courage, the vigor of your free will, and your readiness to absorb anxiety. It was not idly that Kahlil Gibran said, "Work is love made visible."

I have seen factory workers on the assembly line struggling with a malfunctioning lathe, plant managers trying to avert a strike, accountants poring over their tax charts, account managers scurrying from airport to airport, board members anxiously huddling in meetings facing the deadline of the analysts lying in wait at the telephones, a planner who feels ignored in a lonely cubicle, come to life when the consulting conversation turns to the topic of where you find your courage in your body.

Are you ready for courage?

You Are Unique

In order to open oneself to courage, one key point must be understood viscerally. It is the intersection between the inner and the outer worlds in my own body. My body is unique. That is where I exist. Through perception the outer world enters the inner, and, conversely, through willing or volition, through self-initiated action, the inner world reaches beyond itself to the outside. Once we see that, we have the key that unlocks our ultimate strength, our definitive power: It is that of choosing to exist as a body in this world. It is to surrender to our fate. That too is a choice. That is why it is important to connect athletics with being an executive, just as it is important to connect education with the leadership function. Education amplifies the inner world and athletics amplifies the outer world. The intersection is what matters, for there we find you—no one else, only you. And you are unique, you are not someone else.

This discussion about courage and the body, your personal and only body, to be precise, is an attempt at revolution. Once and for all we realize that we are not a thing, something observed, but that we are both observer and observed at the same time, for we exist at the inner-outer intersection.

Is your cheek warm and soft? Use your forefinger to test it. Touch the skin over your cheekbone. Your finger is the inner world and your cheekbone, the outer world. Presto, you reverse this: Is your fingertip coarse or smooth? Well, one way to find out is to feel it with your cheek. At that moment, your cheek is the inner world and your finger the outer. This is the body, your body, my body: It is both subject and object, inner and outer, at once one and the same time.

This is a kind of experiential proof that my body exists at the intersection of the inner and outer worlds.

Now, if we can develop this point to its fullest, we can experience the reality of our existence, which is the ultimate power of being grounded, of feeling secure, of savoring what it means to be you—body and soul combined. And if you are there, then you have become once and for all and for all time the solid leader that you have always aspired to be.

To get to this point in human self-development took hundreds of years of philosophy and a century of warfare. This is what the 20th Century amounted to in the larger scope of universal history: the discovery of the existing individual.

Throw Yourself into Your Work

Here is where good performance breaks through to great performance: How much you throw yourself into what you do, how much you commit yourself to discipline, how much you push beyond the comfort zone. How much you surrender your soul and your body to the task at hand is the measure of your talent. And these are choices, decisions about who you are and decisions about how you live. And they are choices for continuity—not just an inspired week or month, but a dedicated lifetime. This surely is well beyond mere language and words. But if we talk about training, we start with language and words, so that people can after that make the personal lifestyle and identity choices to be the kind of living person that they describe in the language that they use. That is why it is important to learn to talk intelligently about freedom, free will, responsibility, and accountability—and the anxiety that surrounds it—and now also we add the body, the inner-outer intersection, the will, and the energy that you can both create and release. Let us turn to those themes.

Live at the Center

Here, as you explore the intersection between the inner and outer worlds, is where you find your unique individuality. But there is more.

Some of the crucial elements of existence are found at this fulcrum: your source of energy, your capacity to choose yourself to go from ennui to energy, from depressed to joyous, from passive to active, virtually from dead to alive. Summoning your own energy, mobilizing your own vigor, arousing your own enthusiasm, these miracles of the soul all exist mysteriously at that center that is you.

We often use the word "will" or "will power" or "self-discipline," to designate that central vortex, the geyser from which all action springs. You hear it in the heaving of the weight lifter, to overcome one more pound of resistance. You see it in the marathon runner, overcoming the limit of the first ten miles. You see it in the high-tech service company that takes pride to have its people be up all night fixing the malfunctioning equipment in the client's business. This capacity and the choice to activate the will beyond anything one would normally expect is the good news of the power within, brought across the line, past the intersection, into the real world outside.

The key is to know that this part of you is mysterious, that the categories of the outer world are not sufficient to explain it, that it is real, and that above all IT IS YOU! The meaning of life is to make this discovery. The significance of leadership is that this point becomes clear. And your life will be better than you ever imagined, for now you are in touch with your true power.

Transformation

You have a tragedy with your business. There is an ethics lapse, an accident, and you are hit with a catastrophic lawsuit. The owners, the venture capital company, are overwhelmed, alarmed, at the end of their wits with you. You have been defeated. But you don't repress your feelings. You allow your feelings to be what they want to be. You cry. That's OK. In fact, that is the best part of you. It's good because it is genuine. You are living a tragedy. That's reality.

How do you recover? How do you come back? How do you choose to rise out of the ashes? You find where in your body that loss resides. You work on that locus directly: Let it be, let it speak, give it a voice, treasure what it says, listen to it. And then transform the distress and the despair into power and resolve.

You consciously transform yourself from a youngster to a grownup, from an immature child to a mature adult. Can you see that? Experience it? Can you feel your character change? Can you feel that what was grief becomes meaning?

And it is here and at this moment that you achieve transformation without insight, change without planning, transition without technique. Here is the moment of therapeutic transformation—the concretization and embodiment of a thought—and then shift this thought-matter complex from running away to taking responsibility, from hesitation to stepping forward, from no to yes, from denial to accountability, and so forth.

This is the spiritualization of athletics, the "physicalization" of mental activity, the decision for extraversion, for extruding your inwardness out into the real world. All are acts of embodiment—decisions to translate a thought into an action, an idea into a reality. And that is the secret of implementation. To capture it and transmit it is the heart of leadership.

Sometimes this attitude is expressed in hostile and asocial phrases such as "When the going gets tough the tough get going" or "Those who say it can't be done should get out of the way of those who are doing it." But let not these hackneyed expressions tarnish the beauty of the transformation.

Application?

The key question now becomes, the one that I cannot and should not avoid: How does this apply to me, now, in my work and private life? How can I apply it to running my company or my team better? And how can I apply it to the way we manage this company, the way we run this organization?

Push the Limits

A couple of my friends—Fred Kofman and Ricardo Gil—in 2001, scaled Mount Aconcagua, in the Andes, between Chile and Argentina—the tallest mountain in the world outside of the Himalayas. What was their motivation? *To test their limits, to find out what they could endure, to challenge the extent to which they could mobilize their free will.*

It was an unconscionably arduous undertaking. They told me that the last two and a half hours they had virtually climbed semi-conscious. But they made it and cried uncontrollably when they reached the top. One of them had a fall and dislocated his shoulder, which was wrenched in place again by one of the guides. Can you imagine the pain and the anxiety, up there, closer to the sky?

The purpose of any adventure like this is to experience the interface between thinking and doing. This "transsubstantiation" from thought to reality is something that has to be understood, felt, internalized. It's like learning how to read and write, how to do arithmetic, how to drive. It has to be experienced. It is the crux of being a self-starter, of *taking care of your own emotions or feelings,* of knowing that indeed *you are in charge.* It is pushing conscious-ness—a feeling, a hope, a desire—into the world, into the city, the business, the mountains, the road, the car, the market. It is important to know that liv-ing at this edge is sometimes painful and sometimes exhilarating.

Experience is where the focus lies, sensing the full richness of being the bodymind intersection—living there, realizing it is *sui generis,* of its own kind, fundamentally different from either of the other two poles of human exis-tence, mind and body, consciousness and matter.

The mind said *go,* the body said *stop.* The will made the connection. The will made the body transform from stop to go. The will made the *difference.*

For how long, under how much duress? That was the test and that was the motive for the climb.

It all adds up to one thing: Understand the will, and realize that the will is not an idea or a feeling and it is not a physical thing. It is the experience of the combination, the blend, the intersection of the two. As is the case when you add hydrogen and oxygen, you do not get another gas mixture, but water instead, something with entirely different qualities.

Climbing is to ask, "What is my endurance? How do I get a second wind? When do I push too far?" Those who have not tasted such experiences of the embodied free will cannot meaningfully talk about it. It is an inner clarity, having moved into the new world on the other side of exhaustion, a certainty and certitude that more, much more, is possible and awaits you. It is the feel-ing of full integration between mind and body, thought and reality, self and world, now and eternity. It removes anxiety and uncertainty, doubt and con-fusion. It is a feeling people get when they first fall in love. It's a new world!

Change Negatives into Positives

Another formula for capturing the embodied power of the will is to change negatives into positives.

We are told, for example, that stress is bad. No. What is bad is one's *philosophy* of stress. Stress is the feeling of being alive. Enjoy it, allow yourself to be invigorated by it, be it. Feel its drive. This is the Olympics. Anxiety, guilt, and conflict are bad only to the person who has a bad philosophy.

How does the inner world-outer world intersection feel? What is the experience of embodiment? It is stress, properly understood. It is power, properly understood. It is will, properly understood. It is guilt, anxiety, and conflict, properly understood.

The so-called *right* philosophy is to cultivate the experience of power in the face of the anxiety-guilt-conflict triad that is stress. Our challenge here is to put into words an experience that defies words but is nevertheless essential to get to the nub of what it means to produce your own energy. And is not the biggest problem in organizations to persuade others to take responsibility for the whole, to change their personal commitment to the objectives of the organization, without building the deep resentments that often accompany culture change efforts?

Explaining this to your team before there is dissent, not after, is the underlying prescription for holding people responsible for their actions and for the consequences of their actions without creating a situation of bad manners and even fights in your team's work.

The biggest complaint of team members is that saboteurs are not confronted. We can motivate only ourselves. We cannot enter the freedom of another. All these are truths. But the bottom line in real life is that we need to influence other people.

Leadership is the capacity to make things happen through people, often large groups of people. And that requires access to the freedom of another. The greatest problem is presented by uncooperative people, people who undermine a group's work, often no doubt for good reason, but who do not take responsibility for the disruptive character of their behavior. You cannot access their freedom. In an extreme form, this is civil disobedience. Non-violent resistance is to disrupt the system, not be violent, and to accept the consequences. But this is not what occurs in organizations. There is sabotage, but without responsibility and minus accountability, and that leaves behind often irreparable bitterness.

No wonder we live under the new sword of Damocles, yesterday's word for stress!

The Edge

You generate your own energy and your own hope. Your powers for that are virtually limitless. But guard yourself against pathology, against going over the edge, not using judgment or reason, not listening to experience, not learning, and getting yourself into a stupor which then will have its own life and plunge you *over* the edge.

This is the meaning of living at the edge. It is dangerous, powerful, the answer to your questions of living, and the heart of leadership. There you are alone, but also in the company of all the great souls who have striven to take what God has given them and carry that to the next level, the next stage, acting responsibly. They are all alone; but they are alone together. An interesting solution of the isolation versus intimacy polarity!

◆ Activity

For your personal reflection and journaling:

- Can you get in touch with your center?

- Do you hear an inner voice that is uniquely you?

- Can you feel the intimacy of your freedom, that is, that you are that freedom?

- Can you claim the power of that freedom, deliberately be it?

- Do you feel how your inner self and your freedom are connected with your body?

- Do you see these questions as invitations to experience the intersection of mind and body?

- How will this change your attitude toward your work?

- Does throwing yourself into your work have now a different meaning?

From your organization's perspective:

- If you felt free to have conversations about these deep topics, how would your business culture be affected?

- What difference would it make to how business is conducted?

- What difference would it make to the results that a business expects and requires?

The central activity for developing and using inner strength is to be skilled in the technique of following the Cartesian principle of transforming doubt into certainty, despair into hope, pain into meaning, betrayal into power, anger into caring. Deepening the negative can give rise to the positive, tragedy can lead to resolution, and even death to resurrection. The snow of winter fertilizes the soil of spring.

CHAPTER 14

Pain and the Tragic Sense of Life

The Phoenix Factor

THE PREVIOUS CHAPTER *concerned the core of physical energy that you are and over whose expression you can exert a degree of control. That may be the most concentrated self-starting power that you will ever command. It may hold the secret of your health and longevity, of your success in love and work, and, in general, of becoming the person you were meant to be.*

The other side, the Shadow Diamond, is when this great feeling of the joy of being alive leaves you, gradually is dissipated, lowers your level of energy—as the waters of an ebbing tide retreat backward toward the horizon.

What about not the glory but the pain?

Depression

The antithesis of energy is depression. There is clinical depression and there are moments of ordinary sadness and ennui, listlessness and inactivity. Psychiatrists and the *Diagnostic and Statistical Manual, Edition IV (DSM IV)*, published by the American Psychiatric Association, will of course differentiate—as they should. But it is neither healthful nor authentic to take an exclusively mechanical view of depression.

Calling depression an illness may be useful and simple. But where is the talk that it is something that I myself am doing, something for which I should hold myself responsible, and something that is not caused by internal chemistry or external stress? It ignores my best defense: the armor of a good philosophy of human freedom and free will, personal responsibility and accountability. Here we see science used not to tell the objective truth but to give us fuel for avoiding the anxious feeling of responsibility for the co-creation of our existence. When we go that deep, we also have answers. The annual price tag of mental illness, including depression, to U.S. businesses is about $70 billion, figuring in medical expenditures, lost productivity, and other costs.

Without being insensitive to the obviously useful conception of depression as an illness, we can also establish a philosophy in which people take very large doses of personal responsibility for how they deal with their feelings. To make the decision that my feelings of either euphoria or depression are in substantial measure under my control—either by manipulating my environment because I know the causes or by my inner drive and will or because I am in touch with my freedom—can indeed be a strengthening and healing worldview. It is not the only way and it is not always applicable. But it cannot be ignored and must be seen as our first line of defense.

Self-mobilizing your courage is one answer to depression. Knowing that it can be done is half the battle. Feeling responsible may lead to needless guilt, true, but it also can lead to much-needed self-rehabilitation. There is no harm in giving it a try.

Counteracting Evil

Coping with evil is the ultimate act of courage. What ennobles the human race is not necessarily the ability to do good business, important as that may be, but to stand up for what is right, continue to create civilization, and see the existence of evil as the ultimate test of our courage.

There is evil in this world, and it is our destiny to make free and energetic decisions—to use our will power—to stand up to it. Those who do become our heroic figures, the models of what human existence can be.

People like Timothy McVeigh, the Oklahoma City bomber, and Adolph Hitler—who said that he freed Germany from the burden of the Versailles Treaty, which had ended World War I, by means of his will power alone—give will power a bad name. But will power is also used by people who do a great deal of good, people who use power to perform the most heroic ethical acts, who willingly sacrifice themselves to save others. In my day, it was the Protestant priests who valiantly opposed Hitler, and lost their lives, who exemplified using will power for good. We know of Anwar Sadat, the remarkable Egyptian president, who had the will power to sign a peace treaty with Israel. For it he was assassinated. A lesser known example is Dietrich Bonhoeffer, who, from his safe haven in the United States, returned to Germany—because he felt that was his place to preach. For his work in the small Protestant resistance movement, he was hanged in the concentration camp at Flossenbürg on April 9, 1945.

Thus, rule one for calling on our will power is to filter every decision through the intelligence of *ethics*. To do that and abide by it is in turn a free decision to make ethics paramount.

We want to make certain here that we are free to talk about the vigor of the will without at the same time supporting outrageous and evil behaviors. And the proper application of all four corners of the Diamond makes that amply clear.

> How can we honor representatives of fierce resolve and power-ful will and condemn others? We do not want to throw out free will at the same time that we throw out evil. The answer is sim-ple. First of all, courage is not the only leadership virtue. There is also, and fundamentally so, ethics. There is polarity. Ignoring polarity can be poison. And unless courage is firmly entrenched in the direction of ethics, used in the service of ethics, in support of and tempered by the fundamental principles of ethics, there will not be any authenticity.
>
> These are stark issues, never to be ignored.

An Inner Struggle: Job Change

Courage and ethics meld well together. We talk of moral courage. We might say that all decisions have a moral component. For example, changing jobs is a big issue in most people's work lives. It applies to decisions that leaders at the top frequently make, and it is the substance of much executive counsel-ing and coaching.

> You are in a dead-end job. You are middle age. It's either now or never. Are you going to risk greener pastures or are you going to hold on to what you know is secure? You don't like your boss, you don't like your co-workers. You

are a bit ashamed of yourself every day you go to work. But you like the steady paycheck. You are needed. And you can pay the rent and take your vacations.

On the other side you see people talking big. They hide their failures, but many are burned taking chances. They receive good pay, and are out of a job in nine months. Is the risk worth it? Are they in denial, having illusions about the market's interest in them? Or are you just a plain cowardly stick-in-the-mud?

Whoever said that a job is meant to be easy and fun? That's empty talk. A job is your duty. Work is your duty. Marriage is your duty. Going to church and paying your tithe is your duty. It feels good to do your duty. You feel clean. Your feel right. The burdens of guilt are lifted. That indeed is freedom. And when you have a steady job you are simply doing what is right. Stick with it and be proud of your steadfastness. Anything good that happens to you will immediately interpret as confirmation, validation, and reward for doing your duty and what is right.

On the other hand, there are those who live on the edge, who are always anxious, never know what tomorrow will bring, and prop themselves up artificially with all of the new business aphrodisiacs that are pandered by too many business magazines and business advertisements.

They lean forward, often fall, but some start running. Can you be the one who starts running? What's stopping you? From the July 9, 2001, issue of *Fortune,* here are some pronouncements from these business runners:

- "We're driven by innovation. What drives you?"
- "Individuality sets us apart. Our vision brings us together."
- "You could have more solutions than problems."
- "Hire minds."

- "Your customers are cutting their orders. Is it the economy? *Or is it you?*"

Will you choose yourself as a self-starter or as a conservative plodder? These are the inner struggles known to those who face their own inwardness.

It is a choice between two self-definitions. It is a choice between two definitions of what it means to be a human being, what it means to be alive, beliefs about risk and security, about ambition and adaptation. No one knows who the winner will be, for we will rationalize our choice to the end. And there is no answer. Gertrude Stein said it well, "There is no answer: There never was an answer. There never will be an answer. That's the answer."

The Rule of Reason . . . or Passion

One way to conceptualize this polarity is between duty and passion. Or there is the old-fashioned way, between reason and unreason. Reason will tell you to do your duty, to do what is consensual, to do what logically conforms to consistency and keeping promises. Unreason will tell you to follow your passion.

What about your free will? Your free will is neither reasonable nor is it passionate. It is pre-rational and pre-passionate. We have to understand this. We have to feel this. And when we do—and stop trying to solve the polarity between reason and unreason—we act.

There is no way to think your way out of this dilemma. You can only *choose* yourself out of it. And when you do, you understand the meaning of "Life cannot be lived without courage," "Free will is surrounded with anxiety," and "Throwing yourself into your reality, into free will and anxiety, is the only way to move forward."

That is embodied free will and can be experienced physically. It's a knot in your belly, a cramp in your heart, a twitch in your foot. But the result is that you let it be. You change fundamentally how you feel about being human, about being an individual, about being isolated, about being in community, about needing others, and about being emotionally available to others. This occurs because you allow the voice of your unconscious to speak up.

You learn to take pride in your freedom and independence, in your individuality, and in your choice of community. You feel a pull and a push, you feel a drive and a tendency, and your freedom, liberated from its solution-riveted shackles, will in the end carry you on its waves of intensity to some kind of a conclusion that will spell greatness.

Shakespeare wrote that "flights of angels sing thee to thy rest." Allow yourself to be wafted by your unconscious, subtle as that may be.

Crazy-Making

In the transition—from one personality to another, from one value system to another, from one self-definition to another—you will go through a period of crazy-making, a sense that you are insane. The decisions you make you will have to continue to make. But this perilous period of pseudo psychosis has also given you a goal, an objective, that organizes all your agonizing experience into one massive thrust toward your objective. You will know you have earned it. And you are surprised how smoothly the earth supports you. Leadership is the capacity to live in that realm of pure and anxious freedom in which decision making is continuous—very much like the birth of life itself, which did not occur just once but which continues to come about in the special areas of this world where God is still kissing this earth.

You can let your unconscious do the choosing. It's like asking, "What is the will of God?" You have to allow life to gradually move you in the direction in which it wants to go, knowing you will feel inadequate and weak, scared and doubting. You need plenty of practice in making difficult choices.

For as you do, you also learn how to implement them, how to stay with them, how not to lose your nerve.

That is how you decide to change jobs or to stay put, to opt for diversity or stay the same, to expand or to contract your business.

You think you want to keep your job, so you enroll in a mind-expanding seminar. Why? Because you allow your unconscious to push you in that direction. Or you forget about ambition, enjoy your evenings and your weekends with your friends, and look forward to retirement: mortgage paid, health insurance guaranteed, use the gym at the plant, save enough to buy a new car every two years, one vacation in the summer, and visit the grandchildren with gifts at Christmastime.

Who can ask for more? What is health? What is the good life? What is regularity and predictability? What is serenity?

The Choice

Here is how you deal with the eternal conflict between choosing reason and choosing passion. Once you know that you are free, you can never unlearn this insight. Justice Oliver Wendell Holmes said it well, "Man's mind, stretched to a new idea, never goes back to its original dimensions." To stretch the mind or not to stretch the mind, "to be or not to be—that is the question. . . ." Which is it, a life of pain or a death of peace? Does it matter? You now know that you are free, and you can allow yourself to let your unconscious streams go where they want to go, and you choose that path, every time. And you choose to hold yourself accountable for having permitted this unconscious choice to take place.

Is this your last job? Or have you just begun to dream? You have come to your fork in the road. It is not a choice between courage and cowardice, but rather a choice of two different acts of courage: to risk or not to risk? That is the question!

In Sum

Freedom of the will is not an emotion nor is it a thought. Quite the contrary, the freedom of the will is a "pre-predicative" state, before emotion and before thinking. We, as free will, choose reason and we, as free will, choose emotions. We choose how to respond to that which overwhelms us—rationally or emotionally, calmly or excitedly, thoughtfully or spontaneously. When it comes to the edge, we need to choose *both* reason *and* emotion. Emotion alone is dangerous, and reason alone is hollow. Together they bond for authenticity.

Energy is a funny word. In ordinary parlance, it is the capacity for vigorous activity. It is the sum of available power. In physics, it is the capacity to do work, which diminishes as one system does work on another (for example, batteries). In a colloquial informal way, energy describes that geyser inside the soul, at the center of consciousness, where something mysterious called "I" initiates action, generates activity, makes decisions, chooses, perseveres.

This point is difficult to define because it is doing the defining itself. This point is difficult to see, even with the inner eye, because it itself is what is doing the seeing in the first place. The camera is studying the camera that is doing the studying. The capacity to lay claim to that spot is the heart of leadership. That point is the *will*. And it is not *the* will, or *a* will. It is not even *my* will. It is much deeper than that: It is *me*; it is *I*. I *am* the will. The will *is* I.

That said, the ability to create my own energy, the fact that I can energize myself, the reality that I can also inspire others to energy—that is a commercial product, a business entity, an enterprise event. The will to energy has business value. On the marketplace, the decision for courage has a price.

In the end, it is the commitment to vigor, the drive to intensity that is one, perhaps the primary, component of a company's, or an individual's, stock price. That is the hard business application of what some people may think of as a soft philosophical idea.

Freedom and *will* are inseparable in their location within the inner self. And free will cannot be distinguished from the source of *energy* that I am. That is why we use the expression *free will.*

Those who grasp this point are authentic humans, who understand that we are not only rational animals but also the people of the will. This is the true heart of leadership. That's where we start. We are now bullet-proof, ready to take on the most onerous tasks with equanimity.

Here is their mantra:

> Leadership is about *energy,*
> generating it *yourself*
> and *transmitting* it to the organization.

> It is a decision, ongoing,
> that only *you* can make.
> And you make it for your *own* sake—
> it being the source of your *dignity* and *nobility* as a human being.

> Free will originates deep *within* you,
> as mysterious and *miraculous*
> as it is also clear and *powerful.*

> The *time* it takes to make the decision for leadership can be
> either one *nanosecond,* or a *lifetime* will not be enough.

> How do *you* choose?

> Now *spread* this message
> throughout your organization,
> by *example* . . .

> for you are the application.

◆ Activity

Participate in your favorite sport, be it walking or jogging, working out in the gym, tennis or golf, skydiving or swimming, whatever, and think of it as a meditation exercise, something beyond fun or healthful, something being the very meaning of your life. As you do it, do two things:

1. Focus on your free will. Every step, every motion, is a decision, every movement a choice. Say it to yourself: "I am choosing this movement and I am choosing that movement, I am choosing one more set."

2. Focus on the intersection. Your awareness is entering your body and your body is entering your consciousness. Say it to yourself: "I feel my consciousness filter into my body. I feel my body change the way I am conscious."

This over time will give you a sense of wholeness. Extend this feeling over your daily activities. You will be more relaxed and more centered. This is the *real* fun; counting calories and reading the sports page is not.

Then consider your business as your body too. Try to have the same relationship with your world as you do with your body. Your mind enters your work just as your work enters your mind.

Select a business task. You are planning for the quarterly meeting with your team. You are preparing your mind to do the necessary business and also be an inspiration to the team.

You plan after you have prepared your mind. For it is not only the content that matters, it is the manner in which you present yourself and relate to your people. Your focus is then on your people and who they are and what they need, not on your own self-consciousness. To yourself you put it all into words: "I am here for you. I am here to make you successful. I am here not to talk from me to you but to help you talk from yourself to yourself. I am connected with you, my mind is inside you, understanding you, joining hands with you, and then moving forward together." These words can structure how your mind thinks. This is for you only, but they will feel the connection. You do not necessarily do what they want. You have come to lead. But you connect with them inside themselves to hear what you as their boss need from them.

Write it out beforehand. The best preparation is not only to work on the messages you want to pass on but on the way your mind will function when you are face-to-face with them and present to them.

Remember to focus on your free will throughout. Everything is chosen all the time. You feel the weight of responsibility, you feel everywhere the exhilaration of being, and you feel the power and the accountability that come with it. And to reinforce these leadership truths you say to yourself, internally: "I am there and not only here. What I choose here impacts what happens there. I am responsible for how I think and choose and I am the cause of what happens elsewhere. That is how I am connected but that is also how I am tied down."

As with changing your diet, results will show up over time.

Are you now ready, are you now prepared, to dialogue with your stakeholders about courage? Will it help your purpose for being in business?

We have visited the continent of ethics, the zone where you submerge your being in the intelligence of ethics, that is, service, empathy, and principle. For it you need courage, moving over to submerge yourself into initiative, anxiety, and free will. By now you are a rather powerful individual, a leader, or a leader's coach, someone to be taken seriously. It is now time to move over to sobering reality. It's like a new world, a new continent, and a new way of being. The organization expects that the leader must have it all, or at least the potential for that.

REALITY

We live at a time that must be lived through us.

ADRIENNE RICH

I have nothing to offer you but blood, toil, tears, and sweat.

SIR WINSTON CHURCHILL

A conquering army on the border will not be halted by the power of eloquence.

OTTO VON BISMARK

A corporation is an entity to make money for its stockholders. It's not an entity with a heart—and it's not supposed to have a heart. It is what it is. And to get a corporation's attention you take their money, or threaten to take their money. It's real simple.

JOHN COALE, ATTORNEY

I could hear the angels sing and the cash register ring.

MELVIN BELLI, ATTORNEY

Bliss like thine is bought by years
Dark with torment and with tears.

EMILY BRONTË

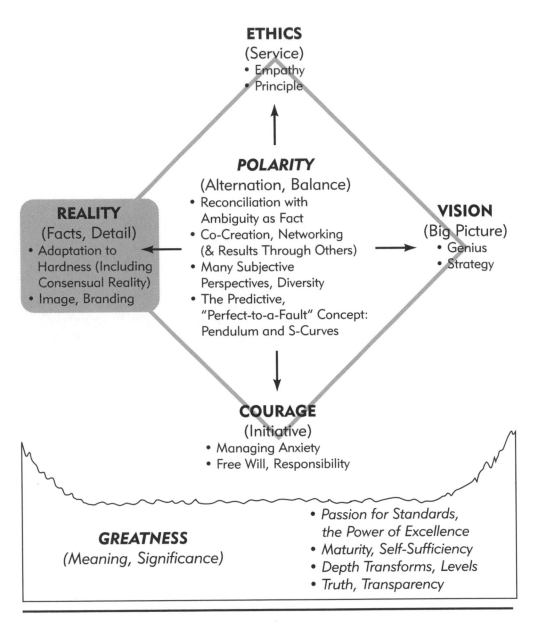

Figure 15.1. The Leadership Diamond®: Reality

CHAPTER 15

Reality

The Zone that Gives No Quarter

DEFINITION: Facts and No Illusion

ELEMENTS: Adaptation to Hardness;

Image, Individual and Organizational

O N LIFE'S JOURNEY, *reality is your merchant, always looking where the money is. I entered a bakery and asked the owner how* fresh *an item was, and his immediate and automatic answer was "That'll be two fifty." A good mercantile response indeed! The majority of people you are likely to meet are merchants, although in many circles that trait is hardly ever mentioned. But for business, the merchant is the central figure.*

The merchant, to whom the wizard introduces you on your journey through life, is not much concerned with the inner world. The merchant's realm is the outer world of fact and not the inner world of sensitivities.

When we talk about reality we are entering a new land, a new continent. We are talking about an attitude. We call it facts and no illusion. I would say this is the predominant attitude in business. Perhaps it should be. But 9/11/01 seems to have changed all that. But who knows for how long. The message is to pay attention to the facts first and foremost and put fantasy, dreams, sentiment, and the soft stuff aside. Facts and no illusions means numbers, data, statistics, measurements. "This is the result of your blood work and we therefore prescribe this medication and that regimen." Scientific facts and scientific solutions. The realist is the materialist, who has little understanding of the integrity, even the reality, of the soul. There is an interesting interview with Jack Welch in the *Harvard Business Review* illustrating this point. It comes straight from the recent scion of American management. In reviewing the book, *Jack: Straight from the Gut,* Welch, Collingwood, and Coutu make the following observation: "If his book was, as its title claimed, straight from the gut, where was the self-examination, the analysis of his motives, the baring of his deepest drives and conflicts? Welch seemed genuinely baffled by the complaints. Relentlessly focused outward and forward, he's uninterested in plumbing the depths of his own psyche" (2002, p. 90).

I am not placing a value judgment on this blindness toward inwardness. I simply want to use it as an example for a demeanor that for a long time had been idolized by American business. Quite to the contrary, I would say that sentimental philosophers like me are anathema to the business community, and if there is one thing for me to learn it is to make hardness, cash results, the idolatry of financial results, the center of my life. It must be a counterweight to many of the abstract and emotional aesthetic issues that have preoccupied me for so long.

In fact, the article gets even more serious: "Critics have used the occasion of the book's publication to revive their claims that GE under Welch sacrificed people for profits" (Ibid, p. 90).

Many CEOs, by their behavior even more than their words, have reminded me, and many others, that unless you make speed and results, ruthlessness and productivity, that is, the relentless pursuit of strong financial statements—with your EPS and ROI and growth ratio and margins precisely where the securities analysts expect them to be—then, literally, "You are out of here!"

Life in the management suite of many a corporation is no better than boot camp, except for the money.

The point is not that this is bad. The point is that reality as a business orientation must be clearly understood, strongly presented, recognized as an attitude of choice, and connected boldly with the profits and dominance achieved by American business. The World Economic Forum meeting for the first time in New York City in 2002 was a good example of the utter realism of the business community. In the war against terrorism, the United States is taking at this writing a very aggressive stance, whereas the Europeans are much milder and even meeker in their foreign policy. Many of us at this juncture need to say to ourselves, not that we wish to retreat into meditation or proclaim the virtues of the arts, but rather that we ourselves have been negligent in dealing with the utter harshness of reality, opposing it rather than joining it. And that the lesson for us is not to sing the praises of softness but rather to venture out into the cold and steely rigor of the life of numbers and consequences.

Mind you, this is not all. The Diamond demands access to all the virtues, to all the orientations toward life, to all the deep structures of human existence—not just one. If we neglect any of them, we court trouble. And if we develop any one excessively, at the expense of another, make them, as my friend Ahmed Yehia puts it, "perfect to a fault," then we can predict that disaster is not too far off. We can overextend realism at the expense of all the other Diamond corners. At the expense of ethics, which makes us a bully; at the expense of vision, which makes us violent and abusive without a strategy, a plan, or a direction—the kind of accusation we at this writing level against Ariel Sharon in his relentless retaliations against the suicide bombers of the Hamas.

Training in reality boils down to two paths. And in this connection we cover two topics: (1) adaptation to hardness and hard facts and (2) the importance of your personal and corporate image that you project to your markets. On the Shadow Diamond side, we struggle against a fantasy world, lying to ourselves, thinking that the world is soft, and that everyone loves you like your mother and does not perceive you instead as an independent and self-seeking competitor.

Humanity in Danger

Reality is the predominance of the machine, the technical, the mechanical, the materialistic. It can endanger the humanity of the person.

In a recent visit to a city that shall remain unnamed, my wife and I wanted to change the seat assignments on our railroad tickets. We had first class on the way out and did not want the same seats on the way back. They were pointing backwards and had no tables, even though the first-class car was otherwise empty and there was therefore no one sitting at the tables available.

The clerk informed us that the seats were assigned by computer and could not be changed.

"You mean the computer chooses for you and you have no say?" I asked in alarm.

"That is correct; that is how we do it here."

"Do you mean to say that even when we bought the tickets the seat assignment was automatic and the customer has no input?"

"That is correct!" The clerk was becoming impatient with my inopportune inquisition of him.

"I can't believe it!" I retorted in amazement. "The whole thing is run by computer and the human being is but an adjunct, a victim, chattel?"

"That is how it's done." The clerk looked at me as if I had just dropped in from outer space.

I put on my hat of philosophical consultant: "Does this not bother you?" I had fired my last piece of ammunition.

"No, not at all." It was clear that to him my questions were dumb.

It was a small point, but it spoke volumes, and I was aghast. We had not seen a person, but a zombie, brainwashed into thinking that he is a vassal to the technology. I had seen the end of the world and met the last man on earth. That's how it felt. Reality perfect in all respects, at the expense of personal freedom and personal dignity. It was like a funeral, but without people, except the dead, for the living were all gone.

The Nature of Hardness: Do You Really "Get It"?

There are many persons living with an excess of illusions:

- "One day business will pick up and we will all be rich."

- "This is a dynamite business idea. Let's try to get some capital together."

- "We wrote off two hundred and fifty million dollars this quarter, but we know that by the third quarter of next year we will be profitable again."

- "We expect to have an IPO in two years, and we project the price will be around $35 a share."

- "It is virtually certain that I will get my promotion, so let's put money down on a house."

A colleague invested in a franchise because he was friends with the investor. He did not do thorough preliminary analysis, as a consequence of which he lost his shirt! A hard-nosed merchant would have known that the figures did not add up. Reality is not techniques, data, and facts as much as it is attitude, attitude, and attitude—getting sick, physically ill, panicked to the core, when you find someone in a state of denial. The code words that announce the appearance of the reality orientation are "results" and "performance." And they are merciless!

Reality is a deep structure requiring the utmost caution. Reality is an attitude, a demeanor of respect for the Other, that is more powerful than you and doesn't like you. If you ignore reality you are "dead meat" in short shrift. If as a result you overreact, you lose yourself altogether. You become hard and callous yourself and lose all chance for real intimacy and true human values. For love exists only because hardness protects it.

We all know we must face reality, but when we understand we see the harshness amplified. The executive above who put money down on a house lost it all because he did not receive the anticipated promotion. Reality comes through for you perhaps only 10 percent of the time. We ignore that statistic. In good times people are profligate, not realizing the importance of frugality and conservation while the cornucopia overflows. Business is a series of S-curves, the oscillation of waves, a swinging pendulum. And you never know where you are.

We think we are realistic, but we are not. And defeat, when it comes, makes that clear. We have calluses, but they are not armor enough against the tsunami onslaught of reality. Unless we are viscerally aware of that, so that when caution is indicated we become ill if it is not there, we are not taking good care of those who depend on our leadership.

The Structure of Reality

Realism is essential, but we can never ignore the risks we should take through courage, the love we need through ethics, and the vision we need for hope—all of which fly in the face of the bottomless pit into which reality, like a vortex maelstrom, can suck us all.

Reality is all outer world and no inner space. Hard reality is unforgiving and it attacks and corrodes the tender core of the inner world. Reality tethers us to the ground. Reality is not interested in being nice, not even in what is true. Reality cares only about that which works.

Where do we learn our virtues? Ethics we learn when we are psychotherapists; courage when we are soldiers; and vision when we are artists. But we learn our reality when we are bankers.

Table 15.1 provides definitions for reality and its subsets, hardness and image.

Reality is the fully integrated recognition that there is a world around you that is in essence different from you, does not care about you, but is a world that you desperately need. It comes to you often as data, reports, numbers,

Table 15.1. Reality

Deep Structure with Subsets	What It Is/Definition/ Description	The Shadow Against Which We Fight
Reality	Facts, no illusion; "Face reality as it is, not as it was or you wish it were"	Fantasy, illusion, ignorance, lies
Hardness	"The Other": the world is unforgiving, full of deceit, betrayal, bias, prejudice, unfairness, illness, injury, legal action, aloof disregard	Rationalization, self-deception, naïveté, denial, escape, wishful thinking
Image	Reputation and its fragility; the projections of others; how others perceive you may say more about them than you, but they will act on that perception nevertheless	Excuses, cover-ups, whitewash, pretext, ruse

and so forth. If we can find one word for it, it is *facts*. Reality's respect for facts is not an intellectual recognition, but an emotional one, an existential one, one that involves your whole being and changes your personality—usually from soft to hard.

Where Is *Your* Reality?

Each of us has his or her own unique reality issues that must be confronted, are evaded, and may be inherently irresolvable:

- "If I could only get rid of my non-performing unit," says a manager, "we would show a profit every quarter!"

- "Sales are dropping, the market is saturated, the economy is slowing, and I am feeling it in my business and I am hurting."

- "If I had been just a tad more attentive I would not have crashed the company car. It's now too late. It's happened and cannot be undone. Now look what I am stuck with! My boss is going to have a fit. It's the result of the stress on our team because of the project's short deadline."

- "Our department is late with our taxes. What's worse, we have no funds to cover what we owe."

- "Our accounting department is late with our bookkeeping and accounting. Why do they have such a hard time keeping the financials in order?"

- "Before we go to trial against our unhappy customer, we will need to have all the depositions carefully studied and analyzed. This takes forever. It seems our organization is no good at dealing with complex details."

These are typical complaints about being overwhelmed and inundated with reality. "If I were only to feel better, have more energy, and not ache so much, I could handle my job quite well and efficiently. I'm just so tired. I am no longer doing good work. Is there no way out?"

Can you see yourself here in any of these not uncommon examples? *What is your own biggest reality issue?*

Step one in managing these is to adopt an attitude toward reality that it *is* reality. This change in attitude is the crux. There is, of course, technical help. To take advantage of that requires financial assets. "I don't have those financial assets," you may say. Well, then, there is attitude. Attitude you can change, instantaneously. You are never defeated. You only defeat yourself. But should you be what you call defeated, you can handle that well. If you so choose. Then you are not defeated.

Hemmingway said that a person can be destroyed but not defeated. Adopting a reality attitude means being willing to see reality for what it is, early. Personalizing reality, focusing on your reality and not on someone else's—that is the attitude to cultivate. And the earlier we do it, as in the treatment of disease, the greater our chances of recovery and survival.

The sooner reality has entered our bloodstream the sooner we can become leaders. The longer we wait the harder it becomes. These are the kind of intelligent leadership conversations we need to have about reality, with ourselves and with our people. It changes our character. It affects our personality. And it is the critical success factor for results!

Make it a project with your team to instill the basic reality attitude in them without destroying their more tender values.

Life Can Be Hard. Are You Ready?

I worked with a car company executive who was in charge of prototypes. His division designed and built the new models. Some cars on the road even today were his technological and economic success and are tributes to him. He was invited to lecture at prestigious universities on how to engineer competitively.

Celebrating the millionth car off the assembly lines, he, nevertheless, on the flight back to headquarters in the company airplane, got into an argument with the boss, mostly on cost overruns. I saw him in his office, immediately after his arrival, visibly upset. He said he wasn't feeling well and lay on the couch, and I asked his secretary to call his wife. Right then and there he had a massive heart attack.

This is reality. It hits hard, it hits suddenly, it wakes you up, and it transforms everything. It tells you there is more than what you think, and it has more power than you do. Suddenly you can muster the energy to act rationally and maturely. Things you could not do before, like balance work and health, abruptly fall into place.

Don't wait for your heart attack to wake you up. The smart leader is awake before, not after.

The Hard Personality

The Diamond describes different personalities that you can become. Ultimately, you make a choice. You are responsible for who you are, for down deep in your nature you do always have a choice, limited as that may be and difficult as that might be to carry out.

Leadership is situational, so the choices may vary. And for these choices you are also fully responsible. One of these choices of personality is to totally absorb in yourself the toughness and the hardness of life. You grow nerves of steel. You can be icy cold and calculating, not because you are born that way but because you *choose* to see the world that way. Circumstances in your childhood made it logical, perhaps, to be cold. But the choice was always yours—sometimes more clearly than at others.

The choice for being hard and cold will have fashioned a mechanical and distanced, detached, life for you. You can cut people off, perhaps because they cut you off. You are prepared to make enemies. You can dismiss another human being. Some find this difficult, for they will equally be dismissed themselves. Others find it uplifting to be strong and tough. It can be exhilarating to some. You feel your power, your muscles.

In an extreme application of the principle of reality, you are prepared to destroy people, families, and lives, if it is right for the business. That does not bother you. People call you an s.o.b., and you take pride that you present to the world such a cold and hard front. Many an executive and many a general has become famous for precisely this political and business presence. You value the business effectiveness of this uncaring stance. You enjoy being stern. It makes you feel strong and powerful. And you are convinced that it makes you effective. Such is the realist, a central figure in business leadership and in other types of organizations. Books such as *Management Secrets of Attila the Hun* and nicknames such as *Chainsaw Al* for Al Dunlap and *Neutron Jack* for Jack Welch cater to this taste. Even if you yourself choose not to be this way, you will have to deal with many who do make that choice.

The point here is not to evaluate this choice. It is instead to call attention to the fact that being cold and hard is a choice of personality. It may have good or bad consequences. Its value surely is situational. But the leadership part of it is that you *chose* it and you *continue* to choose it. And that you *teach* others that this is the way to be as a leader. The focus is on the *choice* of realism, more than on realism itself. The message is that realism is part of the business and organizational scene, and if you ignore that reality requires a powerful response, you are not a leader. The result is that you will be ineffective and lack credibility.

Teaching

Your job as a leader under the deep structure of reality is to teach the people over whom you have responsibility "to face reality as it is and not as it was or how you wish it were." And you do that by redesigning language and, with it, the attitudes, feelings, and behaviors behind it. As suggested before, some overdo reality at the expense of *vision*—which makes them coarse, crude, boring, unimaginative, and unrefined. Some overdo reality at the expense of *ethics*—which makes them rude and we call them bullies. And others will overdo reality at the expense of *courage,* in which case we call them bureaucrats and bean counters.

"You are not highly regarded in this organization. It's a painful realization. It's a fact. You are in denial. Face it. Acknowledge the consequences. You won't last. Take action." Harsh words, but they are the language of reality. Combine it with the language of courage, ethics, and vision, and you have leadership: "Go for it! Get more training. Don't waste time. Sign up before you change your mind. Show some initiative!" "I understand how you feel. It is not easy. I will stand by you." And "There is a better future ahead for you and your family. Be ready for some frustrating and lean times, but you can expect a whole new life for all of you." This is all-around leadership language.

But the kernel leadership message here is that reality literally "means business." Some philosophers have referred to the reality part of experience as that which is totally unlike you, that which resists you, that which limits you, that which has a mind of its own. A thing, an object, is different from consciousness; indifference is other than love. You want the world to say *yes* to you. Instead it says *no.* Every salesperson understands this point. Every CFO trying to raise the stock price understands this point.

And reality is powerful. To have that awareness, to have come to terms with these limits to what is possible for us as human beings, to have accepted the consequences, lived the implications, that is the leader strong in the deep structure of reality or realism.

Civilization has removed reality several layers from the daily experience of most people. We are soft and flabby, so that when reality strikes, we are unprepared. The leader is ready to stare down reality and make peace with it—

whether it is the stock price that collapses, a product that must be recalled, an ethical lapse in fulfilling a contract, or a plant shut down by a wildcat strike. Whatever the problem, managing it begins with being able to accept the inevitable no-saying "otherness" in your life. In the absence of this bittersweet realization, we are in danger of being led on a primrose path toward never-never land.

What decisions with respect to facing hardness have you made and are you prepared to make in the future?

TLC

In contrast to stark reality, there is a place inside everyone's soul that longs to be dependent, trusting, understood. We want to be taken care of, accepted unconditionally, valued, included, and heard. Yet reality can easily deny all these values to us and get away with it, without any allusion to justice, compassion, empathy, or understanding. And we have to take it.

It is therefore not easy to operate in a "realistic" environment. The humane purpose of *science* and *technology* is to do something about the recalcitrance of the "other": to tame it, to manipulate it, to force it to do our bidding. This is the function of medicine. In primitive times, disease was a scourge because no protection against it existed. Free will cannot attack directly the reality of an illness. But the will toward science and technology, the circuitous route to effectiveness, does work. The pyramids were built by people, directly using their brawn. Skyscrapers today are built by machines. That is the difference. Technology has circumvented the overwhelming power of reality and has helped us harness it. Instead of being limited to walking and riding horses, we can now drive cars and fly airplanes. Rather than having to be mystical about the stars, we now have super-telescopes and spaceships to take a look. These are all instances of maneuvering "the Other" into doing what we want it to do in spite of its overwhelming resistance to direct confrontation. It's an end run for us around intractable reality.

Reality As the Will of Other People

Possibly the most pernicious of all forms of reality is the will of other people. They use their own free will to say "no" to you. They can rob you, kill you, reject you, ignore you, betray you. And science cannot change the way people exercise their will toward you. That would be magic, like love potions. And they are not available.

As an executive, manager, or consultant, it is your charge to guide people to cope with reality as they find it. You need to deal with intransigent employees, callous bosses, reticent markets, conniving customers, offensive bureaucrats. That is your reality. You need to help others learn these skills.

The Leader's Task

It is essential at all levels of leadership and under all circumstances to be able to deal with this severe "otherness" of reality. To manage this successfully, without being a moral and emotional casualty in the process, may be the hardest task of life: not to be degraded by a degrading workplace, not to be made callous by being treated cruelly, not to take out on others the deprivations and injustices that you yourself suffered. And to manage this with grace and effectiveness, with results and honor, that is the task of a leader. And you do not manage these affronts for your own sake but to help those who depend on you and those you serve.

How to be psychologically strong without becoming morally degraded, how to endure unfairness without losing empathy, to be abandoned and remain a rock to others, those are the optimal leadership traits. The reward is that you do your duty, that you honor yourself and the human race.

How much reality can you take? How much truth can you manage? How much can you take of guilt, vulnerability, insignificance, values denied, meanings unrealized, death? You take it in doses, titrate it into your soul. This is your authentic source of empowerment, maturation, "characterment," or "encharacterization." People tell me not to be so pessimistic, so cynical. Focus on the positive, they say. Proponents of Appreciative Inquiry, such as David Cooperrider, say, wisely, that the topic of your conversation crafts your environment. Emphasize your strengths, that which is positive.

That's great indeed, for what we here emphasize is the most positive of all, namely experiencing what is real. And beyond that, of course, finding it difficult to not involve courage in the discussion of reality, we make as subject for conversation our free will. That's our strength, that's indeed positive, that's healthful.

Thus, to emphasize the positive would not be to say that I am good at math and should therefore become an engineer or an accountant. It would be to acknowledge that I am free—I am a freedom—no matter what else I am good at, and I must perforce appreciate that freedom and make it the primary topic of my conversation. My environing world will change to become responsible, to not blame others, and to understand the profundity and the burden, but also the opportunity of co-creating the world in which we live.

The Rules

Commitment to reality is the implementation phase, where thought becomes reality. No amount of planning in leadership will suffice if managing obdurate reality as a personality trait, as the hardiness of the soul, has not been mastered. This needs to become part of the organizational culture; it is what managers need to learn to teach. And learning to cope with reality is not only good for the organization but also for the soul of the employee, and with it, the individual's family.

David Whyte (1996) says it well: "Despite everything you have achieved, life refuses to grant you, and always will refuse to grant you, immunity from its difficulties" (p. 27).

Here are the standard processes to cope with stubborn reality:

Stand firm. Be strong by making a choice, standing firm, and being ready to die for the choice you have made. Examples are William Wallace, whom many now visualize as Mel Gibson in *Braveheart,* or the lone student dissident facing the Chinese army tank in Tienamen Square in 1989.

Do you know someone like that at work?

Join the opposition. Be strong by becoming hard as the enemy itself. This is bonding with the enemy in the spirit of "If you can't fight them, join them." In extreme examples, the abused child becomes a child abuser, the daughter of an alcoholic turns to drink herself.

Some of the more difficult people you meet at work may be hard as nails. Do you know one of them?

Dialogue. Be strong by dialoguing with evil, internalizing the shadow, creating an empowering synthesis. An example would be the scientific breakthrough, where opposing theories are resolved by a genius, as was the case with Einstein, who resolved the paradox that light travels at the same speed no matter whether the source moves or not and regardless of whether the observer moves or not with respect to the light.

Do you have an unfinished conversation with someone regarding an issue that has to do with facing a reality in the workplace and avoiding its denial—either about you or about the other person? What still needs to occur?

Learn the hidden message. Each time you must face reality, you have that same challenge: *What is the hidden message that you can read into a personal catastrophe?*

Bill Clinton's dalliance with Monica Lewinsky, made public by Linda Tripp and Kenneth Starr (and ultimately by Congress), led him to deny in public that it occurred. Rather than admit at the beginning that he made a moral mistake, it took no less than impeachment proceedings before he would tell something like the truth. His external reality was that he had been found out under very embarrassing circumstances. His response was to lie. He discovered later what a serious mistake that was, instead of facing the reality that he had deceived his family and the public, and that he needed fundamentally to redefine the meaning of what it was to be Bill Clinton. That way of dealing with reality—which would have been far more effective—was not in his character.

Is there any reality currently in your life that requires an act of leadership to address? Is that act of leadership choosing a new you that, whereas temporarily pained, will improve your work life forever?

Act on vision. On the business side we have an example of managing reality not so much with courage as with vision. In his article in the *Harvard Business Review*, "Moving Upward in a Downturn," Darrell Rigby (2001) distinguishes leadership responses from fear responses. The idea is to call on your power of vision to move from the panic reaction of "Cut costs like there's no tomorrow" to "Treat your stakeholders like fellow combatants who happen to be stuck in the same foxhole" (p. 99). In such a mindset, you might scoop up acquisition bargains that bolster the core business. He mentions Emerson Electric, which shifted smoothly and slowly to add people and R&D investments to add to their capacity for growth.

What's the Cash Value?

Where is this all going? What's the business purpose of such a lengthy discussion of reality? Consider this: In the mental health professions, contact with reality, a correct perception of the consensual world, is the single most significant criterion for *mental health,* even for sanity itself.

And what is the cash value of a targeted discussion on the importance of facing reality? What is the return on training the mind so that whenever we think or perceive, or feel or do, the focus is fully on being in touch with the immediate reality that we are facing? If this point about the meaning and the centrality of reality is made repeatedly and emphatically in an organization, and with customers, the results can be to greatly strengthen the resolve to act on the basis of an intelligent appraisal and a comprehensive database regarding what is really happening, what the facts are, and often, control over the exact numbers. And resolve translates into dollars.

To start the discussion, ask:

- "What is the cash value of this reality conversation?"

- "What are the savings?"

- "What are the sales implications?"

- "What is the implication for customer satisfaction?"

- "What project succeeded that would otherwise have failed?"

Herein lies the payoff.

Hard as it may be to quantify, we nevertheless ask our clients to tell us what Strategic Intervention Moments they have had, what the Diamond content was in them, and how well-equipped their people are in carrying out Intelligent Leadership Conversations within the Diamond context.

And then we ask, "What have been the financial returns, long-term and short-term, locally and globally, from this effort to change attitudes and behaviors by installing a new respect for leadership language? Has culture implemented strategy realistically in your organization? Do the numbers confirm that?"

Remember that focus on reality is one way of being intelligent, but not the only way. Seen in total context it may be out of proportion. There is danger in excess, as well as there is danger in not being dominant enough.

Too much reality, often carried out at the expense of ethics, makes people crude and arrogant. But not enough reality quickly undermines a person's leadership credibility. It is important for you to examine your personality structure to check how you manage when you are confronted with an irrevocable NO from the world: A relationship that is important to you has ended. You find out that a contract has been violated. Your trust has been betrayed— you desperately want a relationship in which you can trust, so you trusted too soon only to taste the harsh bitterness of betrayal. You thought you stood on firm ground and, as in a nightmare, the scaffolding suddenly collapsed from under you. Your associate has been badmouthing you behind your back, stealing clients away from you.

◆ Activity

Think of occasions in the past when, in your opinion, your company's business plan has been out of touch with reality.

- What blinders did top management use? In other words, how did they rationalize their path away from reality?

- What were the consequences for the company?

- Over the years, what have been some of the great illusions in your business life?

- What has happened to the business as a result?

- What should you have done differently?

- Is there a current illusion under whose spell you are doing business?

Whereas facing hardness is one way to come to terms with reality, a second is what we call *image.* It is to be aware of how others perceive you, how you affect others, what happens to others in your presence, and what others say behind your back. This is a most useful part of realism, for people act on these perceptions and you would be much damaged if you acted in blithe ignorance of these facts.

CHAPTER 16

Image

Multiple Perspectives

A GOOD MERCHANT DOES NOT LIVE IN THE INNER WORLD *but in the outer. Thus a key concern is what others think of you. Your image on the market, as person or company, is your currency. It is reputation, trust, identity. It is your most precious possession and your greatest commercial value. The realist lives outside in the world of public opinion. And the latter is not fashioned only by you, but it is heavily co-created with the client system. Don't think your culture is your customer's culture, and don't believe that your values are your customer's values. Be prepared to think differently, especially on the global market.*

Narcissism

I once saw a cartoon in *The New Yorker* of Narcissus sitting next to the pond, morose, with his girlfriend. She looks over to him and asks, "Narcissus, you seem depressed! Is there someone else?"

Most of us are narcissists. The narcissistic premise that the way I see myself is how others see me is outrageously naïve. I may think I am important and have an *exalted* view of myself. Or I may think of myself as insignificant and have a *depraved* view of myself. I may wonder how others see me: exalted or depraved. If I were attentive, I would discover that, far from being seen as either exalted or depraved, I am not seen at all! As far as others are concerned, I have disappeared in the woodwork. Or worse, I never existed in the first place. I am a non-entity, a non-being, at best a number. Others have zero interest in me.

Well, that may come as a surprise. As a business person or a politician, my success is based on how people vote for me—literally with their votes and symbolically with their pocketbooks. Both are buying decisions. Polling is not necessarily at all a measure of myself, but more a measure of the people voting and purchasing. The exact same thing goes for employees and managers. The difference between polls and the Diamond is simply degrees of depth.

> In business you need to learn how to place yourself into your customer's mind better and more deeply than the competition. The hidden danger, greater than most people realize, is that you *do* believe that the customer thinks like you, although in truth the exact opposite is more likely to be the case. For one, your boss, who is your most important internal customer, wants you to think in terms of the entire organization and not just yourself. You may believe you already do, but your boss thinks you do not. And your supervisor will act on what he or she perceives. That's reality.

Diversity: The Cure for Narcissism

Enormous numbers of issues can be discussed under the topic of reality: facts, data, information, numbers, details, statistics, research, history. After hardness, perhaps the most useful issue to reflect on and to make use of for purposes of leadership is the theme of *diversity*. In the last analysis, diversity means to choose to see the world through the eyes of another and, in particular, to see yourself through the eyes of that other person.

Diversity means that, whereas the world is full of people like you, and whereas it is most meritorious to talk about the brotherhood and the sisterhood of humankind, people are also very different from one another. People have diverse world views. These diversities are expressed foremost in ethnic and religious forms. And people are *extremely sensitive* about having the value of their unique way of being diverse called into question—or even just brought to their attention.

Diversity reaches far beyond the rational and deep into the unconscious. No conflicts are more bitter than those based on divisions of views regarding the nature of reality and its nucleus of values. And no bonds are closer than the ancient tribal drums calling us to action on behalf of our private ancestry. Emotions run high and it is often excruciatingly difficult to find common ground. The world's trouble spots, those that can ignite a major conflagration, are ethnic, tribal, and religious: Northern Ireland, the Middle East, the former Yugoslavia, Chechnya, Afghanistan, Indonesia, Kashmir, India, and so forth.

It is easy enough to say that we must value and welcome diversity. Of course we must. It is ethically right, and, from a pragmatic point of view, it can be challenging and creative. Appreciating diversity is also a modern necessity. In a global world, we have no choice in the matter. But diversity also means that I am not understood. It means that others do not see what I see and value what I value and prize what I prize.

We can overdo the toleration for diversity, as when we lose all absolute values and all sense of personal pride and identity. We can also overdo jingoism, and be biased and prejudiced, which has lead to some of the most ugly episodes in modern times. It's a genuine polarity.

Diversity is a fact, and your task as leader is to *teach* those who depend on you the nature of diversity and ways to cope with it. Above all, it is your responsibility to show them how to *integrate* these insights about diversity *into the way they do business.*

Image

You are not your image, you are *you.* And you barely know yourself! But everyone else thinks you are your image. Whether we talk about a corporate image or how people perceive you, as leader you must come to terms with two stark realities: (1) You help create the reality of your image, so you need to find out your contribution to it and make the decision to change it and (2) you are a victim of the unresolved internal conflicts of your customers. It's really their problem and not yours. But their customer status makes these problems yours. You must come to terms with that unfair but unalterable feature of your business.

The service industry is a good example. The hotel clerk is there to check you in. Housekeeping is expected to have the room clean and orderly. But the traveler after a long trip is cranky, anxious, and frustrated—and worried about tomorrow's sales presentation. The underpaid, undertrained, and understandably immature clerk is expected to play the role of psychiatrist, providing what Carl Rogers called "unconditional positive regard" and demonstrating all the skills of "active listening."

The deeper role of the hotel staff seems to be to provide emotional support and a kind of nursing understanding of how the world looks and feels to the customer. For the staff is not a person but a representative of the whole business, and the clerk is seen as the projected image of the unresolved needs of the worn-out customer. That is the image issue. And the reward for the staff is to experience a higher level of personal skill, namely, emotional intelligence and to learn and gain personal growth from the business transaction. These are the brutal image realities that people face in business. I wonder how clearly these are understood and how well people are able to realize that growth, personal character, is what is required and is what they gain from their jobs.

You perceive them as hotel representatives, there to give you what you paid for. You do not see them as individuals in their own right, nor should you, for that is the social contract with which we all live. Conversely, they are paid to see you as a needy customer, not to dump their issues on you. Then they would have to pay you. If the expectations of the social construct are not met, then tempers fly.

Projection is really a form of abuse. Emotionally the hotel employees too need human approval, but they are rebuffed instead. They need to feel liked, but they are derided instead. They need to express their feelings of frustration, but instead they smile and serve. That is how they have been taught to deal with negative projections. It is in the face of that rejection that they have to be effective and not slacken. When you feel the projections of others you know that you are not a real person to them but an extension of their perturbed unconscious. Image is a painful reality. Responding to it is a heroic skill. You can't be in business without understanding that.

A good example is a flight attendant I spoke to on this topic:

> "Never mind me. Tell me how *you* feel about your work."
>
> "Oh! Don't ask!" she replied. "Our managers are demanding and show little compassion." So began the flood of her unburdening. "Some pilots treat us like servants. They claim we don't know our business. The passengers are often hostile and irrational—as if everything were my fault! I am to blame for everything! And at the end of a long flight I feel like screaming! And my colleagues are also on edge—politics, gossip, favoritism. Too much, if you ask me!"

"Do you have any training and ongoing support for this level of emotional frustration and stress?" I asked.

"Not much regarding people skills, mostly safety," she continued. "Few care, few acknowledge good work, and the pay is low. But I work for the love of it. I like helping people."

What better example is there of a person who has confronted the hard reality of projection, the hazard of one's public image, and still takes responsibility for the whole. She does not receive much more than internal rewards. If you ask me, I say that this is a hero's life: facing the reality of projection, of people responding to one's image. Whoever thought that business required such internal leadership maturity!

Business Application

The business application of diversity has to do with understanding how I am seen by others, what happens to others when I enter in their field of vision or arena of consciousness. People will not tell me what I must know most:

- Do I have bad breath? How will I find out?

- Am I rude? Do I annoy people? Will they avoid me? I think I am pleasantly aggressive; will people take to me as I display this executive virtue?

- Am I cool? Do others think I am ridiculous?

- Do I come across as weak and not believable? Do I make zero impact? And yet I remember my mother telling me how powerful I was.

- Are my rationalizations blatant, transparent even to a child? Do I pontificate magnificently on why one never needs to take risks in relationships?

- If I feel that my boss has humiliated me in public, do I just take it? Do I fail to affirm my dignity? Do I not have the skills to assert myself graciously? Do I tell myself that is OK? Am I simply turning the other cheek, but when I go to sleep I have nightmares?

- Do I not know how to close a sale? Am I embarrassed to confront? Yet people are lovely to me and I reciprocate by being nice. Do I keep trying more of the same, yet my sales record is abysmal? Does everyone know I am scared, except for me?

Knowing how others perceive you is of special importance in all forms of management, in sales, and in recognizing the role of the company image, the branding of the product. We ridicule the politician's endless polling and focus groups. Yet if you are in business, including the business of politics, your entire existence depends on how you are seen by your market. Knowing that, objectively is transformational. A 360-degree feedback assessment is a great idea, especially if it is from your close associates and they are honest.

Learning, without asking, how one is perceived in light of the prejudices and biases of others, is one of the great marketing tools. Occasionally we do need to interpret ourselves to other people, customers, bosses, and peers in particular, cautiously and considerately to be sure, in order to avoid damaging misunderstandings. Frequently it comes to me that one role of a consultant is to interpret one person to another: boss to subordinate, subordinate to boss, customer to salesperson, and even salesperson to customer.

What can we infer from actions? Actions often reflect attitudes. But behaviors may start out phony and gradually reinforce themselves to become also attitudes. Your gruff behavior as boss may please you. It's how your father was and you admired his demonstrable strength and you received praise from imitating him. You are surprised that your subordinates do not react as your father did. They cry instead, avoid you, and make nasty comments behind your back. They work less. You have a bad 360-degree and your supervisor reprimands you! It's all downhill for you!

So you change your behavior. You do not raise your voice. You no longer criticize bluntly. You tone down your language, making it more mellow. You count to ten before you open your mouth. And you remember once in a while to acknowledge and validate the people who work for you. They take to you. They talk to you. They seek you out. Productivity actually goes up. You wouldn't have admitted it earlier, but you like the new attention! Your attitude too changes.

Good Business

It is very difficult for us to learn how many of our failures are the result of negative and unflattering perceptions people have of us, perceptions we could remedy if we but knew, but perceptions they will never mention to us. We have to figure this out all by ourselves.

The rule is: Don't be *paranoid,* but don't be a *fool* either. Do you think you have been subject to ethnic discrimination, sexual harassment? Is that really what happened, or are you making excuses for your own inadequacies? This would make you paranoid. On the other hand, are you taking personal blame for what is really discrimination? Have you been excluded from something or lost a sale, not because of your own incompetence and inadequacies but simply as a result of a customer's racial bias?

The message here is: Be realistic and not a fool, don't accept blame for what is really insidious and illegal immorality. The sword has two edges; the knife cuts both ways:

- "We are letting you go because you are not a reliable worker. You overreact to every attempt to guide you toward improvement." You may cry discrimination, or the reason for dismissal may be spot on.

- "We are sorry to have to inform you that your performance on the test and interview were not of the caliber of other applicants." You say to yourself, "I must work harder at being better. Or was it bias?"

Have you managed to manage this ambiguity about reality?

Integrity

You need to know how others perceive you, but that is not to say that you should lose your integrity or conform to consensual parochialism. Don't become a puppet. What it does say is that you need to take charge of the decisions that you make on how you are in the world, how you present yourself to your environment. And these decisions must be based on reality and not on fantasy, on the courage to see reality as it is and not on the cowardice of changing reality to suit your tender feelings. Your values are part of your reality. And being true to your values, making the tough choices, taking the courageous stands, that is all part of how you confront your reality.

Nothing here says you must agree with what the market thinks and adjust to it. The only authentic leadership requirement is that you not be blind to what others think of you and that you not act in blindness.

How I extend myself into the world, that is reality. How people respond to that extension of self, that is reality. Recognizing the gap between what I think of myself and what others think of me can be painful. I don't like others shooting down my comfortable self-image. I become nervous when my self-concept is undermined. I have worked on it laboriously for many years, so I am not going to abandon it now! Nevertheless, making intelligent adaptations to the world's perception of me is a dynamite answer to intractable stuck points in my management career.

The leadership step is to adapt deliberately, by design, and not automatically or passively. If I am stuck, it is because I do not know how I am perceived and because I would not be able to manage how I am perceived if I did know it. I may well make the decision not to care about what others think. And that may be a decision of great integrity. The integrity itself, if known as such, will impact the perception people have of me. If they don't hear of me or see me, then I do not exist. Since I do exist very much for myself, I find it difficult to get the point that to some this very much alive human being simply is not to be found, as they say, on their radar screens.

In sum, it is important to know what others think *of* me. But this is not to say they think *for* me. In the last analysis, I am responsible to think for myself, for that is true integrity.

Subjective Perspective

Most important of all, perhaps, in analyzing the implications of diversity, is the question of what the *subjective* perspective is in terms of which a problem is examined and resolved. *Everything we say comes from a subjective perspective.* It is a point of view. And the point from which the problem is seen is different even in my own versions. I can see myself as a victim, which is passive, and I see the other person as the agent: "It is your fault!" Or I can see myself as agent, which is active: "It is your fault, but I choose to do something about it."

There is always an observer who is talking:

- The CEO is an embarrassment to the company and to the industry. So says the postal clerk.

- The CEO is trying to do the very best under very difficult circumstances. No one else could be more devoted or do any better. Criticisms are very unfair. So says his wife.

- The stock will go up as soon as the CEO is replaced, says the securities analyst.

- We live in a period in which CEOs are fired as one technique of capital management and manipulation, says the business historian.

- The CEO is a very friendly and considerate person, says his chauffeur.

- I hate the guy, says the main competitor.

- The CEO is a cheat and a liar, says the recently fired vice president of human resources.

- The CEO is rude, says the Japanese visitor.

- The CEO is humble, says the investigative reporter.

- The CEO is in over his head and I am not wasting my work time on a nothing company. I am going to take a big risk, have faith in myself, and start my own company. So says the entrepreneur.

- I appreciate people who recognize how difficult my job is and who are loyal in supporting me, says the CEO.

Who is right? Could they all be right? Could they all be wrong? It's a bit like Aesop's famous fable about the donkey and the father and son. The leadership issue is how to navigate smartly, sensitively, and with integrity in this sea of many currents.

Reality means to awaken the executive from his or her self-centered slumber. A seasoned executive will always be able to say, "This is what people say about me behind my back. And this is how I have chosen to respond."

The secret of a successful organization is to help diverse people to reach jointly this one conclusion: Diversity is the heart of human reality. I must know how others perceive me, especially in areas where I am very sensitive. I must learn to understand their point of view, hard as that may be. I must maintain the dignity of my own point of view. This is particularly true in the public sector, where issues of race and religion, political party, union membership, chamber of commerce affiliation, level of education, ethnic back-ground, and socioeconomic class can make a huge difference. Attitudes toward education, welfare, health care, taxes, crime, law and order, privacy, drugs, abortion, marriage, raising children, and on and on touch the most sensitive and delicate regions of the soul. Here people are supremely defensive and can be irrationally explosive in how they protect themselves.

In fact, the angrier you become, the closer you are to your point of ulti-mate vulnerability, parts of you where you clandestinely agree with your worst enemy.

If people can agree on this foundation, finding common ground, most social problems are on their way to solution. But can it be done? Are vested interest and prejudices so strong that they supersede any attempt at reconcil-iation?

Understanding the generalities—*Otherness* and *diversity,* in this case—makes the intractable manageable, the stuck point movable. This is then the leadership power of deepening.

Keeping Distance

Freud talked about the *transference neurosis*: The client in psychoanalysis expe-riences the therapist as a significant person in the client's past. Its business application is to practice the therapist's skill of learning what it is like *to be cast into the world picture of another.* In fact, that is the realism with which each marketing person must begin his or her strategic thinking. Beyond that, as in therapy, you together explore the world from within the other's subjectivity, including the role that you play in that person's private world. This is true realism, to understand that you are not seen as who you are but as some other person. Your feelings do not matter and do not count. You allow yourself to be the projections of another. You as a person are utterly discounted. As in psychotherapy, not only must you perceive yourself through another's eyes, but you also do it sympathetically, seeing the reasons and the logic of why you are perceived in this peculiar way. And then you ask yourself, objectively, how to best serve the greatest and most genuine interests and needs of the other—the customer, the co-worker, the boss. *This is the ultimate in objective realism about yourself and how others perceive you.* There is also a self-sacrificing dimension to this kind of realism—how others use you for their own private purposes—that is a good lesson to many an excessively ambitious businessperson on how to relate to a customer.

> The opinions that people have of you is more an indication of who they are than of who you are. The more you know about other people the more you will be able to understand the images they have of you. This is useful business information. Conversely, the more you understand about the images they have of you, the better will you understand who they are. This is even more useful business information.

The experience of having a relationship with a person who appears to connect with you and who is sensitive to your needs—but who in actual fact sees nothing of the real you, is incapable of seeing you, sees only part of himself or herself—is quite extraordinary. To be able to operate in that distanced fashion and keep up your ethical principles and your moral convictions is indeed a rugged calling. And that is the nub of realism for the business executive or the politician, especially when they are high in the organization and visible to a large public. They must live in the isolation of being *used* rather than *met,* and must retain under these conditions the highest ethics and the highest professionalism.

It is superb practice to go through this process as a training session so that you gain the skill of relating to a person who is not relating to you. You learn how to be decent and responsible toward a person whose interests lie in an entirely different direction. That is the realism of knowing what it is like when others perceive you (this, of course, is a radical example) in purely utilitarian and exploitative terms, in the context of which you have a duty to fulfill, an objective to reach, a service to perform. Police officers often find themselves in this position, and so do teachers, physicians, and clerics. That is realism with respect to human relations.

Your proposal was perfect for the prospect, you put into it everything you had, and you really cared about the guy. In the end, he bought from his brother-in-law! Remember: You are a vendor and not necessarily a person. The customer is always right, for the customer is king. How much degradation can you take? How often can you be used rather than met? That is the hard part of life. What does it take from you to be cheerful in defeat, happy in being ignored, serving when you feel kicked? Those are the mental acrobatics required for dignity and self-respect, for maintaining values and making a profit for the company at the same time. How do you manage this? Do you explode? Do you manage rejection with aplomb and without injury to your psyche? Can you be abused by one customer, as many salespeople are, and then be cheerful and friendly to the next?

Business requires it. In accepting your salary, you in effect sign a contract to do it.

To be prepared to operate in that isolated realm, working toward a goal that will neither be recognized nor rewarded, is the fate of the leader functioning in the intelligence of *realism*. That point needs to be understood, assimilated, and translated into simple language. And that language is to be taught to those of your subordinates who are expected to carry out the strategies of your organization. *Without realism there is no implementation.*

Leaders often are called on to act in total solitude and from a position of complete withdrawal, serve others, be given no recognition or emotional rewards, and be required to be motivated by the purest of ethical principles, and without supervision and evaluation. The cynic will say this is never the case. The optimist, however, will let you know that there are many unsung heroes among people in leadership positions and many unsung moments for people with high levels of responsibility. This is not only realism. It is also high *ethics* based on principle and rational motivation.

When you act on this reality prescription, how much are you worth to your company? Think of yourself as a stock. What is your current market value?

◆ Activity

Here is a journaling exercise for reality in practice.

1. Name an important business relationship that is difficult for you, and explain why.

2. See the urgency by focusing on the emotional and financial cost to you both.

3. Using the Diamond, diagnose how the two of you are different.

4. Are you approaching this individual from the point of view of *your* Diamond or from the perspective of *that* person's Diamond? Pay special attention to reality, because there one often finds severe and irreconcilable differences. This requires not a fast and simple answer but an answer from a deeper part of your personality. A good friend can help you here.

5. Examining these two diagnoses, what changes in how you present yourself to that individual will move you past the stuck point of your relationship? These changes are likely to be in more than language and behavior, although that is a good start. In the end, circumstances will ask for changes in personality, in character. You are likely to be required to go more into a materialistic and opportunistic survival mode than into an aesthetic and loyal relationship mode—more courage and reality and less vision and ethics. Or perhaps the reverse? You may draw the line and say it's not worth it and it's not the way you want to go. That's fine. Just be clear about it and take responsibility.

6. As a result of this analysis, how will you now redesign the conversations you have with this person? You should compose some practice themes and sentences and try a fantasy psychodrama to play out what you think would likely be an ensuing conversation.

We have now in our travels on the journey of life traversed three continents: the land of *ethics,* the territory of *courage,* and the civilization of *reality.* We are on our last leg, embarking on the voyage to the soil of *vision.* We need not live everywhere, but we need to have traveled there, so that we can make judicious choices when the moment of leadership truth arrives.

VISION

All things are to be examined and called into question.
There are no limits to set to thought.

EDITH HAMILTON

And when we allow freedom to ring, when we let it ring from every
village and hamlet, from every state and city, we will be able to speed up
that day when all of God's children—black men and white men,
Jews and Gentiles, Catholics and Protestants—will be able to join
hands and to sing in the words of the old Negro spiritual,
"Free at last, free at last; thank God Almighty, we are free at last."

MARTIN LUTHER KING, JR.

To see the World in a Grain of Sand
And a Heaven in a Wild Flower,
Hold Infinity in the Palm of your hand
And Eternity in an hour.

WILLIAM BLAKE

Then on the shore
Of the wide world I stand alone, and think
Till love and fame to nothingness do sink.

JOHN KEATS

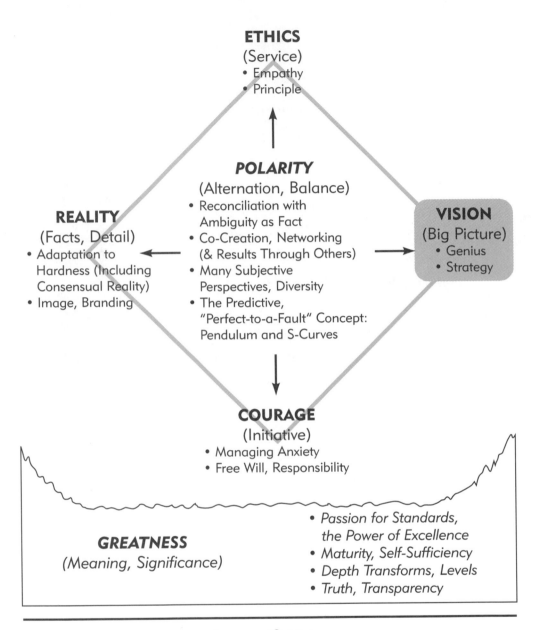

Figure 17.1. The Leadership Diamond®: Vision

CHAPTER 17

Vision

DEFINITION: Big Picture Thinking

ELEMENTS: Genius, Strategy

T HE LAST HELPER TO WHOM THE WIZARD INTRODUCES YOU *is the seer. And the seer lives not only in this world, the outer world, but also in the world of pure thought, such as mathematics and speculation, as in science fiction, that is, preeminently the inner world.*

Vision, the capacity for it, is the crowning achievement of human evolution. In the knowledge economy, vision is what is most valued, treasured, admired, rewarded. It is the capacity to always see the larger context, the big picture. It's a key leadership habit. It's a core leadership sign. When John Kotter, formerly of Harvard, distinguishes between managers and leaders and tasks the latter with giving directions and managers with executing them, he makes the same point.

"The future enters into us, in order to transform itself in us, long before it happens," wrote German poet Rainer Maria Rilke (1923).

There is more. It is not just the future that transforms itself. It is the future in us that transforms us now so that the future itself can happen to us. What a discerning description of the mindset of many of today's executives one meets! This is the deep side of the definition of vision.

Vision is an exciting topic. That is why philosophers become philosophers, to delight themselves in expanding the amplitude of the mind's capacity and operations. It fulfills the promise of the archetype of the seer, drawn from our initial journey metaphor. Vision uses inner space and inner time to master better outer space and outer time, which makes vision perhaps the most powerful application of the two-world theme.

In this chapter genius and strategy are intertwined. Conceptually they are distinct, and it is important to make both of them our attitudinal objectives. We want to think that way. But in practice they are like two sides of one coin and it is difficult to discuss one independently of the other. Genius is the quick mind, the spontaneously creative thinker-artist. Strategy is the ability to see new patterns in your market, to think with facility about very complex data, and to grasp the distant future to where we are all going but many just don't care. You want to train yourself in both skills. It can be done. It is an ideal. And it is the secret of success. With it, life is easy; without it, it's a rusty wheel.

Kant

It is here where the discussion of the two worlds, the inner and the outer, is particularly relevant. For vision means to understand the role that the exploration of the inner world plays in the construction of the outer world. For example, the German 18th Century philosopher Immanuel Kant held that the truth of geometry and mathematics is established by exploring the inner world, that is, inner space and inner time. But he also believed that the truths of mathematics apply universally to outer space and outer time as well. He said that you discover inside your head that 5 + 7 = 12, and there you prove it, but you also know that in distant space, beyond where you can see, five galaxies added to seven galaxies give you twelve galaxies. And you know it with a certainty that scientific experimentation cannot offer. That is not where you learn the truth of mathematics. The truth is learned inside. It is not only mathematical truths that we find located there; it is also leadership truths—free will, God, the purpose of life, morality—which for the average person may be the most important of all. Kant concluded that the person, the human being, with a body and a mind, stands between these two worlds. In fact, for him, it was the mind that projected inner space and inner time, with all of its mathematical and geometric insights, onto the external world. The effect of all this was that he understood the great power the mind—that means you and me—has over the construction of the world. And that, of course, is leadership, leadership from the point of view of vision. You have the capacity to see the world as it might be, what is possible, and you have the guts and the realism to actually work on making it happen. This is the glory of the entrepreneur, the builder.

The Importance of Visionary Intelligence

Vision means seeing the big picture, far into the future, far into space. The roominess thus created is not only physical space, but since vision is in the mind, it is also mind space, thought space. The exploration of that thinking expanse is in itself conducive to enhancing the power of the mind. We call that capacity, that attitude, nothing short of *genius.* And part of genius is to see into the future, and that is where brilliant business *strategy* comes in.

"Strategizing" is sometimes called "futurizing"—the unique capacity to look ahead in time. There is no way to know that it is accurate. But a mind pointed in the direction of the future, even the distant future, is a visionary mind.

Exploring this realm of pure vision can enhance the quality of your thinking. Literally, it can raise your intelligence and will give you a grasp of how to think about the future and how to live ahead of yourself without at the same time losing your footing in the grounded here and now. It is OK to dream about how one day you will own your own business. But the dream needs a connection with what you do today, such as enrolling in a program on the basics of how to run your own business and being hard-working and diligent in the pursuit of that goal.

What we want to do here, under vision, is to develop what we might call in ordinary parlance your "pure" intelligence and to help bring about a truly intelligent organization—ruled by reason, made profitable by concept, and rendered productive by logic. That is what we are about here: supporting you in being clear about the thinking powers of your mind, pursuing that objective for its own sake, for its wholehearted joy, and then applying this knowledge about your mind to your business for the sake of greater growth and profitability and for more prestige and significant accomplishments.

You cannot run a successful business without people with brains, people who have command over the power of thought. I fear this is often not valued enough, especially when compared to brawn, in today's enterprises. Some cultures give more respect to intellectual brilliance than others, which may actually deride it. And genius is then applied to strategy for the whole. This is the formula for a company's visionary success.

Raising conceptual intelligence by changing your mental models about what really matters, that is the kernel point of this Diamond concern with vision.

How manifest are these attitudes in your organization? How much is facility with concepts a value for you that is worth pursuing for its own sake?

Table 17.1 describes both vision and its elements, genius and strategy.

Reason

Vision is that zone of the leadership mind that is also known as *reason*. What is reason? Where is that skill located? How can you enhance it? Is it something that exists in the world as well as in the mind? What does it take for someone to say to you: "You have a really good mind. You are a smart person"? And

Table 17.1. Vision

Deep Structure with Subsets	What It Is/Definition/ Description	The Shadow Against Which We Fight
Vision	Big picture thinking; systems and systemic thinking; manages complexity, mastery in multilevel mental operations	The dull and stagnant mind; cultivating the mind is not a value
Genius	Brilliant, vast scope and range; fast; immensely creative and innovative	Passive, gullible, lethargic, depressed, inactive mind; "Ignorance is bliss"
Strategy	Thinks in large units of space and time, geography, and history; has a passion for strategic thinking: how to look far ahead and how to get there, as a dominant habit of mind; promotes the strategic thinking organization: interests a critical mass of employees in strategy development	Can't see farther than their own noses and don't want to; not interested in the more comprehensive picture; provincial, narrow-minded

then how do you put that to use in the service of your organization and of your clients?

A visionary person, as the term is used here, finds reasoning and logic easy and is usually an outstanding learner and a gifted conceptual thinker. A visionary is also a Renaissance person. Can we enhance, not only emotional intelligence, as we tried to do with ethics and courage, but also conceptual intelligence, mathematical intelligence, and research intelligence, as we try to do with vision? No doubt we can, even if all we talk about is attitude. To support you in making yourself smarter is one of the noble steps in achieving a leadership mind.

> Use the power and the courage of your freedom to change your
> own internal culture to such a degree that you become fixated
> on superb intellectual achievement. That is your first step to
> becoming a major visionary leader.

Modeling

Much of what gets you ready to vastly increase the powers of your intellect are matters of culture. What your culture values, how your culture has evolved, your faith in yourself, your attitudes, your expectations, your ability to imitate bright people, and how much you contribute to enhance the virtues of your culture have impact on how much weight you give to the inner world of intelligence formation.

When it comes to courage, for example, we can say that a person raised in a culture that emphasizes free will as the final truth about human existence, and drums into you from early on that the world is full of opportunity and that success is the direct consequence of your autonomy, self-confidence, determination, and persistence, will have a far better chance to get out of poverty than one with a fatalistic and dependent view of the world.

The same is true of vision. A person with high-minded models in his or her youth, with high aspirations, with an accurate image of how bright people's minds work, and of how that affects the rest of one's personality and life, and who also has a solid foundation in the case for free will and responsibility, will more likely become a brilliant intellectual, than will someone whose environment never had such elevated expectations of the next generation!

If you do not have this in your background (and who really does?), or if you neglected to take advantage of it (and who really did?), then now is the time to "re-parent" yourself—to create your own image of that background, those distinguished roots. For, no matter what your birth, you are entitled to fulfill your potentials as a leader.

You can take responsibility to re-parent yourself, to imagine such a background for yourself and act accordingly. You, of course, need enough realism in order to avoid self-deception. But with the right kind of determination and with an adequate image of what a brilliant mind looks like and feels like from the inside, you are already half-way there. Our job here is to challenge and support you as you ignite for yourself and for your organization the spirit of vision.

We are talking here about intelligence in general and strategic thinking in particular, the latter being *grounded "futurizing."* This is what we call *genius* and *strategy* respectively, the two principal components of the orientation toward business that we call vision. We want to develop a series of tips on how to develop genius-level thinking. The mind's study of how it can improve itself is the highest calling on this earth. Strategy is here used not in the ordinary sense of making plans but in the more psychological and subjective sense of a mental capacity and proclivity: looking for the long view, expanding the space, such as the geography, in which one makes plans, gaining a feel for history, managing complexity, searching for trends, coming up with new and creative connections, and so forth. A good mind can think strategically. This skill, which follows an earlier attitude of interest, can be trained, enhanced, practiced. That is a key leadership function. We all can benefit from this commitment to practice.

Vision is the struggle against living with blinders, being shortsighted and narrow. The Shadow Diamond does not only mean living with blinders, but it is to deprecate a sharp and creative mind and to be focused on detail and on tomorrow and not on strategy for the days after. And in your business, you have an improvising and reactive organization instead of a responsibly planning and strategically thinking organization.

Vision in the context of strategy means getting the big picture, setting the long-term goals. But when we implement vision, we talk about developing the thinking capacity of the mind and bringing about what we call a *strategic thinking organization,* where strategy has become a culture project and phenomenon.

Where is your organization in valuing strategic thinking? How satisfied are you with what is happening strategically in your company? How much of a hearing do you receive, and how much of a contribution do you yourself make? How much interest do you display in understanding the company's grand strategic design? How eager are you to take part in its execution?

What happens in your company when a customer asks about the long-term strategic objectives of your enterprise?

◆ Activity:

Speech

The purpose of this activity is to translate an important ordinary and regular daily activity into a vision-building one, a way to raise conceptual intelligence. It is practice to change your speech to authentic leadership language, from negative or neutral to positive speech.

It could be about such simple actions as how you greet your colleagues in the morning at work, how you talk to your boss or subordinate about a project's progress, how you answer a customer complaint on the telephone, how you present the latest financial figures to the audit committee, or how you help increase the effectiveness of your team's sales talks.

Divide a sheet of paper into three columns. In the first column, write down what you actually said, the language that you used. In the second column, write down how you might have done the same thing in a much more visionary way. The key is to see what is possible and how you can change habits of thought, talk, and behavior. In the third column, write down the anticipated and actual changes in results.

It is even more effective to do this as a team. Following is an example:

Column 1: Non-Leadership Speech	Column 2: Visionary Language	Column 3: Anticipated Results
I complained to my boss that I was not happy in my work. The stress of deadlines has been too great. Also, I said that I had some unpleasant friction with my principal co-worker.	A visionary response would be, "I can see how the market demands a strategic increase in productivity. Both you and I know how difficult it is on our people. I have made the decision that when the pressures build up I will keep in mind our larger perspective and our bigger goals. Also, I told my difficult colleague that I understood his feelings and I am working hard to help everyone finish the project properly and on time. Do you have any advice for me on how I might do my job better?"	Complaining to my boss, I fear, was a career move. So is the positive speech also a career move, but they are certainly steps in opposite directions! In the negative comments, I come across as a very mediocre employee with little future in the company. In my positive statement, I give the message to both my co-workers and my boss that I am a good team player and promising leadership material. Furthermore, the positive visionary attitude gives me energy. Complaining drains me of energy.

Tips for Developing Genius

There are certain specific steps you can take, attitudes you can assume, language you can use, to foster elevating your own intelligence and that of your organization to genius level (i.e., greatly enhancing creativity). And to the degree you see yourself as a coach, teaching leadership, these steps are content material for your strategic leadership teaching moments.

Persistence

Recall the quotation from Rilke at the beginning of this chapter: "The future enters into us, in order to transform itself in us, long before it happens."

Developing a genius-level strategic thinking mind will not happen in a day. You raise your intelligence, as you improve your muscle tone and reach your ideal weight, by adhering to a plan, over time. It becomes a daily routine, and you may well find group support very helpful. We have body gyms; why not mind gyms?

A fundamental support for improving your mind is to make the free-willed commitment to stick to it. There can be no high-powered intelligence without courage. That is how these polar opposites are intertwined. Read the newspapers; look at the latest merger, the last bankruptcy, the currency exchange rate; read editorials; keep your mind active. That's vision. But to do it daily, to brief yourself every morning on the most relevant news, to scan a couple of papers, to make a couple of notes, to do it fast, and to do it as an ongoing process, that's courage, that's initiative, that's will power, that's persistence.

Making Business Your Practice Field

Redefine your business as the golden opportunity for you to practice raising your visionary intelligence. The success of your enterprise is in direct proportion to the ability that you develop to use every one of your business activities as an exercise and as practice to think ever smarter and smarter.

For example, you visit a customer—and you immediately think that this is your occasion to sharpen up your sales strategy. You ask yourself, from the perspective of being in business, how should you treat this person so that the customer will be so *satisfied* with your work and at the same time so *motivated* that you will be quickly recommended to other potential clients? What intelligent ways of managing this account must you come up with in order to make this visit the beginning of an avalanche of new clients? In this way, you use your business as an opportunity to do some creative, innovative, reflective, and strategic thinking. In the end, even though your goal is to do good business, developing your mind's intelligence is a higher objective.

Every step you take is practice in being visionary. Assess how you are working on your computer. Are you too slow? Do you not keep up with the latest software? Think of better ways of doing your current task. Could you be clearer? Could you be more accurate? Do you always reflect on what you do and make a visionary leadership lesson out of it.

Using what you take seriously, namely your business, becomes a practice field for leadership if you do it in the spirit of a vehicle to reach a destination: to become stronger and better at what you do. For leaders this also becomes a habit. And so should be the teaching of it.

Witnessing Genius

How can we promote genius? One answer is to live in the presence of creative genius. How is genius different? You can find out by watching genius in operation and by dialoguing with a real genius. What do you need to do so as to embody genius? Imitate. Above all, ask, "What is in the way?" Laziness, timidity, ignorance? Always ask what the resistance is—and what your decision role is in that resistance. You invented the resistance. You put it up. You came between you and the answer. The most common source of resistance is the escape from anxiety.

Here are your questions. All you need to do, as the German poet Rilke said, is to "live the answers."

One client said, "I had dinner with a genius last night. She was a MacArthur Fellow and now she is a professor at the ____University Graduate School of Business. She specializes in venture capital. She has amazing insights. Even during our dinner conversation, she displayed many traits that made her a business genius to me.

"I made a list," he continued:

- "She was *energetic*.

- She was cheerful, *excited*, and pleasant.

- She was *curious, listening* attentively to what I was saying. By being an *interested* and *active listener*, she gave me the chance to speak my *voice*. In other words, she was *alive, alert, responsive*.

- She was well-*read* and well-*informed*. She said she always carries a book with her.

- She gave evidence of a high degree of what we call *cultural literacy*. She knew a lot; she had an ample reservoir of *general knowledge*.

- It was clear that she loved to *learn*, had good *retention*, read widely, and showed deep interest and *curiosity*.

- She was in that part of the university where the *environment* welcomed and appreciated her. That seemed important to me, for it is a factor that many business people I know miss sorely in their own work.

- She had a *grateful audience* in the lectures that she gave. I think she took personal responsibility to be well-positioned in her 'market.'

- She had her pockets of immaturity. She enjoyed showing off and being the center of attention, but her charm won us over. I felt she had earned her right to do so. In class as in private conversation, she said interesting things in an interesting manner. *I enjoyed her presence and I learned from her.*"

Most of these are "mind muscles." If you keep yourself alert, you can flex them and grow them. Others represent the professor's ability to connect, to link one conscious center with another, to create the right chemistry among people. *These all have a core of choice in them; they are in the last analysis decisions, decisions, and more decisions.*

The steps my client exemplified and therefore taught by adopting the genius professor as a model are

- Seek out people who can serve as models of vision. Observing them and interacting with them to the degree possible—or vicariously if needed—is always helpful.

- Start by imitating their behavior.

- Try to adopt the attitudes that stand as foundation for the behaviors.

This is not unrelated to coming up with an expert system, observing how geniuses handle matters that we ourselves would like to be able to manage well. In the financial area people used to feel that way about Ross Perot, Warren Buffett, George Soros. How do they think? What are their attitudes? How do they obtain information? From where come their "instincts"? What commitments about self-definitions and values must they make, what personality characteristics are required, in order to achieve the level of financial success that they have attained? What sustains them in their dark moments?

These are not one-time questions. The process is a lifetime of focusing, interest, and exploration. It also requires that we examine the web of resistances that we put in the way of achieving the genius in our field that we believe ourselves capable of being.

How serious are you about introjecting vision into your way of thinking, feeling, speaking, and doing?

There is no reason that you cannot redefine yourself in this fashion—and choose to do so in a sustainable way. For only then will you obtain results. Your environment and significant others may be surprised. But the greatest surprise of all is the benefits you will accrue.

◆ Activity

Traits

Ask yourself:

- Can I imitate these genius traits?

- Do I have the brains to place myself into an environment in which acquiring these traits would be supported?

- Am I currently in a restricting environment partially of my own making?

- What do I need to read? What conferences shall I attend? How do I build my networks? How do I deal with competition, with jealousy and envy? With dismissal? With betrayal?

To take action on these items is up to you. It will be done if you do it. It will not be done if you don't do it. It won't be easy. But you can do it if you so choose. There is no law that says you must choose. Start with changing your speech from non-visionary to strong visionary. That you can plan and measure.

"Re-Parenting"

To change your parents in fantasy and to redesign your childhood in imagination can go a long way to re-choosing who you are at your roots. This is the project of Diamond Reverse Engineering. Find out what configuration of your root Diamond creates a world for you that you want to change—for example, you find your job boring—and then choose those changes—an exciting job.

In the case of vision, you make the development of your intelligence and that of your organization your highest priority. You use a thought experiment to put you in the mood in which intellectual achievement becomes the highest value to which you can aspire. You then reconstruct your image of your heritage as being a lineage of distinguished intellectuals. You "re-parent" yourself as if you were raised in a household with regular soirees for artists, thinkers, scientists, and diplomats. You engaged in sophisticated conversations at the dinner table. Reading, travel, concerts, museums, lectures, and especially *education* were high priorities in your family.

This new automatic way of thinking, this elegant self-concept, becomes a habit. As you think of yourself so you will become—especially if you make it endure and if you see to it that your practical life manifests this shift in self-definition.

This is the image that you carry in your head and that you teach those whose leader you are. It is your mental model, your index of aspiration, the template against which you compare the imaginativeness and sophistication of the strategy that your company needs vis-à-vis what you actually have.

Encouraging Analytic Thinking

There are rules you can follow to divide what is before you into manageable component parts and then deal with each separately. It is an effective and efficient way of thinking. What starts as one complex and worrisome problem system becomes a chain of simple steps to solve. You change your task from overwhelming challenge to a simple piecework.

Can you think of a current circumstance in which applying this principle would make a lot of sense, for example, improving the effectiveness of the task force of which you are a member? Following are five specific ideas for doing it.

1. Distinguish Abstract from Concrete Thinking and Understand the Difference Between Universalizing and Deepening

Concrete thinking is in terms of things and objects: "I live in a house." *Abstract* thinking is to elevate your talk to the level of concepts: "I live in a world that I have created myself." *Universalizing* is to say, "Requiring shelter is what humans have in common with the animals," connecting it with a principle from the science of biology or anthropology. And *deepening* is to think that "Moving into an abode is like returning to the womb or surrendering into the folds of God's arms, as in the Basilica of Saint Peter in Rome," restating in terms of depth psychiatry, mythology, and theology.

Charles Darwin, as suggested already in Chapter 5, is frequently quoted as saying, "It is not the strongest of the species that survives, nor the most intelligent; it is the one that is most adaptable to change." Going from concrete to abstract, from universal to deep is like a warm-up or stretching exercise for the mind, for it makes it nimble, supple, and adaptable to whatever circumstances the particular tasks at hand demand.

You submit your budget for next year. You prepare your presentation to the finance committee of the board. What kind of thinking have you used in its preparation—concrete, abstract, universal, or deep? What combination is appropriate? What have you done? What might you still do? What does your audience require? How will this monitoring review sharpen the effectiveness of your presentation, both in terms of content and of form?

Can you educate your audience without talking down to them?

2. Get into the Habit of Being Prepared to Give Reasons for Everything

The purpose is not to be right—because reason is not always the solution. The purpose is to gain practice in reasoning itself. Your mind is always thinking, reasoning, arguing, inventing. That is the active mind of the genius. A continuous well-lubricated reasoning process is what makes you intelligent. And that is what you want: practicing conceptual, systemic, and creative intelligence. Whether you are right or not is not an issue as basic as being in the habit of always finding reasons and arguments for what you believe and for what you do.

Essentially, you learn to be an effective *debater.* But being a good debater is not your objective. It is to lubricate the mind. *It is to hone your mind for better strategic thinking.*

Think of a conversation you just had. You made an assertion:

I think your issue is not scientific but political. Scientists know what to do to save the environment; it is the political quagmire in which environmental issues are entangled where the leverage for results and actions is ensconced.

If that is all you say, you will be ineffective. Vision demands that you present instances and arguments as well. For example:

It is not so much a question of replenishing the depleted bird population as it is to understand the emotional needs of the political opposition: Their pride is injured by foreign intervention, as is Brazil's sensitivity about foreign pressure on their forest fires, and Ecuador's concern over world pressure on their Galápagos policies.

To move from vacuous generalizations to giving concrete reasons, arguments, and examples may be extra work, but that extra effort earns you credibility and gains you results.

Can you make up your own examples from your own current experience?

3. Get into the Habit of Stating Opposite Views, Contrary Positions

Again, very much as you learn in debating, you train yourself to be able to pick any side and do a good job defending it. This is good for people for whom the art of persuasion is an important aspect of their assignments, such as selling, managing a partnership, recruiting difficult prospects, and the like. For example:

> We believe in civil rights, including freedom of speech, for all people at all times. This is the cornerstone of our view of what it means to be a human being. We cannot budge from that position, for, by making us into hypocrites, it would totally dishonor us as a people. Therefore we cannot condone what is occurring today in China, and our policies toward that nation must reflect our values.

A person of high intelligence will also allude to counterarguments:

> We should not be unsympathetic to their point of view. They are a big nation trying to enter the modern technological age for the benefit of the entire population. They are not practiced in democratic institutions. The choice they must make is between upgrading the prosperity of an originally extremely poor nation, which requires a degree of regimentation, and instituting the kind of democratic processes that work well in the West but are likely to be dangerously destabilizing in China. If we view their position with compassion and see them as well-intentioned reformers and not as an evil race, they will be more receptive to constructive coexistence with us.

The point here is not "who is right and who is wrong." It is, "Does your mind function in such a way that you will bring up counterarguments to your position?" Preparation for stating an opposing view is excellent training for thinking more expansively and more clearly and speaking more persuasively with your enhanced leadership mind.

What useful counterarguments have you overlooked in your recent leadership conversations and how would the results have been different had you been more comprehensive?

4. Practice Parallel Constructions

While your proposal may be the best path, there are alternatives and it is wise to bring them up. For example, one superintendent argued as follows:

> We need to make sure no students come to school with a weapon. We must therefore search them and their lockers. But this may be too severe an approach, sowing the seeds of distrust. It might be better to involve them in monitoring weapons, asking them to create the proposals, and even putting their suggestions to a student vote. It would show our trust in them.
>
> There is still a third alternative, which they tried successfully in the district south of here. They left it up to the parents. They brought them to school and presented the security problem to them, with lawyers talking about who is legally accountable. And then the parents took on the task of monitoring and patrolling for weapons. The more alternatives we have, the more constructive our thinking on this delicate and charged problem.

Does this generate any new ideas for how you can increase your leadership credibility by sharpening your thinking?

5. Practice Using Metaphor, Analogy, Symbol, and Simile

This can be clever and creative, and a felicitous metaphor can make quite a literary figure out of you!

Shakespeare is of course a master here: "We are such stuff/as dreams are made on, and our little life/is rounded with a sleep." (*The Tempest*)

But there are others, such as Adelaide Crapsey, who in *Cinquain* says (Bartlett, 1992): "These be/Three silent things:/The falling snow. . . the hour/Before the dawn. . . the mouth of one/Just dead."

Or consider Keats' (1848) evocation of the empty space of pure consciousness from which springs all enhancement of genius potential: "Then on the shore/Of the wide world I stand alone, and think/Till love and fame to nothingness do sink."

But, of course, not all metaphors need be derived from literature. Business metaphors abound, such as, "We don't sell software; we sell solutions."

Ford and Warner Brothers cooperate on a fifteen-episode adventure television series called "No Boundaries" showing that an automobile is not transportation but it means freedom and global thinking.

Agilent Technologies shows a man's profile, eyes closed, with the caption "Our customers dream the dreams of giants," a clear reference to greatness and the power of inner space, when the advertisement says, "And the world they see with the eyes closed." We cannot help but think of Wagner's reference to Beethoven as a "Titan wrestling with the gods."

Porsche advertises "What a dog feels when the leash breaks—instant freedom."

Crystal Decisions advertises "What kind of decisions are required in today's business climate? Smart ones." They show a man running and a man swimming, both thinking—wearing the company's logo dots around their heads. A clear challenge through metaphor for clarity of thought and easy use of free will. It is through metaphors that we see the world clearly.

What is your favorite metaphor? How can you use it in your work? What difference would it make?

Are personal problems business problems? An advertisement sponsored by the National Anti-Drug Media Campaign plays on the guilt of children by writing, "When I do drugs, my Mom and Dad spend their days worrying instead of working. And that's got a bunch of guys in suits somewhere all stressed out because it means kids like me are robbing companies blind." Need more be said? (*Business Week,* Feb. 25, 2002)

Illustration: Summing Up Analysis

Your visionary leadership conversations—sales talks, reports to the board, leadership conferences, stockholders' meetings, analysts' forums, and so forth—will then contain topics or sentences such as:

- "Here is the *strategy* we propose. Here are the *diagrams* that illustrate it."

- "And we have a *story* to tell."

- "Here are examples of how this would affect *your* particular *organization.* There are five principal *reasons* why we believe this will work well. And here are five *counterarguments,* problems that might arise."

- "And here are our careful *answers* to these counterarguments."

- "Here is a very different strategy, an *alternative.* And here are the *reasons* one can give in its defense."

- "In *comparing* the two possible strategies, we here give you the reasons why we believe the first is better than the second."

- "You may have the following *objections* and questions. Here they are. And here is an *analysis* of each one of your anticipated reservations, with pros and cons clearly listed."

- "We can put this in the form of an analogy. Take sports, for example. When Tiger Woods. . . . "

- "In sum, this is our most honest *recommendation.*"

- "This is something *we* are doing for *you*."

- "What would *you* like to discuss with *us* now?"

This may be a good time for you to carefully redesign and rephrase the next major speech you are planning to give.

Up to this point, our central concern has been to invite you to visit the spacious expanse of your mind. We continue this process in the next chapter, hoping to suggest more practical ways to achieve that so that you and your organization will have a culture that supports powerful strategies of innovation, assuring you competitive advantage.

CHAPTER 18

Genius

Ways to Expand Visioning

T HERE ARE MORE MASSIVE ZONES *of the atlas of the mind to explore in order to gain access to the full genius and strategic potential of the leadership mind. This chapter surveys practical ways for developing* strategy grounded in genius *and* genius grounded in strategic applications.

Creativity

Creativity means to try new paths, to shatter old patterns. It is to perform psychological karate on your old molds, models, and crates. It is to break the routine, to get out of the box. It is to assume the outrageous—or the random—to believe in it, and then to let your unconscious do its work. You keep the faith that you can innovate. You cultivate the imagination. Keats (Bartlett, 1992) put it well: "I am certain of nothing but the holiness of the Heart's affection and the truth of the imagination."

Incubating and recording dreams always helps. Think of dreams as starters for creative thought. Assume that the dream is a deep truth about yourself, a profound unconscious insight about the hidden nature of the universe, and the mysterious ways of fate. It doesn't matter if it is literally "true" or not. We know that it is useful. You can combine your dream analysis with your business needs.

> You dream that you are redesigning from the inside an elevator door that has problems opening. You know that in real life you have mild claustrophobia. You worry about elevator doors not opening. You quickly deepen and generalize this dream by saying to yourself, "It's a birth experience. I am still in the womb and I want to get out. Perhaps my mother had difficult labor with me." Then you fantasize and free-associate further: "Birth is the basic metaphor for life. We get born periodically, as we move through stages. Each *birth* is preceded by a *death*. Do I know how to *grieve* the death? Do I know how to *celebrate* the birth?"
>
> "Am I ready for rebirth?" you ask. "Do I need to redesign my environment before I can change more readily? Do I need to redesign how I approach change in my current position? Is that what my deep unconscious is trying to tell me?" Coming in this fashion from yourself, as self-discovery and not as vacuous pontification from another person outside, you invite yourself to embrace willingly this conscience call to authenticity, rather than digging in your heels with obstinate rationalization and defensiveness.

Your business question is, "What does redesigning the elevator door mean in the current context of my team? What changes does my team have a right to expect from me that they are not now receiving? What anxieties must they feel of which I am not aware?"

You can make a deliberate effort to be more creative, to think "outside the box." It can become a game, a way of life, a style of being. You always ask yourself, "Is there a better way?" You never slacken.

Here are a series of wider questions, translating your vision virtues into the company's cold cash:

- How much are your answers to the above questions worth to your company or organization—in terms of savings, revenues, profits, and growth?

- Would someone else have gone down this route of questioning had you not been there?

- Will you collect? Do you want to collect? Is there a place for generosity in competitive business?

Subjective Research

Subjective research is a most effective way to access best practices, for these practices come straight out of your own experience and have made a life-long impression on you. You are an expert on your own best and worst experiences.

Describe a time at which *you* were/felt most creative. Evoke also a time when your *organization* was most creative, a time when you came up, fast, with new ideas, better insights, improvements to what had never been questioned before. What else was occurring? What was the explanation? How was the cross-fertilization? Can you duplicate that today, even improve on it? Can you be this way with your co-workers?

Conversely, it is constructive to look at dry periods in your life, when you felt stunted and did nothing creative. The questions to ask are how you got there, whether being uncreative bothered you, and how you stepped out of that sterile mode. What were the triggers? Then you are ready for the more important question, namely, "*What are the implications of knowing how to promote creativity for building a strategic thinking organization?*" For not only do you want to develop your own genius, you want to promote long-range and intelligent thinking over a critical mass of your team and organization.

Systemic Thinking and Systems Theory

The capacity for systems (or systemic) thinking as a habit of thought is the very essence of what the leadership mind wishes to accomplish when it refines its *vision. Take off the blinders!*

You look for the big picture. You study history. You pick trends. Looking for the characteristics of systems began in early Greek philosophy with the search for the so-called "categories" of being. These were the ultimate and most universal "trends" in the universe.

But you must do your own search for the categories because it still is the smartest training of the mind that you can possibly do. It is the most demanding challenge that your mind can handle.

How do we find categories? Take an example: We talk in a subject-predicate language. Most sentences are of the form "A is B": "Clouds are white," "Gravity is a force in nature," "Our stock price is down three points," "Shakespeare was the greatest playwright in the English language," and "We are an organization that needs a new CFO, one who has more credibility on Wall Street." This is a trend, one way to describe the nature and structure of reality. It may not be the only one, but it is ubiquitous indeed.

Or take another example. We can argue that our world of experience is made up of three different types of phenomena: (1) *Events* (things or substances), with their (2) *qualities,* and (3) *relations.* We then say that "the *blue* (quality) *box* (event, thing, or substance) is to the *right of* (relation) the pen," "The *best performer* is *next in line* for promotion," "Our *product line* is *outdated* and lags *behind* the competition." It appears that all we can say fits into one of these three categories, and, conversely, that each complete statement contains all three of the elements of being.

What's the business point? Study philosophy, detect trends? The point is this: Learn to think really big, not in terms of untrammeled and phantasmagoric ambition, but in terms of characteristics and trends of being and of experience, of history and of politics, of economics and of society. This kind of practice and training in wide-ranging thinking will set you up to be creative and innovative about the larger patterns that govern the world. And once you own this skill you are also in a much better position to plan ahead, set direction, and be keener in making strategic decisions.

Strategic and systemic thinking starts with valuing the training of the mind. You strengthen your mind so that whatever you will do you will do better. It is the same with strengthening your heart and lungs through aerobic exercises. After a good workout and getting into shape, everything you do will feel better and be better. The mind, which may be good at detail, needs to also be nurtured to become good at overseeing large systems.

Where in your organization is there the greatest need for thinking big in a meaningful way? What is the cash value to the company, given its particular market, if thinking big becomes a cultural habit? How many additional stock points is a strategic thinking organization worth?

The Koan: Paradoxical Thinking

Paradoxical thinking is the key to enhanced systemic thinking. If you can think in terms of opposites, you can see trends in systems. Many people are familiar with koans, the provoking questions of the East. "What is the sound of one hand clapping?" is a familiar example. They are meant to provoke innovative thinking, to instigate change in how we see a problem, a radical transformation of who we are as leaders and how we approach our work.

The koans are part of a general creativity tool. Paradoxical thinking stretches the mind. It is the application of polarity (see next chapter) to enhance the intelligence of vision. Progress in the Olympics and marathon training occurs at the stress point, the second-wind edge. Progress in vision occurs at the paradox interface. Learn how to distend the mind, and then let it integrate, as in dreams and alternation (such as recreation and sleep), and be sensitively attuned to collect the results. Many scientific breakthroughs and technological inventions arise in precisely this way. The idea is to present you with an ambiguous stimulus, one that makes no prima facie sense, and then "hypnotize" you, or strongly suggest to you, that there is an answer, that a solution exists, but you just don't see it. You can push your own mind in this way to transformation, to see things you did not see before, to contact a logic that usually appears to you only in the penumbra before sleep and the haze of a dream. This is how originality in art can be generated. It is that part of vision that we harness for change and innovation in business.

What matters is not the accuracy of the prediction—that has to be revised daily. What is important is the habit of thought to look ahead, move forward, feel the pull. To be always "ahead of yourself" is the visionary leadership formula.

Take as an example these words of a frustrated partner in a once well-known advertising agency: "Business is bad, the market is dry, our products are uninteresting to our former customers. I can see no way out." This is your koan, the assignment from your guru for the week of meditation. Convince yourself that there is an answer, a solution, a better way. Trust what you begin to see. Don't dismiss it. Take the process seriously. At first what you see may seem bizarre, but you can gradually fine-tune it to reality. Allow what first is a nebulous mist to become a sharper image, perhaps a picture telling you that there is a next generation of public relations consulting beckoning you. You consult no longer about soft drinks, but about consulting itself. These are not solutions, just prompts for you to go your own way.

Practice the habit. See your business and your practice change and grow.

Pushing the mind into impossible corners, and expecting answers, is the same trick Edison used when he challenged his co-workers with "There is a better way; find it!" Pushing polarity is definitely a vision aphrodisiac, stimulating the mind into new ways of thinking. It induces a new paradigm to be born. It is the fuel for scientific and technological revolutions. Sometimes, however, "thinking out of the box" is discouraged in companies, sweet words to the contrary notwithstanding. *The New Yorker* featured a cartoon in which a dog admonishes a puzzled cat near its sandbox, "Don't you dare to think out of the box!" The polarity theme proper is discussed in the next chapter.

Example: Software Security

The paradox message is to always seek forever larger contexts in which you can understand and frame events. Trends can be expressed in paradoxes, conflicts, opposites. Polarity is one of the great aids in helping people think in large strategic strokes. Be alert; always expect the other shoe to drop.

If, for example, your concern is ending runaway stealing of your software secrets, you acknowledge that you have tried most everything and still the goal of security is not within reach. Einstein-like revolutionary thinking is all that is left for you to do. Your company's interests and the competition's interests are still in conflict, and you require a synthesis beyond them—a resolution that no one has yet thought of. A friend once told me that everything is free on the Internet: data, information, and knowledge. What remains is wisdom. That is then your product—not the software itself, but practice and support in using it. And here only you and your company with your experience and expertise can make the difference. Again, this is not a solution for you, but encouragement for ongoing visionary thinking for you and for your organization.

Example: Naming Assignment

Another way to illustrate the strategic importance on thinking in terms of paradox is to do a simple assignment: Name the five major paradoxes that govern the world political arena today and how they impact your industry at this time. Make a game of it with colleagues and determine whose list of conflicting interests is more encompassing and more useful for molding strategic direction.

Here is a try for five—for illustrative purposes only, as thought starters, to provoke you to improve them:

- Religious and ethnic standoffs and confrontations. The Catholics and Protestants of Northern Ireland are one example; Islam and Christianity in the Middle East is another.

- The rich versus the poor, the growing "Digital Divide."

- Freedom versus dictatorship, the authoritarian versus the democratic personality structure.

- The individual versus the team, entrepreneurship versus socialism, rule by majority versus protection of minorities.

- Change versus stability, the new versus the old, adventure versus security.

Practice for yourself finding large-scale paradoxes. Evaluate those of others. What are the implications for your business? What surprises lie ahead? What is the unexpected for which you need to plan?

Global business is concerned with cultural diversity. For many it is the contrast between a democratic and an autocratic government, and an entrepreneurial and welfare economy. These represent deeply held beliefs. As leader, your task is to kindle your workforce's ambition. You would do that differently in each of these systems: personal responsibility, commitment to the team, adherence to bureaucracy, and the legitimacy of cutting legal corners—all these issues will emerge as ethical dilemmas. How much will you compromise your own principles? How much will you proselytize? Are your personal commitments absolute? Do you acknowledge that in fundamental matters of human relationships and political and economic values that a crevasse of differences is acceptable, or do you look for converts?

Example: Great Changes

Look at history. How have the great changes of history occurred? In my lifetime, some great questions were: How was World War II won by the Allies? How was the Vietnam war lost by the United States? How did the anti-war movement in the United States prevail, from total agreement that communism in Southeast Asia must be stopped, to electing a war resistor, that is, Clinton, as president? How did the environmental movement reach such prominence? And then we can ask, "Is change instituted from above? From below? Is it co-created? And what has succeeded and what has failed?" We can apply this analysis to union movements, to anticommunism in Russia, and so forth.

The way these conflicts have been addressed—and innovatively can continue to be addressed—are the way you must address your conflicts with the competition. Patience, reason, perspective, a sense of history, faith in the future, coexistence, recognizing common interests, these are the formulae used in politics and they are an improvement over "kill the competition" that has characterized, for example, the bitter battles Microsoft has waged with competitors.

What can you learn about achieving your goals—business and otherwise—from the history of these mass changes, changes that have taken place in the lifetimes of many people active today? These are among the most fruitful questions you can ask to cultivate and apply visionary intelligence to the core issues of your leadership responsibility.

Redefining

There is also the matter of *redefinition,* starting with realizing that you are not in the *movie* business but in the *entertainment* business, and not in the *railroad* business but in the *transportation* business. For example, we start talking about jobs and being *employed.* Then we say that this is an outdated way of thinking and that in truth everyone is an *entrepreneur,* the so-called "employer" representing simply a consulting arrangement. As if this were not enough, we now say that every person in business is a *stock,* and the people you thought employed you are really *investing* in you. You go from doing your job, to creating wealth via an IPO, to making yourself marketable globally.

Again, the focus is not on whether these redefinitions are true or false, but on how useful they are. It was the pragmatists in philosophy, preeminently the great American thinker William James, who represented this position: Truth is what works, what is practical, what is instrumental to achieving a value, not what corresponds to an actual state of affairs. And for business, the value is to raise the stock price. This is known as "pragmatism."

Redefinition occurs through redesigning language. The business significance is to recognize that language builds reality, and then to take control of this situation for your business purposes. We must have a value that we pursue, and we look for vehicles, which are in the forms of words and concepts, not that are true but that are pragmatic and that work. To ask you what really is your business is to use the deepening tool of philosophy to intensify the marketing process.

We can then say that your true business objective is to influence the free decisions of a set of people whom you have determined are the stakeholders in your way of doing business, the people whose decisions matter to you.

This is different from simply saying that you market by using direct mail and that what your customers want is quality. The latter may be true but naive. However, to say that you have a target audience whose free decisions you want to influence and then to start studying the intricacies of free will—that is the new way to go about setting up marketing strategies. You will have found that managing people's decisions reduces really to managing people's *anxieties about making decisions* and to collude with them in their effort to escape from their freedom. However, when this happens you quickly arrive at ethical considerations.

Redefinition is another way to pressure the mind to expand. If you push too hard, you may go crazy and snap into hallucinations. If you do not push enough, you have zero change and results. If you push just right, provoking the proper amount of stress, the mind creates a breakthrough synthesis. That human end is the eventual value, not merely the business. Here business serves a higher function. Strategic demands are a practice field, an opportunity, for the mind to reach new heights of development. Literally speaking, this is not business, nor the science of business, but the *art* of business.

What does Diamond Theory recommend? That the free choice of morality—combining courage and ethics—be the foundation of the new values for the new economy.

There are technologists who design and run the modern NASDAQ companies. There are psychologists who do focus groups on how buyers make decisions. You could use the Diamond to increase the effectiveness of manipulating people's choices, once you know which leverage "buttons" to push. But then there is seriousness about ethics. The honorable way to market is not to exploit people's weaknesses through the Diamond but to be their allies in the legitimate pursuit of authenticity—real values, true values, not substitutes or subterfuge. This is the ultimate business idea, true Philosophy-in-Business. It means to talk sense to your customer.

Futurizing

We are talking here about how to seize control over how you experience time. It is to understand time, especially the dimension of the future. Get into the habit of seeing everything as a function of time. For example, depression is the end of time. Frivolity is the emptiness of time. Hope is the continuity of time. The future attracts you—when it moves into the light. Or the future frightens you when it moves into darkness. Where is your focus in time: past, future, or present? Closed, open, or active?

Units of time, chunks of time, in terms of which you experience time, can be small or large. In general, the longer these units of time are, the more leadership capacity you have.

Let's look at some examples:

What is the unit of time lying at the base of the following line of thinking or of experiencing the world?

- Your preschool daughter, says to you, in the morning: "Tomorrow is my birthday party." After her noon nap, she asks, "Is it tomorrow already?"

  The unit of time is half a day or a couple of hours.

- Your adolescent son has a conflict between a test in school tomorrow and a party with friends tonight. With a one-day time frame—where he misses seeing clearly the future consequences of his irresponsibility—he goes to the party. He is impulsive. But with a one-semester time frame, or longer—where he focuses on long-range consequences—he acts responsibly and he does his homework. The time frame does not follow the decision, it precedes it. Leadership training is not in the logic of postponed gratification but in enlarging one's time frame, really, the space-time frame. It all has to do with consequences: a short time frame does not make a person aware of the implications of his/her actions and inactions. A long time frame does. Leaders think in large units of time, non-leaders in short ones. Leaders-to-be practice thinking in long-range terms when they may have been used to thinking only narrowly. The results are immediate!

- As you go to work, what are you thinking?

  "How am I going to make it through the day?"

  "What shall we do this weekend?"

  "When will I be ready for promotion?"

  "Should I look for another job in a different company, where there are more opportunities for advancement?"

  "How are the funds accumulating for the children's college fund?"

  "How shall we think about retirement?"

  "Did we ever think of our family as a dynasty?"

  "When has a CEO lost his or her usefulness?"

  "What are the historical roots of terrorism?"

  "What is the future of making anti-terrorism the primary national policy?"

  "Am I in the right line of business or has the market left me behind?"

In each case your operative time or space-time unit is different. The unit used builds as you go down the list. Thinking about how you will manage through the day at work implies a much smaller space-time unit than thinking about the implication for history of terrorism. These are not just different questions; they are manifestations of how your mind grasps and utilizes differently the categories of space and time underlying all your experience. The sequence of growth roughly follows this progressive pattern:

> What is your present unit of time?
>
> Can you change that?
>
> Does that modify your expectations?
>
> Do your values change accordingly?
>
> Does it impact your results?
>
> Does the change spill over from private life to business life, from specific to general, from turning back an unsatisfactory meal at a restaurant to you, as board member, firing the CEO?

The objective is to diagnose more or less accurately the unit of space-time in terms of which you perceive, think, analyze, plan, and live. The assumption is that the unit is specific to the objective, but that in general terms, the larger the unit the greater the visionary leadership potential of the individual and the team. In selecting visionary leaders you look for the size of their space-time unit. But even more important, in growing greatness in your visionary leadership, you work directly and deliberately on enlarging the space-time units you bring to the task. In proportion that you enlarge it, your leadership capacity will equally grow. This is the operative and useful principle and tool on which you base your growth and that of your organization. In the end, that is what you offer your customers.

One business significance here is to create principles for structuring organizations. People who think in terms of short time spans should be placed low on the hierarchy, and people with a long time span deserve to be placed high. Then you have, what some people call, a naturally structured organization.

There seems to be little doubt that time span—and I would add "space span" as well, since space and time are closely linked in physics and in personal experience—influences leadership success in income, status, education, health, effectiveness, and accomplishments. This is important leadership information.

If we place free will at the base of the leadership mind, then we concentrate on the choices we can make on configuring and reconfiguring the way we want our minds to work. We can control the time span—and space span—units in terms of which we think, perceive, plan, . . . and talk. And there is high leverage in that effort at mind control. The mind here functions as a genuine servomechanism, like the strength enhancers in power steering and power brakes.

> The business prescription then is to make the effort to approach all tasks, from detailed record keeping to installing wide-ranging IT systems, with a large time span/space span, or, for short, the time-space-span (TSS) of the leadership mind. We increase and stretch the TSS. It is a skill that we can master.

Eternity. There is another way to view the units of space-time: eternity, which, spatially, is infinity. It is the eternal here and now. You are always at your goal. You are clearly focused, and the goal does not change. Perhaps it is to build a sterling company. Perhaps it is to write a great symphony or the great American novel. Perhaps it is to have the best medical practice or legal firm, a model for others, respected by the world. Perhaps it is to find God, period.

If the goal is single-minded, if it does not change either over time and based on location, the sense of space-time stops, as it were, on a point. Rather than to say the space-time unit is small or large, one can argue that it is everpresent.

To honor our need for consistency, we can say that the eternal here-and-now is the largest possible scope of space-time. It then does not matter if we lose the past, for we have always been at our destination, so that what we do today is not different from what we have done before, except perhaps better. The future is going to where we will do more of what we are doing now. One's work is not made up of different parts, but each day, as it were, is an improvement of the previous day, containing them all, so that discarding the past presents no problem, and we are confident about the future.

We critique work that we see done, strategies that are presented to us, editorials that we read, opinions that people hold, in terms of the scope of the TSS with which they are fashioned. Discerning the long-term consequences of our attitudes and actions—from relationship habits, financial habits, and health habits to study habits, punctuality habits, and driving habits—gives us a clue to life's prognosis: success or failure, greatness or mediocrity, achievement or collapse. Caesar and Napoleon, Jefferson and Roosevelt, Gandhi and Martin Luther King, Jr., went as far as they did because of their dogged determination to keep that visionary TSS going. You can do it too, and, more importantly, you can teach it to your people.

◆ Activity

Mensa

Work a Mensa puzzle and, at the same time, examine how your mind tries to work and how you think it should work. Engage and reflect concurrently.

Look again. Decide that your first two-tier approach—work the problem and reflect on your mental actions, describe them—was only ordinary. You need to sharpen it by two degrees of genius. Measure what you do by using "genius units" (gus). Lift up your thinking at least two more gus.

Do not delegate the genius work to your brightest people. What you need is to hire genius teachers, for yourself and for your team: people who will challenge you and train you to think more sharply and more innovatively.

There are verbal, numbers, and spatial tests, also referred to as intelligence test segments. Taking these tests is to use the engaged consciousness. Reflecting on how your mind works and how you can improve that is shifting over to the reflective consciousness. Here are examples of verbal and numbers tests. (There is no spatial test in this sample.) The answers are provided at the end of this chapter.

Verbal

In each line below, underline two words that mean most nearly either the opposite or the same as each other. (This is part of a fifty-question test, for which you have exactly fifty minutes to complete.)

1. liable, reliable, fluctuating, trustworthy, worthy

2. foreign, practical, germane, useless, relevant

3. relegate, reimburse, legislate, promote, proceed

4. window, lucent, acrid, shining, shady

5. lucubrate, bribe, indecent, spiny, obscene

Numbers

The numbers in each row in the figure on the next page run in series. Write the two numbers that should appear in the blanks on the right-hand side double square. In the example, the left-hand number increases by one at each step; the right-hand numbers are multiplied by two at each step. (Maximum time is one minute per question.)

Ex:	1	2	2	4	3	8	4	16
1.	3	4	4	6	5	8		
2.	2	8	3	12	4	16		
3.	5	7	4	8	3	9		
4.	49	7	36	6	25	5		
5.	2	3	5	6	11	12		

Reprinted by kind permission of Constable & Robinson from Victor Serebriakoff's, SELF-SCORING IQ TESTS (Barnes & Noble) derived from *How Intelligent Are You*, published by Robinson Publishing, 1995.

Thoughts and reflections that come to mind as you try to work the test:

- To take the test is to be *engaged*. To use the test as a means to understand how the mind works and what we can do to improve it is *reflection*. This distinction between the engaged attitude of consciousness and the reflective attitude is a fundamental distinction in the theory of knowledge. The capacity and the willingness to make this shift, and make it many times over, is the mark of a leadership mind. We discussed this important point earlier, for to solve a problem is to be engaged, whereas examing how we did it is reflection.

- The presumption here is the disciplined control over the mind, which is a highly regarded religious and monastic virtue. It is also found in artists and athletes, chess players and thinkers—concentrating, focusing, that is, total absorption—on how the mind functions at any one moment. This practice must first be valued and rewarded before it can be practiced sufficiently to actually be effective.

- We clearly see the difference between taking the test cold, as it were, unprepared, and after practice. Practice gives us insights that cannot even be verbalized. Remember when you learned how to drive, how frightening it was? Now it is natural. So it is as we gain familiarity with words and numbers. The latter are universal, the former local. If we think globally it is indeed difficult to use verbal intelligence tests.

- Experience clarifies, but so too does creating your own examples.

- We can answer by looking for the pattern of the numbers in the first cell of each pair, and then the second cell of each, and then do the same with each second cell. But then we also have to ask about the relationship between the numbers in both cells of each pair. These are two separate operations. They are different. Only when we see what is before us in some kind of larger perspective can we have thoughts like these. The mind adapts its sight to this and kindred issues. Suddenly we see clearly. But it takes a visit to that region of the mind where these matters are illuminated. It is not a question of not understanding or not having skill with numbers. It is a question of achieving the illumination required, literally, in a land of numbers. Students good in math do exactly that. Here as elsewhere, cliché or not, practice makes perfect. But practice without understanding has no staying power.

- We quickly see that decisions about values enter the picture, and that general health and well-being are associated with alertness and quickness of recall. Doing mathematics with speed is an Olympic athletic endeavor.

- Speed is a key factor. Some deep thinking is hindered by speed. I.A. Richards, one of my teachers, wrote a book on how to read a page. His motto was that you cannot read slowly enough. Intelligent people, he used to say, are measured by how slowly they read a page, not by their speed. But today in the business world, speed is everything. To run against the clock is the most common form of stress and pressure. Leaders adapt themselves to speed and learn how to perform well. This is a true Darwinian adaptation to reality. It can be done, and it can be done as fun and not as stress, as learning and not as punishment, as a game and not a life-or-death issue, no matter how serious the context may be.

- To work with speed means to have cultivated the art of concentration, which is positively and negatively affected by rest, environment, mood, fear, distractions and distractibility, physical well-being, mental discipline, competition, self-image, and the like. These are powerful peripherals that require consideration.

- But the underlying attention is toward your whole life and your whole personality, your character and what we call your overall "being-in-the-world"—just as with the real Olympics. You prepare for them over a lifetime, and the preparation is continuous, making you rusty very quickly. And you maintain yourself in shape long after the games are over. Then you are ready, always prepared, to think clearly and see sharply with your inner eye.

- It is easy to become upset when taking an intelligence test. Then, when panic strikes, uncertainty and guesswork take over. You address that issue not with a few test-taking techniques but by cultivating your serenity and your health, your world view and your leadership—continuously, over your lifetime. Then the positive results come in. This shows the intensely contextual character of intellectual brilliance: It is a result of personality structure and lifestyle choice. This is true Diamond Reverse Engineering™, in which pragmatic results are tied directly to decisions you make about how your mind is to work. Lifestyle and health impact performance, including strategy and creativity.

- The answer is not now but continuous. If you always hone your mind then, like your body, you are ready when the need strikes. That is really the undergirding lesson!

- How do you reconcile the fun of this with the anxiety? Entertainment is the shibboleth of today's generation. Tying together fun with intellectual brilliance, in the form of puzzles, rivets the attention of most people.

- What are the fears? That your ego will be dramatically undermined? We are aware of the anxiety of diminishing our self-concept. But we are also aware of the decision to face the truth, which leads to the possibility of transcending the present state. It is a clear case of moving from anxiety to hope, from paralysis to smooth going.

- There are inherent problems: By accident there may be more than one answer or there may be contradictions not noticed by the test makers. How do you deal with that type of frustration, when the system tells you it works but you know better, you have found out that it is flawed? This is the generic issue of being managed by people who are less smart than you are, less mature, and who know less. That is the best motivator to run for public office, said Socrates, to prevent lesser beings from governing you.

- What are the economic consequences of sharpening your mind? Is it the depth, the speed, the alertness? After all, we want to apply these philosophic leadership insights to change and innovation. How does your ability to think clearly, to improve your visionary intelligence, relate to introducing change initiatives, creating innovative products, or unraveling the Gordian knot of strategy in an uncertain and confusing economic landscape? Is this acquisition a good idea? Is this investment in research smart? Is it time to pull in your advertising— or to increase its budget?

- What about the concept of a strategic thinking organization? Would it help to make the promotion of visionary intelligence the priority in your company? Is that what is needed to move into the future, to sustain your profitability during unclear times? Is this the time to prepare for the future by investing in research and in training?

- But there are gaps in intelligence tests. Where is the practice for creativity, innovation, finding novelty? And where is the systems test to help you with trends? And how do you test for and then enhance the capacity for seeing with the inner eye ever larger space-times, more ample geographic and historical expanses?

- This is the development of vision. Now combine that with courage and you have the configuration of the entrepreneurial leadership mind, needed to fuel the free-market economy, anywhere in the world.

It is important to continue this list. Then we must ask the question of how we can train for genius-level intelligence and how can we apply it. We then can strive to become intellectual athletes, conceptual Olympians. The applications, of course, extend far beyond business. Everything we touch will be smarter and more creative. Truly here practice makes perfect and, following Aristotle's original insight, we learn by imitation, patterning our thinking and behavior on people we deem to be particularly bright.

What are your thoughts, insights, and reflections? What can you teach us?

Example: Widening Vision

Let's take a look at how coaching vision works in practice. Following is the account from an OD consultant of how she has used the Diamond principles in the area of increasing the vision of a top executive team.

In Practice: One Executive's Experience

First you tune up your mind. These are desultory thoughts, to stimulate your imagination. You create your own. This is the warm-up. You limber your mental muscles so that the future may be clearer.

Joan, an account manager at one of the large international client firms, engages in a kind of meditation exercise. She takes the time-space-span scale seriously, and she developed one that makes specific sense to her client, dealing with the situations that concerned the customer firm at this moment. She meditates on locating and expanding vision before she addresses the business context. Having done all of the above, she creates the following statement for her client, the CEO:

"Our clients are apprehensive about three topics, all at the same time, and they are segmented or stratified in their awareness.

"*1. Global warming.* The chairman just attended a conference on the subject of Global Warming: Business as Cause and Remedy, and he came away convinced that this is a critical business issue, that there is much special-interest lobbying and deception pandered about this topic, and that indeed there is danger to Earth and to mankind's future. He feels strongly that, from his vantage point as a high-level business executive and with the power that he has in his company, he needs to do something substantial to make a meaningful contribution to solving this problem—not with clichés but with science, ethics, and high-minded actions. When it comes to cars, chemicals, aluminum, steel, oil, and plastics, the environmental question looms paramount. He, working in some of those industries, feels the 'green' pressure, the bite of the laws, and the conflict with commerce.

"*2. Financial worries.* Ecology may be the first issue, but financial troubles is a close second, if not the real priority. Our clients do not see their business prospering as they had expected. The market is drying up, on top of which the competition is threatening to put them out of whatever business is left. They never thought it would come to this and they have a hard time keeping up their optimism and the enthusiasm of their employees, not to speak of meeting payroll. They need something new.

"*3. Employee concerns.* Their last item is the matter of their employees' *dignity* as human beings. They feel an obligation here that transcends the requirements of the business. But we have been telling them that attending to self-respect issues is indeed part of good business! They had been proud and successful, and they now see their power and esteem slipping away from them. Should they prepare themselves for 'death'? Is it not much too early? Are they going through a transition, suffering all the ills that go with it? Or is it all over? Can they turn this around into a new beginning? Here we are helping them deal with the subject of hope, of grandeur, of meaning, of significance, of dynasty, of doing something of true importance with their company.

"We have concluded with them that each of these three concurrent concerns requires a different visionary futurizing mindset for the leadership of the company and eventually for the culture. Let's make some assumptions about them. We discussed the following:

"For you, the money is short-term, global warming is medium-term, and destiny is long-term. From the outside in, it is the reverse—destiny, global warming, money, in that order (see Figure 18.1).

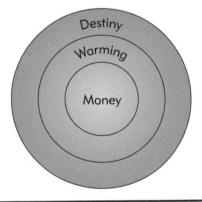

Figure 18.1. Goals

"You decide that dealing with the financial issues is a three-to-five-year proposition, and statewide in scope. If your strategic thinking is good enough and your energy mobilization powerful enough, you think you can take care of this in three to five years. That is how you believe you must think. Global warming as a business issue is a major political topic, and you make up your mind that you will devote the next seven to ten years to giving it your best and your all under the circumstances that you have available. You are committed to making your contribution to solve this problem. Even though global warming is global, and your business is global, you have decided that your effective concern will be only for the nation of which you are a member. And you do not lose sight of your bottom-line business realities.

"Finally, the destiny issue is an eternity issue, an immortality-project matter, for you and for your employees—those who identify with your business—that requires a legacy you leave to the world and a legacy you leave to their families, and that your plan will take you the rest of your days as CEO. And here your spatial scope, of course, becomes then the entire globe (see Figure 18.2).

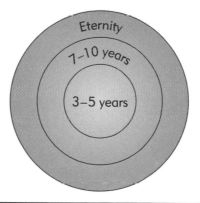

Figure 18.2. Time Frame

"And while you think of these matters, you realize that every stake-holder's good health is a prerequisite for making that happen. General health then becomes your underlying instant priority.

"You make a real effort to make these three mindsets your own, together with health, and to instill them cooperatively and co-creatively into the culture of the organization. *You literally reprogram your mind in terms of time and space to think like that, to bear yourself like that, to talk like that, to plan like that, and to have faith in the reasonableness of that.* This is your commitment to yourself, in your full loneliness and isolation as a leader.

"Now remember the key: The solution is not to work only on the business issues but on controlling TSS, the time span and the space span in terms of which your mind perceives your reality, conceives of directions and answers, and energizes itself for action. You think in three tiers: three to five business years and your nation; seven to ten business years and your continent; and all the business time you have and the full globe. You modify your space-time sense and you move from out to in, from all the time to three years, and from globe to nation, and you have in your possession a clear outline of how your mind is to be reframed, your thinking reconfigured, and your units of time reconstructed in order for you at all times to be working with maximum efficiency, maximum hope, and maximum energy on the concrete and practical issues that you feel need resolution. You begin big and you end small, rather than the reverse. (See Figure 18.3.)

"These thoughts are not absolute. They are illustrative only. You design what works for you. The key to remember is that in order to make true progress toward making your vision a reality you start with a clear future. But vision is looking far ahead. Rather than start with today and work on the details, you start with the future, which is a destiny theme, and work your way backward, which is income. You do not ignore the present details. Quality is in the details. But without the overarching issue in the back-

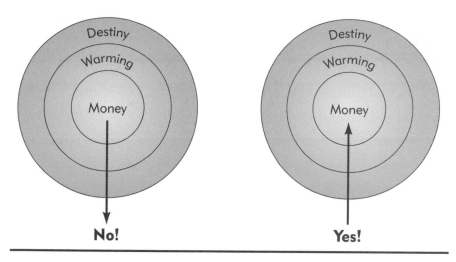

Figure 18.3. Direction

ground, nothing significant will ever happen. The vision itself is the magnet that will exert the pressure and the pull to see to it that you will not be deflected."

> *If you wish to build a ship, do not drum your men together*
> *to bring wood and distribute the work, but teach them*
> *to long for the wide and endless sea.*

Antoine de Saint Exupéry, *The Little Prince*

Joan's confidential message to the CEO continued:

"What you immediately discover is that if you see all three space-time zones together they support each other. The larger hope that your destiny is under control will involve you more readily in politics and in learning more about global warming. This concern with social responsibility will take you out of the funk or depression into which your company's financial situation has thrown you, making it easier to handle the latter. One of the results of this analysis is that you reverse the normal process of control. Ordinarily we would say that you start by putting your finances in order. Then, if there is any time left, you will worry about global warming. And then, much later, if at all, you will address the issue of destiny, greatness, and perhaps what heritage you will leave for the generations of your family that will follow you. And then, only then, will you worry about time-span issues and space-span issues, the kind that is foundational for enhancing vision.

"Your money will come, if your company should fail, not by looking as an ex-CEO through the help wanted ads in the classified section of the local paper, but by harnessing your destiny theme to the political theme and making a new business out of the bonding. It could be by writing an inspiring book, for that is how inspiring books are written, and then turning it into a business, because it will give you name recognition and bring you into public view, helping you in the marketing of whatever else it is that you are doing.

"Or you can invent new products or set up a business with other people's inventions, such as importing inexpensive solar batteries from China or India and building them into sets you sell in the West, as one of your directors did as a sideline.

"Or you may sell this very idea, how to reconstruct a life, and how you have done it, and write about it, speak about it, give seminars about it, and use that as the springboard for a whole new series of entrepreneurial enterprises to produce income for you. If you are looking for employment, this looks good on your resume."

Resisting: A Final Word on the Obstacles

When you bring up the possibility of increasing the time span and space span, as Joan did, you must be alert to identifying the resistances that people put in place to avoid facing their guilt about unfulfilled potential. The resistance is a choice, an unconscious decision, we might say, having its roots deep inside the inner world, to engage in self-deception. We choose not to dare because daring causes anxiety. We also choose not to look seriously at the consequences of not daring—those being the loss of life itself, of meaning, of identity, a value in our existence. Misconstruing anxiety as evil rather than empowering, as pathology rather than as the vestibule to greater health, is the final choice of self-deception, the final nail in the coffin of an authentic existence.

What are these resistances?

- Paying no attention to these vision tools, seeing people's eyes glaze over and wander about when the topic of increasing conceptual intelligence and the capacity for visioning are brought up.

- Having no ambition, no sense of greatness, thinking that a life dedicated to fun and maintenance is not an escape from authenticity but is the meaning of life.

- Thinking that one just does not have the capacity for finance, or that one is not destined to be a significant leader. These are resistances in that they deny our potential.

- There is unwillingness to reprogram our thinking and change our mental models, so that we find it difficult to move people without vision to be people with vision instead.

In general, none of these genius-level strategy-producing mental characteristics are written in stone. They are possibilities to most people, and they can be practiced, learned, and cultivated. What is important is that we know it can be done and what the alternatives are. Herein lies true leadership power.

And your task as a leader is to practice being a genius and to apply the lessons, results, of what you have learned, strategically to your *business*. Here's how: *You apply strategic thinking to how you plan to run your organization—better than the competition, with more innovation and more efficiency.*

The secret is not only to understand this effort to expand the intellectual and conceptual capabilities of the mind, nor even just to practice them—but to become a conceptual athlete, an idea Olympian, a three-time winner at the innovation Wimbledon.

We start with ethics and we end with vision. Each corner of the Diamond is a different way to encounter the world. Your client and your customer have needs that must be met. They are not just food and shelter, but they are the Diamond points: the capacity to cope with the boundary situations of life. People need to have access to their free will, to that part of their personality where decisions are made, risks taken, and commitments delivered. Leaders must be aware of that region and they require the capacity to talk intelligently about the issues that arise in this context. Human beings have ethical needs, and they are fundamental. There can be no life that works if it is not guided by keeping promises, communicating, sensitivity to people's feelings, and a deep sense of equity and justice, fairness and honesty. Too often people lie to themselves, hiding from view the harsh reality and losing out massively as a result. We need to develop an attitude of deep respect for what in the world cannot be altered and does not suit either our values or our whims—an abiding recognition of what is real.

And people need to train the mind to think more innovatively, in larger units of space and time, and with increasing analytical acuity. A residue of leadership topics remains. And the latter are basic. Rather than to refer to these also as ways of being intelligent, we call them modes of mastery. For one way to cope with the Diamond corners is to sensitize ourselves to *polarity*, the inherent ambiguity of the world. We recognize that the mind is always more than any theories about it and that the world also is bigger than any theory we can develop about it. For a product of the mind comes from the mind and cannot go back to it and in turn encompass its own source. The same is true of the world. The world cannot produce a theory that then turn around to encompass the full world from which it came as but a part. Awareness of polarity is a crucial modifier of the leadership mind. And so is *greatness,* the second mode of mastery discussed here. We end on that note, for the heart of leadership is the pledge to make a difference, in oneself, true, but, more importantly, in one's clients and in the world into which we are thrust—or out of which we came. Human beings have the capacity and the will to continue the process of creation and therewith to make this a better world than they originally found. Therein lies the nobility of being human.

Answers to the Mensa Activities

Verbal

1. reliable, trustworthy (synonyms)
2. germane, relevant (synonyms)
3. relegate, promote (opposites)
4. lucent, shining (synonyms)
5. indecent, obscene (synonyms)

Numbers

1. 6, 10 (the first number in each domino is one more, and the second two more, than in the domino before)
2. 5, 20 (the first number in each domino is one more than in the domino before; the second number is four times the first)
3. 2, 10 (the first number in each domino is one less, and the second one more, than in the domino before)
4. 16, 4 (the second number in each domino is one less than in the domino before; the first number is the square of the second)
5. 23, 24 (the second number in each domino is twice the number in the domino before; the first number is one less than the second)

PART FOUR

The Main Body of the Leadership Mind

Two Mastery Tools

POLARITY

O serpent heart, hid with a flowering face,
Did ever dragon keep so fair a cave?
Beautiful tyrant, fiend angelical,
Dove-feathered raven, wolvish-ravening lamb!
Despised substance of divinest show,
Just opposite to what thou justly seemst—
A damned saint, an honorable villain!
O nature, what hadst thou to do in hell
When thou didst bower the spirit of a fiend
In mortal paradise of such sweet flesh?
Was ever book containing such vile matter
So fairly bound? O that deceit should dwell
In such a gorgeous palace!

SHAKESPEARE, *Romeo and Juliet*

And we thank Thee that darkness reminds us of light.

T.S. ELIOT

Dreams are necessary to life.

ANAÏS NIN

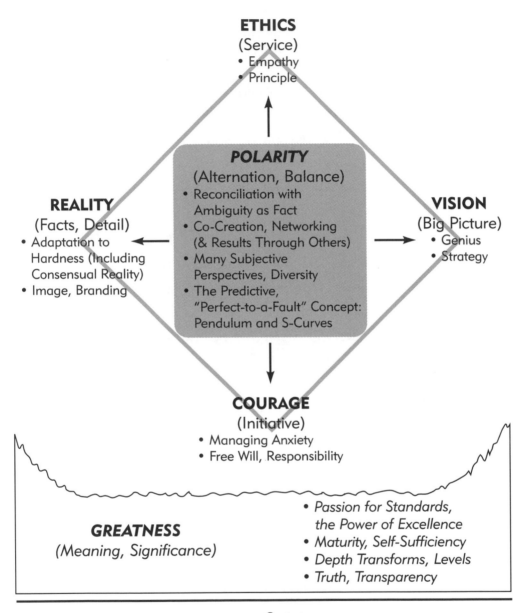

Figure 19.1. The Leadership Diamond®: Polarity

CHAPTER 19

Polarity

DEFINITION: Alternation and Balance

ELEMENTS: Reconciliation with Ambiguity,

Co-Creation and Networking,

Subjective Perspectives,

Prediction

PREPARE YOURSELF: POLARITY IS HERE TO STAY!

Polarity is a deep structure of human existence that we do not call a way of being intelligent but a way of *mastering* the four intelligences. Each intelligence is in itself ambiguous, paradoxical, conflicting, and comes as a polarity. What is the right position to take in this union-management dispute, such as the strike of airline pilots, disrupting the economy but having legitimate grievances? When and where do I take my ethical stand? When values and profits collide, how do I choose? We can burn off the gas that comes out of our drilling for oil, or at extra cost we can inject it into the underground deposits again. Which vision is right for my company—shall we expand or consolidate? What is really going on in the stock market—is there a shakeout, so that only the very best companies survive? Ambiguities are built right into each one of the principal tools of leadership, the ways of being intelligent.

There also is polarity *among* the various ways of being intelligent. Ford Motor Company, for example, had in the 1990s as chairman Alexander Trotman. He was a good example of a full Diamond leader, competent in all four ways of being intelligent. Under Petersen and Poling before him, one could argue that Ford's focus lay on product and attention to the workforce—that is, *reality* and *ethics,* respectively. However, the strategy of a world car and the boldness required for its implementation had been neglected. When Petersen and Poling retired, the business requirements of Ford clearly were *vision* and *courage.* They needed to be added to the Ford leadership Diamond. Alexander Trotman clearly filled that bill. He was a full Diamond, clearly emphasizing the latter two intelligences.

I spent time with Trotman earlier, when he was president of Ford of Europe. The day of our meeting, in Brentwood, near London, I came to his office. There was a wildcat strike in the midst of ongoing negotiations. The plant managers were there, agitated and worried. Trotman went to the phone and called in to his negotiators, barking in an order: "If by afternoon the workers are not back, then all so-far negotiated concessions will be null and void." He turned to me, "Peter, let's drive to my house and talk about vision and courage." Which we did. And we made plans.

My interpretation is that the Ford board, at the time of Trotman's impending retirement, in effect divided the Diamond between two executives. William Clay Ford, a member of the Ford family, took the job of vision and ethics—the environment and the soft side, as chairman, whereas CEO Jacques Nasser, who was then affectionately known as "Jac the Knife," was given the job of reality and courage—the tough things, the operational and survival factors, such as the Explorer SUV with its mammoth Firestone crisis. In the end, the Ford Diamond became destabilized, Ford lost money and prestige, and Nasser was let go.

There is conflict, inherently, between courage and ethics on the one side, the more intellectual and human issues, and between reality and courage on the other, which is the tough action-packed operational leadership presence. There is polarity between vision and reality, and there is polarity also between ethics and courage. Vision looks far ahead; reality looks to the next quarter. Ethics considers people's feelings; courage can ride straight over them.

Polarity and Adaptation

Reconciliation to the uncertainties and ambiguities of life is a good expression. Perhaps the most powerful use of that term in recent history was Archbishop Tutu's application of it to the moral task of post-apartheid South Africa. Reconciliation was the Republic's primary political assignment. So is the word *adaptation* appropriate, for it comes out of the context of biology, where the species on this earth become what they are by adapting their physiological characteristics to their unique and changing environmental circumstances.

Adaptation, in the philosophical sense, is not biological, in that you make do and survive under new environmental circumstances. Here, adaptation means both accepting and overcoming. It has ethical and rational components as well.

Adaptation means that you make up your mind that chaos, ambiguity, uncertainty, conflict, paradox, diversity, and, in a word, *polarity*, together represent one fundamental aspect of human existence. It is the aspect of confusion and pain. The world is ambiguous, whereas I may prefer to think of it as having clear answers, being black and white, digital. It is in my perception where the problem lies. Demanding monism where there is dualism, that is where the problem lies. Ignoring the truth of polarity stops me from making leadership progress. That is the problem with people who have trouble making decisions. They think they must have answers before they can decide. Little do they know that they create the answers as they choose. First I choose and then that becomes the answer.

Let's take an extreme case: You have a serious car accident on your way to work, which results in your becoming a paraplegic. At some deep level you gain the unforeseen insight that it doesn't matter that you are paralyzed. What matters is not your circumstances but your underlying maturity and character. That becomes obvious only over time, as life moves forward. It is only when it fundamentally does not matter that you then have the power to deal with polarities. Because then you are free to choose.

Working with the same company for fifteen years, you realize that you are a woman of thirty-nine, never married, and very much wanting a child. You adapt yourself to the fact that at some deep level it really does not matter whether you marry or not, have children or not. That's tough to say, but it is human reality. It happens in real life! On the one hand, of course, unfulfilled potential is always tragic, and we must taste the tragic element. But it is even more tragic when you cannot make the adaptation, be mature about defeat, gain substance from frustration. What matters is your character and your maturity. Not luck. My mother, who died at forty-three, was happily married. Her sister, my aunt, died at eighty-three, happily unmarried. Reconciliation, accepting fate, identifying with your destiny, those are the possibilities that make value out of despair, solutions out of problems, and fulfillment out of emptiness.

Adaptation means we recognize the harsh truth, the fixed fact of polarization, the lack of definitive answers, that many answers are not logical conclusions but courageous acts, free choices, under conditions of significant risk. And that is the leadership facet.

◆ Activity

What are your fundamental values? Here's a good list to choose from: truth, beauty, love, wealth, power, and unity, representing respectively the theoretical, aesthetic, social, economic, political, and religious person. Create an activity around this list and ask these heuristic questions: (1) What are your fundamental values? What matters to you? (2) What are the culture's fundamental values? Where lies the power in our society? (3) Where is the alignment or engagement gap? What are the feelings of unease? and (4) How do you manage the gap? How do you cope with polarity and paradox? The result will be a stronger management of polarity.

Or you can ask the questions below. They will put you in touch with the full spectrum of experiences surrounding the deep structure of paradox and polarity (using here these terms interchangeably).

Write a short statement in response to these questions (or those you find relevant). Share your concerns with a partner. Discuss with that person the extent to which this kind of dialogue helps you manage the paradoxes you face in the workplace. Many people have reported that even a forty-five minute conversation on these points can have a significant impact in managing more successfully one's difficult choices and decisions.

- Can you see your life and work as a series of paradoxes?

- What are your personal paradoxes?

- What are your paradoxes in the workplace?

- What are your career paradoxes?

- What are those of significant co-workers?

- What are the organization's paradoxes?

- What are the paradoxes of the larger context, such as the economy, society, politics?

- Which are important?

- Which are not?

- Which are your role to address?

- Which are other executives' role to address?

- What are you doing to manage the paradoxes?

- What are you not doing but could be doing?

- What are the organization's obstacles to experiencing in depth its paradoxes? And then managing, superseding them?

- How does it feel when in the vise of a paradox?

- What has been (or is) your worst paradox?

- How has it impacted your life?

Discussing these points, dialoguing about them, engaging in Intelligent Leadership Conversations on them, can give you and your team a grip on some of the thorniest questions you are likely to be confronting.

Co-Creation and Subjective Perspectives

These are two important themes, but not much space will be devoted here to these components of polarity. The first focuses on the comprehensive theme of achieving results through others. Leadership is not doing something by yourself, but to change any narcissistic mode into the attitude—and the Diamond promotes changes in attitude occasioned by using leadership language—that I can do nothing by myself alone. I am the leader, yes, but I must find ways to achieve results by motivating, organizing, and influencing others. Nothing can be more difficult, especially since I am part of the system itself that needs to be directed. This is a way of looking at reality that leaders need to adopt, and it is a perspective on the world that consultants need to support in their clients.

The opposite is dependency. I ask; I do not take the initiative. That is not co-creation. It is to allow the system to do all the creating. Thus, the attitude of achieving results through others is to manage well a fundamental ambiguity, in language, in attitude, and in behavior.

The component of subjective perspectives is also the diversity issue. I see the world in my way, I have spent years getting there, and I have certain blind spots, true ones, that I don't even know exist. There are some things that I simply cannot understand that nevertheless are axiomatic to others. Examples include how married couples relate, what kind of manners children have, how hierarchy functions, how important punctuality is, what is appropriate in displaying anger, and so on. All these can be cultural issues. But no one can be a leader who does not cultivate the capacity to see the world through the eyes of another or fathom the legitimacy of language, attitudes, and behaviors that to oneself are not even a concept. We need this tolerance for diversity to be good people, but also to be good businesspeople, be it managing a team or marketing a product. And whenever we lead or we consult, we must be conscious of the subjective perspective from which we are operating.

Prediction and Transformation

A further component of polarity is prediction. Polarity predicts the opposite, the negative, the contrast, the resistance, the push-back. We must therefore be prepared for the other side to show up. The stock is high; we can predict it will be low again. The stock is low; we can say this is natural and with proper strategy we can bring it up again. The economy is slowing down; that is because it had been heated up. And a slow economy is an opportunity for new inventiveness—even if it is profiting wildly from books and tapes about how to survive in a slow economy! That is why we must be both conservative and aggressive, both cautious and adventuresome. And we must be well-informed.

What this means is that polarity does not lead to a solution but to a *transformation.* By being confronted with the truth of polarity, and by recognizing that we are made to live a polarized existence, by nature, by God, by evolution, by experience, by desensitization—it doesn't matter what we bring up as cause—we see life and world differently. We feel renewed rather than burned out when we come off work or when we return the next day. The darkness and the ennui that engulfed our job and made us look gray and drawn now is transformed into a smile, good color, and a bouncy gait.

This insight leads to transformation of both self and world. The key point here is that it is results-oriented. It is a technology, it is to find a better life, in both work and love, business and recreation, wealth and wisdom.

The transformation phase is different in important ways from the adaptation phase. *Adaptation* is to recognize reality. You can choose defeat. Or you can use the data as a springboard to greater and better things. This then is *transformation.* Transformation is the most practical and pragmatic technical outlook on how to change the world—not take it lying down as it is—but make it over so that your values and ideals can be made real.

That is why we say that business is the language of effectiveness. It is a way of seeing the world so that we do not take lying down what it dishes out to us, but rather that we summon the burst of our energies and the razor of our genius to change things to receive what we want—provided it fulfills the criteria of ethics and compassion.

> There is danger in too much adaptation, for it may mean complacency. Look for your driving force. Something you want "really bad." Know that others are like you. Help yourself to transformation, and it becomes your new or renewed business idea. Be

supremely practical. These new plans have to be conceived in terms of organizations and directed at organizations! This is the formula, for that's where your clients are.

Polarity As a Deep Structure

Of the Diamond deep structures that we discuss in leadership coaching, some receive a much stronger response from the public and from executives than others. Ethics and courage are two of them. But polarity is another. There is a really strong supportive reaction, a kind of "aha!" experience, when people are reminded that life is full of paradoxes and contradictions and that it is not really necessary to adjudicate among them; many of them can quite happily coexist.

A manager can have employees who compete with one another and still run a perfectly respectable organization. In fact, many believe that internal competition strengthens performance. Brokers recommend a diversified portfolio, averaging out hopefully to your advantage precisely because purchases are made by conflicting and contradictory stock selection criteria. Any democracy can live successfully with a variety of conflicting political parties, without revolution or conniving. A good symphony is full of contrasting melodies, tempi, harmonies, volume, and rhythms. Accepting polarity as a finality, neither being capable of resolution nor requiring resolution—that is, some problems emotionally must be resolved and yet logically they do not have any answers, at least not if you take the history of philosophy seriously—is indeed life-transforming. It actually changes your fundamental metaphysics, that is, the basic mode in which you see reality. There is true diversity here, right inside your own mind. For what yesterday was impossible today is logical. As is, for example, accepting the death of a loved one:

You love your mother, you are attached to your mother, and your mother dies. It is a shock. You now live in a world without a mother. It does not seem possible. You just spoke with her yesterday on the telephone. You don't believe that she is gone. The world by its very nature contains your mother and now that mother is no longer in your world; your entire world has been changed.

At first you cannot function in that world. And you are proud of it, because it proves your mother was important to you and that you loved her truly. Tomorrow, however, you accept the rightness of the world without your mother, something that today, in shock and disbelief, is inconceivable to you.

It is important to get in touch with this possibility of transformation in the soul. For when we were young and fanciful we thought that contradictions need not be and can be resolved. I used to feel that way when I studied theoretical physics as an undergraduate at Stanford. But as we grow older and perhaps more mellow and more tolerant and can see the legitimacy of quite different points of view, we no longer feel that urge to select. And things work better now. It's funny, is it not, to say that the world can both be logical and illogical at the same time? That is, however, how the great polarities of life are resolved. To apply this practically to our business and to our everyday life is to understand how we manage polarities, and then how we can use the tension among the opposite poles to actually move forward during our most painful times of being stuck.

Polarity and the Bottom Line

Before we go to the polarity mapping activity, a down-to-earth summary statement of what polarity does and how it functions in the workplace is indicated. What really is it and how does it actually work in business? The essence of polarity as a leadership tool is two-fold. One is that we become used to polarity as a phenomenon of existence. The conceptual equivalents for how we use this term in Diamond Theory are such words as "uncertainty," "ambiguity," "contradiction," "conflict," "paradox," "chaos," and others.

To accept polarity in an orderly world, with a logical frame of reference and a rational mind, is difficult if not outright impossible. Polarity provokes once again the hackneyed resistances against all forms of systems thinking. Polarity is the key paradigm shift step from problem solving to transformation, from linear thinking to global thinking, from stasis to process. It is today a common language, but do we really understand it? We are inculcated with demands for clarity, which is understandable. But simplicity is not evisceration. Simplicity is to see the whole as a unit. That is already the result of experienced systems thinking. Systems thinking is a mind shift, a new way of viewing the world. The system has its own ways of behaving that are not explainable even by detailed analysis. And not because it is impossible, but because it is a different way of viewing the universe. It started with Einstein: Space is curved and time slows down. In common sense, in linear thinking, this is not false, it is worse—it makes no sense. Today, we are used to this kind of thinking, just as after the Middle Ages people changed to thinking of the earth as spherical rather than flat and the sun rather than the earth as the center of the solar system. So it is with polarity. We grow used to having two children making contradictory demands. We become used to husband and wife having different temperaments. In the end, we are used to living happily in a democracy, where citizens have different opinions and still manage to live together not only in harmony but even with pride and patriotism.

Now we do the same with aspects of the inner world, such as polarities of feelings, motives, and decisions. We are used to not seeking solutions but living in ambiguity. This is the paradigm shift syndrome. Staying in polarity is not always relevant, of course. We do make either-or decisions. But we need to know the difference.

In order to make good investment decisions, I need to be able to predict the market. I cannot. But I do invest. This ambiguity is the source of anxiety. At the root of investment thinking is managing this type of anxiety. That cannot be done without fundamentally changing one's attitude toward money, earning, family, career, and life itself. And a broker who is also a good businessperson will pay attention to the anxiety of the client. Understanding the anxiety component of free will becomes a business issue. Here is where deepening the understanding of anxiety is pivotal.

The second key point in using polarity as a tool is that the different poles need each other; they are incomprehensible without each other—shadow and light, consciousness and unconsciousness, good and evil, life and death, matter and empty space, movement and rest. Even the word "define" itself etymologically means to create an object by pinpointing it and carving out something clearly delineated and separate from the environment. But it is the business uses that matter. We would not be aware of individuality if there were not teams, and we would not be aware of change if there were not stability and continuity. If you want to create new strategy, new direction, for your business, you experiment by asking this: Today's general direction does not work, or at least does not work as well as it should. What is the polar opposite of our current direction? Will we experiment with that? For example: We have been too hard and aggressive in our selling. We are also, through increased use of automation, depersonalizing our customer relations. This attitude does not work well. Does this mean we should be even more aggressive and depersonalized? Probably not. Aggression is perceived as such only because we can compare and contrast it with gentleness, kindness, concern, and involvement. Depersonalization is understood only because we have a sense of intimacy and commitment. Perhaps we should try the latter? It would require substantial personality shifts.

The converse may be the case. We are too concerned and kind, too personally involved with our customers, too dedicated. This is painful to say, but it may in fact not be good business. (What a paradox!) Generosity makes sense only when contrasted with being rough and tough. Perhaps people take advantage of our gentleness? We are becoming "perfect to a fault" in one pole of the Diamond. Perhaps it is time to try the opposite! The answer to polarity is mostly the conversion to democracy, which is not either team or individual, neither equality or freedom, but holding the polarity of both. This is a key point and we cannot do business without it. The management of polarity is found also in dialogue, learning in-depth and sensitive communication. Now apply this thinking to real crises in your life. One is to look out for the signs of overdoing one end of the polarity. Always be watchful. What are your polarities at your job? To be judged and to be loved, to be held accountable and to be forgiven. To be friend and professional. If you surrender to either one, you become a vassal. If you hold on to the polarity—even if it were in the Machiavellian sense of "divide and conquer"—you at least maintain your independence. And how do you practice this? In part you change your language accordingly. The outraged subordinate asks, "Are you my boss or are you my friend?" You answer, "The trouble is that I am both. And I want and need to be both. How about you?" You continue, "I am not unsympathetic to how you feel. I have the same ambivalence. What do you think would be the basic behaviors we need in order to make our relationship work, be a success, feel good, and be good at the same time? I could use your help in this effort."

Or take another case. The boss speaks: "I have called this meeting to make a decision. Should we invest in growth and in the future or should we concentrate on the present and pay our debts? We have two hours. I want an answer before the meeting is over." The high-potential on the team volunteers, "This is certainly our issue. The truth is that we need both. We cannot survive without investing in the future, nor can we survive by not paying our debts. Unless we find a way to do both, we are dead meat!"

"How on earth can we do both if we can barely do one?" the boss shoots back.

The high-potential continues, "If you will allow me some words, sir, I will propose to you the following, in the spirit of loyalty to this company."

"Go ahead," the boss concedes.

Reassured, the high-potential proceeds, "First, we must really understand the virtues of both sides. Each of us, before taking a position, must understand both sides fully and acknowledge their value. Then we must also recognize the downside of overdoing each point of view. We then have an overview. But rather than taking sides we need to be eloquent, as in a debating society, to make a good case for our opponent's stand."

He looks around, checking that all are listening. Satisfied, the high-potential goes on, "This is the easy part. The hard part is to retune and retool the mind. The answer is not a compromise but a smarter way to do both. We could vote, but that would be a last resort. The leadership way is to find a fresh, new, innovative approach. We do not want to defeat one side but encourage them both to win. It takes genius and creativity to do that. It literally took an Einstein to do this in physics. It will take an Einstein among us to do this in our company. I would like to ask this team for creative solutions, not compromises, not either-ors, but some profound way of saying both-and. Could it be that more energy, more dedication, more commitment, more seriousness, more joy in our work, a better attitude, would make much more of a difference than we would ever imagine? If we were among ourselves more connected, more supportive, more committed to each other's goals, were in the business to make others powerful, would that not help to achieve both objectives as a unit? We needed to win in Afghanistan, but also to pacify and modernize the nation—all at one and the same time. One without the other is futile."

He pauses, and meekly appends, "I trust it was OK for me to speak to you this way? Do you think there is merit in what I said? I have monopolized much of your time. Nevertheless, I would welcome learning from you."

This is using leadership language: ethics, courage, vision, realism—all wrapped in one package. The team will go nowhere, certainly not in keeping the company competitive, without addressing these issues. When T.S. Eliot was asked about polarity, he said, "And we thank Thee that darkness reminds us of light."

We are now ready to do the work, that is, to map the polarities that give us our greatest concerns.

Polarity Mapping

I am repeating here much of what Barry Johnson (1992) and Ahmed Yehia have said about plotting issues in polarity format. The key insight is to realize that two opposites belong together, such as the individual and the team, but they remain opposites nevertheless. We are forced to change the way we look at contradictions. As you solve the individual-team paradox in favor of the team, as many people do—they say the team comes first, period—you recognize its value but also the danger of overdoing it. As you increase the emphasis on the team, which yields collaboration, the negative begins to emerge, which results in stifling creativity and feeling outright oppression.

We then veer over to its opposite, namely, singing the praises of individualism. That feels good and presents itself as a solution, until too much individualism leads to anarchy and chaos. Then, once more, we see that the solution is teamwork and collaboration. The cycle repeats itself. This is an example of creating an intelligent leadership conversation. The Polarity Diagram in Figure 19.2 illustrates the strengths and weaknesses of each pole.

Many people are inspired and reassured by this analysis of polarity. It speaks to them; it corresponds to their experience. And it makes it clear why there can be no resolution of polarities.

But current reality demands that we accommodate both individualism and teamwork. Compromise is a solution, and that means trying to keep the oscillation in the positive arena—capitalizing on what is positive in teamwork and what is positive in individualism. Then we recognize that the democracy in which we believe, not as mere ballot-box behavior but as a complete personality structure, the democratic personality, has the capacity and makes the choice to live in the tension between these two opposites.

The simplest solution to the individual-whole polarity is this: We, the company, will take responsibility for integrating this polarity. It is our policy to care for our people. We will hold ourselves accountable to find a way to

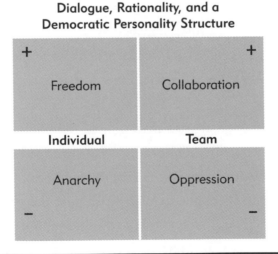

Figure 19.2. Polarity Map

demand good work—we are accountable to our owners—and insist that employees show up at work, fully present and engaged. At the same time we acknowledge their need to be available to their children. Parents have problems with babysitters. We know what we need from our employees and we also know that they have their own family needs. We will see to it that we do the best to accommodate both sides of the paradox.

But we expect the same from our employees' families. They have needs, but employees and their families must understand that the company has major needs from them as well. And the company pays their salary. And this is other people's money. The company is accountable for using it well.

If the company sees the employees' needs and the employees see the company's needs, then an accommodation usually is possible.

Here are three steps to take to manage polarity.

1. Problem solve. Choose among the alternatives. Keep a stiff upper lip about what you have rejected. *Example*: We shall handle the long-term plights resulting from our short-term strategy.

2. Live with it. Recognize polarity as natural and live in its shadow. Polarity, like guilt, anxiety, and even death, is one of the limits to life itself. We can adjust to it. We are equipped by nature to live with polarities. *Example*: You are a single parent and have four children. You have a job and are committed to developing your career. That will involve more education, graduate work. Life would be simpler for you if you did not have children. But you love all of your children and cannot imagine being without any one of them, so you make the best of it and take pride in your struggles. You are a better person for it. You have character, experience, and personal power—and you are wise. There is no other way to have achieved these elevated states of being. You are thankful for your life and for the fortitude that you either have been given or have achieved to triumph in this capacity and to transmit real human values to your children—and to your co-workers. From your depth, you recognize this as a life you would have designed for yourself if the choice were yours. The truth is, it was yours!

3. Be energized by it. You experience the stress and the tension produced by the polarities. You recognize that there is power and energy in this tension. You learn how to make use of this tension-generated propellant. This energy carries you forward to a life that looks different and changes the nature of your present stressful conflict. *Example*: You feel you need to change jobs but do not have the courage. The polarity is between the security of a job without a future and the uncertain promise of a job that starts low but could have a really promising outcome. But you know if you do not choose now you will probably retire in your current job. That makes you feel guilty. But leaving it and trying something else makes you feel anxious. Rather than worrying about choosing, you stay with the stress. You feel the tension and you recognize the energy that it has. You use that energy to continue what you were doing—but now it is vitalized and ignited.

You will soon discover that this renewal of power within you, this surge of excitement, readies you to make the changes you need to make. It is not just a matter of choosing a more promising job. It is to make sure you are ready to take *advantage* of it. For your lethargy in making a choice, your indecisiveness, is really a sign that you were not yet ready to make the change. And you would have failed. But the energy you now derive from feeling the surging tension between the two alternatives, the old and the new jobs, does prepare you both emotionally and intellectually to take on new and more substantive challenges. Now you are ready!

You realize that this tension is the natural condition of being alive, not the result of some localized decision that needs to be made. It's really the "use it or lose it" syndrome. But for what? The new job? Probably for much more.

Perhaps what you really want is to run for elective office. Win or lose, it's a new you—with vastly enlarged potential. Your realm of possibilities is now greatly expanded, and you may end up with something far better than the promising job that earlier you were worried about.

The Conscientious Objector

Early in my career I had a rather curious introduction to the weightiness of polarity. In fact, it was how I became interested in connecting philosophy and psychiatry in the first place. I was a teacher in California when a psychiatrist approached me with a quandary about a patient. He thought philosophy could help, for he was not sure whether the conflict in the life of a young man, his patient, was psychological or ethical. And he assured me that the treatment plan depended on the answer to that question. We had two levels of questions: (1) the conflict or polarity in the life of his young patient and (2) the contradiction in the mind of the psychiatrist between essentially medicine (or science) and ethics (or philosophy).

It was during the Vietnam War, and the struggle was between what appeared to be conscience or cowardice, between going to war or becoming a war resistor. This meant either the then dubious status of conscientious objector—difficult to attain—or to give up his country and escape to Canada or Sweden. This was this young man's view of his struggle. And the psychiatrist's struggle, he told me, was how to interpret this man's dilemma. In thinking Canada, was he a moral giant, a man standing up to his government and refusing to fight in a war he saw as unjust? Or was he a person who had difficulties "identifying himself with his father and the male role in life," which, at its most primitive, means to be ready to be the warrior, the "defender of home and family." Today we may no longer think along these lines, but one or two generations ago that was not uncommon, including in the psychiatric profession.

For the young man, of course, the dilemma was, "Should I go to war or should I go to Canada? And what are my motives? Will I go to Canada because I have moral courage and will take a stand? Or will I go to Canada because I am afraid and therefore essentially a coward? Or, if I stay and join the armed forces, is that because I am afraid to do something countercultural, like leaving my life as an American, a U.S. citizen, or is it because I believe staying and going to war and doing what my country asks me to do is indeed the right thing to do?"

Ambiguity everywhere! This ambiguity—to put it mildly—became one of the "defining moments" in American history.

There is really no way to resolve these paradoxes, for, after all, we are here talking about the decision to define who you are, to set your values, to determine your personality structure, to organize your world view. Even if you work out something logical and conceptual out of this labyrinth, it may be an elegant argument but it will have little effect on what you will do, how you will act, and how you will choose.

The prescription for managing polarity is now not to focus on a solution but rather to concentrate on the dilemma, the paradox, the tension of the polarities between the two sides or among the many sides. This requires respecting the differences, not blurring them or trivializing them. And it includes recognizing that they are incompatible. Either you go to Canada or you go to war. Either you are a hero or a coward. There isn't much room in between.

The real issue is not Vietnam or Canada; the real issue is courage or not. You can choose either option in a cowardly manner, or you can choose either alternative in a courageous manner. Once we realize that here lies the decision, then it is clear it will be in the direction of courage, for we have just now discovered one more time that life cannot be lived without courage. The genie is out of the bottle, and it will never be different again. And once that has taken place, the configuration of the issue if forever transformed. And what's more, now the polarity is manageable!

The "Treatment"

Thus, what is the "treatment"? Ride on the energy produced by the tension. Only when you see the disparity can you feel the tension. The tension is like anxiety. It propels you forward. It keeps you moving. And as you move forward the world changes for you. You have discovered the feeling of courage, the taste of valor. This is the critical point of transformation.

As the psychiatrist rides on the energy of his dilemma—moral courage or inadequate socialization—he will find that he is comfortable now letting his patient himself decide the authenticity of his own motivation. That takes courage, the courage of faith. It is not up to the psychiatrist to decide whether his motives are authentic or not. That is a decision for his patient to make and for him as psychiatrist to facilitate.

As far as the young man's own dilemma goes, he will realize that he needs power to make either choice: Joining the army takes personal power; escaping to Canada takes personal power. And once he has the personal power, the decision itself will not be that difficult for him. He knows whichever way he goes it will be with courage. It is the courage issue that he has resolved himself. Going with the creative tension of his polarity has given him the guts to make either of these two very difficult choices.

It has been my experience that once the courage barrier has been crossed, the remaining decisions come rather easily—with more reflection, more introspection, and more dialogue. But now it is not a choice between courage and cowardice, the army and Canada, respectively, but between two acts of equal courage—the army and Canada. Knowing that, no matter what, he must exercise courage, the young man's self-image and his value scales change sufficiently to make the actual choice a simpler and a lighter one. The choice for courage feels good and conforms to the nature of this world. It is what needs to be, and human existence is not only equipped for courage, it thrives on it. And in this case courage is the outcome of pursuing the feeling of creative tension. The tension between polarities is the birth of the experience of courage. Don't waste this opportunity for growth and renewed health.

The choice still has to be made, and in some sense it isn't any easier.

Nevertheless, clarity helps. So does dialogue. There are instincts and intuitions that are thus aroused. Also, there is the power of insight. The agony of the polarity is also the energy of taking responsibility. Emerson writes, "Do not go where the path may lead. Go instead where there is no path and leave a trail." That is a feeling. That is an insight. That is knowledge. That is the merger of free will and anxiety that makes up courage. That is how big decisions are made. We need to attend the decision Olympics, for that is the game of life. Practice in making tough choices is what, one decision at a time, builds character and leadership. The trick is to know that making tough choices is possible, for it is natural. Once we understand that also it is inevitable, and that our souls are equipped for it, we have unraveled the riddle of existence.

There is then no agony, just thinking. There is then no anxiety, just comparing action steps. Rationalization stops and the young man can then determine where his home is and where his security lies. The worst is over!

The world is polarized; so are you. This is not a problem but it is reality. It is a welcome reality. Leaders are reconciled to that state of affairs, notwithstanding our constant and nagging proclivity to demand to know which side is right. The possibility to make mistakes and the opportunity to learn from them are built into the nature of this world and into the fabric of the individuals and organizations in it. Once we are at peace with that deep truth, we are functional and effective, we feel a new surge of health, and life is changed from frustration to hope.

Polarity is an important theme, sometimes here called paradox, and there is much demand in organizations to find people who are equipped to address systematically the aggravation of managing conflicting positions. A working summary of rules for polarity management is thus appropriate.

Seven Rules for Facing the Paradoxes of Leadership

1. Do not rationalize but feel the pain. Just as there is pain in truth, so there is truth in pain. In a well-known OD exercise, Argyris' right-hand column (what you said) might read, "I can take it like a man, like an adult. I am always positive, affirming." The left-hand column (what you only thought and felt) might contain, "I am scared to death. I don't know what to do. I feel like crying." Only as you move into the depth of the experience will it reveal to you its healing power.

2. Polarities need each other. Polarities require each other to makes sense. In business, for example, the concept of the individual does not makes sense if it is not contrasted with the reality of the team. And, conversely, the concepts of team and organization cannot be comprehended without realizing that the latter are made up of individuals.

Stability is not noticed if there is not change for contrast. Nor can there be change unless there is an underlying reality that remains constant throughout the change.

3. Alternation beats prioritizing. You look for danger signals to detect polarities that are becoming excessive. Too much concern with the short-term begins to create problems with investors, who are looking ahead. Then it's time to think of the long-term. When quarterly returns begin to slide, it's time to reassess grand strategy to see where the problem lies. Catching excesses early is good prophylaxis against polarity pathology. Prioritizing is difficult; alternating is easy.

4. There is power in dialogue. Communication is not two bunkers with short-wave radio stations, but a solar system with two suns (see Figure 19.3). Dialogue creates a common field of awareness, where there is an emotional alliance, a sense of community, and a personal bond, all of which can supersede individual differences and alienating confrontations. Dialogue can settle intractable conflicts.

5. Paradoxes provoke the mind to breakthroughs. Forcing the mind to confront an apparently insurmountable dilemma, such as short-term versus long-term, challenges it to "extrude" as it were, or give birth to, a new form, a neonate, that has as parents these polarized antecedents. Often, the breakthrough is no more than to be happily reconciled with the demand to work harder and smarter, ratchet up the level of commitment, and literally stop worrying about the conflicts. It's not unlike learning to play the piano with two hands rather than just one. It requires a decision, a snap in the mind as it were, to accept that two hands playing different melodies can actually be played at the same time by one person. Learning how to swim, drive, fly, and sky dive are, for the uninitiated, absolutely impossible. Yet once you make up

Figure 19.3. Inauthentic and Authentic Dialogue

your mind that any of them can be done, voilá, you actually accomplish it! You solve a paradox with a dimensional change in attitude and commitment, with a transition from negative to positive evaluation and lethargy to energy— and not just in prioritizing. That is a decision. And that is a breakthrough!

6. Each choice changes your environment. Each decision changes your world. For the world responds. You must make a decision in order to understand what the next decision is to be. This is the nature of competitive games, from soccer to chess. Each time you make a choice, you enter a new scenario. Your next step is determined by this new scenario—and not by the last scenario. This simple and obvious insight can make it more manageable for you to make difficult decisions. Here, indeed, practice makes perfect.

7. Practice democracy. Resolution of paradox lies in the democratic personality structure and the democratic institutions of society. These value diversity and change it to inclusion, from negative to positive. At the center of our political thinking is the commitment to democracy. We deal with polarity not with a public massacre but with freedom of speech. Democracy is a breakthrough transformation on how people experience contradictions and on how they respond to them. Thoreau said it well, "The fate of the country does not depend on what kind of paper you drop into the ballot box once a year, but on what kind of man you drop from your chamber into the street every morning."

These seven rules in themselves can transform employees and managers from dealing with otherwise paralyzing paradoxes and polarities to a way that leads to progress, productivity, and competitive advantage. *How much is that worth to a business and an organization?*

We end the heroic inner-world-outer-world journey by arriving at greatness, the symbol for the hero who now reaches the apotheosis.

GREATNESS

We hold these truths to be self-evident: that all men are created equal; that they are endowed by their creator with certain unalienable rights; that among them are life, liberty, and the pursuit of happiness; that to secure these rights, governments are instituted among men, deriving their just powers from the consent of the governed; that whenever any form of government becomes destructive to these ends, it is the right of the people to alter or abolish it, and to institute new government, laying its foundations on such principles, and organizing its power in such form, as to them shall seem most likely to effect their safety and happiness. . . .
And for the support of this Declaration, with a firm reliance on the protection of Divine Providence, we mutually pledge to each other our lives, our fortunes and our sacred honor.

THOMAS JEFFERSON, *DECLARATION OF INDEPENDENCE*

Death is the enemy. . . .
Against you I will fling myself, unvanquished and unyielding,
O Death.

VIRGINIA WOOLF

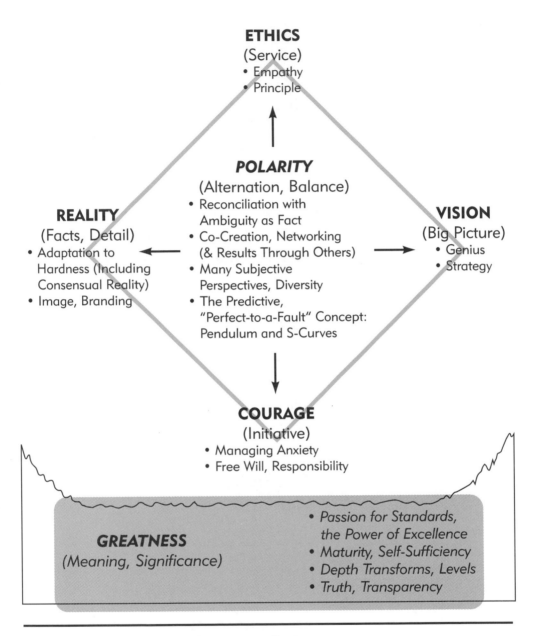

ETHICS
(Service)
• Empathy
• Principle

POLARITY
(Alternation, Balance)
• Reconciliation with
Ambiguity as Fact
• Co-Creation, Networking
(& Results Through Others)
• Many Subjective
Perspectives, Diversity
• The Predictive,
"Perfect-to-a-Fault" Concept:
Pendulum and S-Curves

REALITY
(Facts, Detail)
• Adaptation to
Hardness (Including
Consensual Reality)
• Image, Branding

VISION
(Big Picture)
• Genius
• Strategy

COURAGE
(Initiative)
• Managing Anxiety
• Free Will, Responsibility

GREATNESS
(Meaning, Significance)
• *Passion for Standards,
the Power of Excellence*
• *Maturity, Self-Sufficiency*
• *Depth Transforms, Levels*
• *Truth, Transparency*

Figure 20.1. The Leadership Diamond®: Greatness

CHAPTER 20

Greatness

DEFINITION: Meaning and Significance

ELEMENTS: Passion for Standards, the Power of Excellence;

Maturity, Self-Sufficiency;

Depth Transforms, Levels;

Truth, Transparency

WE END WITH GREATNESS.

Greatness is the sun around which the planet corners of the Diamond are in orbit. For to live requires that we honor this spectacular phenomenon of being alive. Whatever we do needs to be done with greatness. The purpose for these extensive analyses of the Diamond corners is to ensure that each one of them is taken seriously enough to be our homeland, a country we love and are willing to defend. Whether it is love for people or wisdom about the real world or respect for valor or amazement at the work of brilliant genius, a new dimension, a new illumination is added to existence when we surround it with the halo of doing great things.

Thus, we define greatness as seeking *meaning* and *significance,* words that should elicit for many this challenge to honor life. We talk about *passion for standards* and the vigor of *excellence.* Is this not the meaning of the Olympics and the general enthusiasm for sports? Is this not the uncompromising dedication of the artist? Is this not also about standards and the joy they can bring, the dignity, the self-satisfaction, the texture of accomplishment?

Greatness is about the values of *maturity* and *self-sufficiency.* One thing I have learned in my years working with psychotherapists regarding the implications of philosophy is their professional focus on rational living, logic, and the virtues of being truly grown up, adult. Successful living is, in Freud's offhand remarks, about love and work, period. Successful human interactions require little: keeping promises, or renegotiating them, never ignoring them; ample communication, so that there is contact; and focusing on the needs of the environment, both of humans and of nature. Tilling the soil and attending to the weather are simply a way to live—and it is by focusing on that which is other than I am. So it is with business. Business is successful as long as you think about the customer, care about the customer, and satisfy the customer. These are all modes of focusing the mind not on itself but on the other. By giving yourself away, as it were, by generosity, you achieve maturity and self-sufficiency.

Greatness means *depth.* This has been a recurring theme here. Do not believe the surface; trust the depth: instinct, intuition, unconscious, dreams, the peripherals of life—they speak the truth if we listen to them. We will always have perceptions and reality checks, averting the danger of sliding into a fantasy world.

The last component of greatness is *truth* and *transparency.* What a simple life this presages, like spring, like fall, when the skies are clear and the air is crisp! Transparency in human relations is clean and relaxing. Transparency in business allows executives to sleep at night.

But ponder a bit on how difficult it is to tell the truth in business. At this writing, the transparency crises are the Enron debacle, Kenneth Lay et al., the Arthur Andersen catastrophe, the still-alive notorious Clinton shame, Jack Welch's embarrassment with the *Harvard Business Review,* and Percy Barnevik's colossal credibility crash—Mr. Europe himself! When you, dear reader, will read this, the names will have been changed but, sadly, the reality will remain.

True transparency provides serenity! How refreshing! How rare! How smart it is to keep that ideal of greatness always before us, sustainable, beginning with our earliest years!

This undertaking has been the effort to be both a bona fide philosopher and a bona fide businessperson, at one and the same time, and, one hopes, succeeding at both without being untrue to either. This is not a point of view but a journey of life. In a sense, it is everyone's journey.

Business, like politics, is the language of results, and philosophy, like meditation, is the language of reflection—contrast the general and the monk, Margaret Thatcher and the nun.

Greatness is to create the synthesis: Do breakthrough-level better business by becoming a real philosopher and maximize the credibility of philosophy by making it as indispensable as medicine.

We need sensitivity to the inner and the outer worlds. We cannot understand history without recognizing how mankind's thinking over the centuries has woven itself in and out of these two worlds, from the deep religiosity of the Middle Ages to the cold scientism of the Age of Reason and from primitive animism to the merger of giant high-tech enterprises.

The business issues here addressed are change and innovation, for they are connected. Within this context, the Diamond Model stands at the foundation of bringing philosophy into business, both for executives who hire consultants and for the consultants thus engaged. These have been the bonding themes.

Henry David Thoreau is frequently quoted in this regard with these eloquent words from *Walden,* a cornerstone of American literature:

> There are now-a-days professors of philosophy, but not philosophers. Yet it is admirable to profess because it was once admirable to live. To be a philosopher is not merely to have subtle thoughts, nor even to found a school, but so to love wisdom as to live according to its dictates, a life of simplicity, independence, magnanimity, and trust. It is to solve some of the problems of life, not only theoretically, but practically.

This is a practical book. We shall end by reviewing a series of activities that can intensify the application of philosophy to practical business needs, which leaders require and which consultants support. In each case we want to involve as much of the total Diamond as possible. The revised version of my *Leadership: The Inner Side of Greatness* is devoted to an exhaustive treatment of the meaning of *Greatness* as a major topic when we introduce philosophy and the Diamond for results to business and to organizational development.

PART FIVE

Appendices
Using the Total Diamond

The Magic Matrix

THE TOOLS PRESENTED HERE *work for many stakeholders: the consultant, the internal client, and, significantly, the end customer. You get an overview of where on the heroic journey of life today you find yourself and your organization, and how you can integrate the virtues and the powers of both the outer world and the inner world.*

Quick Test, Diagnosis, and Healing

Give yourself a quick test on how well you understand the Diamond material and how much you correspond to its criteria.

Reflect on the following questions and then discuss what they mean to you and how you might wish to respond to them. These are then examples of carrying out Intelligent Leadership Conversations. This activity becomes a diagnostic test with these results: If you show a deficit, it will predict the limits of your leadership accomplishments. If you are stuck, it will reveal how you must change in order to become unstuck. It shows you how to reach your potential.

Instructions: Circle the number after each item that best describes your response.

Ethics

1. Do you naturally reach out to other people? Are you regarded as friendly?

   No, I don't reach out.   Yes, I do reach out.

   1   2   3   4   5

2. Are you motivated by principles rather than by what feels good? Do you act rationally rather than emotionally, that is, do you think first rather than impulsively "shoot from the hip"?

   I am motivated by   I act on principle first and
   what feels good.   foremost, whether it feels
                                                               good or not.

   1   2   3   4   5

Courage

3. Do you worry about anxiety, or is fear OK with you? Does it bother you that you might be a worrier? Are you intense? Do you believe that anxiety can invigorate you?

   I think to be anxious
   is not good.   I welcome anxiety.

   1   2   3   4   5

4. Do you have a really deep and persuasive sense about your own accountability? Do you choose to be held accountable because it feels right—it gives you a "rush" of power, potency, and agency? Does your intense accountability delineate your identity, tell you who you are?

Being held accountable is an unwelcome burden.

Being held accountable makes me proud.

1   2   3   4   5

Reality

5. Do you have inside you a post of steel that, if necessary, will not bend no matter what? Is that also the way the world is?

I am weak.

I am strong.

1   2   3   4   5

6. Do you know your reputation? Do you appreciate how fragile it is? Do you understand that what people think and feel about you is probably more revealing of them than of you? Can you live with that?

I don't care about my public image.

My public image is very important to me.

1   2   3   4   5

Vision

7. Many people go to the gym and like sports. They work out. Do you also work out *mentally*? Do you deliberately try to train and sharpen your mind as you may do your body?

I don't train my mind anymore.			I vigorously and consistently train my mind.	
1	2	3	4	5

8. Do you tell people what to do or do you expect them to see the larger picture and figure it out for themselves based on that? Do you give people the broader economic background and rationale for what you expect them to do? Do you yourself ask for that of them?

I am not particularly strategic.			I am very strategic.	
1	2	3	4	5

Polarity

9. Are you stiff and rigid? Do you have a single-track mind and refuse to contemplate alternatives? Is the demand for logical and adaptive flexibility a threat to you?

I am rigid.				I can adapt.
1	2	3	4	5

10. Are you intellectually, emotionally, and strategically ready for *what's up to come down* (such as perhaps your health) and for *what's down to go up* (such as perhaps your company's debt load)?

I am not prepared for real surprises.			I am prepared for dramatic surprises.	
1	2	3	4	5

Greatness

11. Do you love your job and talk about it with joy?

    No, I don't like my job.   Yes, I do like my job.
    1   2   3   4   5

12. Do people instinctively trust you emotionally; they think you are experienced and wise?

    No, they don't trust me.   Yes, they do trust me.
    1   2   3   4   5

Scoring

In the second row in the grid below, write in the number of times you gave each answer listed in the top row. In the third row, total your points by multiplying the number of appearances (the entries in the second row) by the number you gave as an answer (the entry in the first row). Finally, total the numbers across the bottom row.

1	2	3	4	5

49–60   Superior Diamond leadership

37–48   Good Diamond leadership

25–36   Acceptable Diamond leadership

12–24   Needs remedial Diamond work

Interpretation

On this assessment, scores range from 12 to 60.

Following is a sample:

1	2	3	4	5
1	5	2	2	2
1	10	6	8	10

Score = 35

Mediocre, not bad—but far from truly effective.

I am too stiff, too directive, and don't nurture my network and market image. To get ahead I must work hard on these three sets of undermining attitudes.

A self-test is always a marvelous springboard for insightful dialogues: What does it mean? Is it accurate? Does it trigger other thoughts and feelings? Will it impact your career? Does it require action?

Compensating for the Shadow

The earlier distinction we made between *competence* and *authenticity* also makes for a useful strategic matrix (see Figure A.1; see also Figure 1.1, page 6).

The Matrix

This matrix is a good way to make Diamond leadership conversations the common vocabulary of companies interested in promoting leadership dialogues within their culture.

Leadership capacity or readiness is measured along two axes: competence and authenticity. Some people are competent, that is, they know the business, and others are authentic, that is, they are willing to make a 360-degree suc-

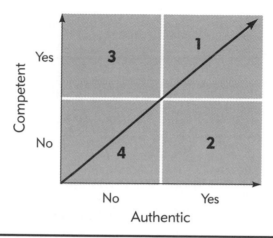

Figure A.1. Leadership Capacity or Readiness

cess of the job that they have. Factory workers need the competence of running a sophisticated lathe. But they also need the authenticity to manage the social relations and their personal initiative on the job. Workers must know how to drive a Brinks truck and follow closely the security routines. But they must also have the character and the autonomy to deal with the unexpected and the irrational. A good realtor needs to know the law, the regulations, and the market. But there is no hope for success if this person does not have the sensitivities required to deal with potential customers in the delicate area of the highest-cost item they will ever purchase—and the convoluted stresses to which this transaction leads.

What is the relative importance of competence and authenticity in hiring, retaining, and promoting? Which is easier to evaluate and to teach? Which has the longest range of consequences?

From the practical point of view of managing, knowing what is ideal is not enough. One must design strategies on how to implement leadership growth in organizations and institutions with variegated populations—in terms of maturity and capacity, interest and values, mental health and belief systems, physical health and experience.

You can use the matrix for making practical business decisions. The reality is that you do not do the work. You find the people who will do it for you better than you could do it yourself. You need to know how to find them, how to attract them, how to cultivate them, and how to keep them. This is a leadership issue.

Those who are deemed to be in quadrant four, that is, incompetent and inauthentic, unable and unwilling, will have to go. You wonder how they ever got into the organization in the first place. Only where there are blanket admissions or hiring mistakes will you find them. Letting them go is what the larger company strategy requires, and ultimately the rigors of the financial markets demand it. Nevertheless, you have to decide how far you are prepared to go along with the market ultimatums and recognize that you will have to address the consequences. It requires courage and risk for you either way: downsizing or not downsizing. Some companies take out the bottom 10 percent of their employee population yearly, hoping in this way to catch quadrant four people on a regular basis.

Those in quadrant three—competent and inauthentic, or able but not willing—are given, from the point of view of what is right for the corporation, one more chance. *The culture is the implementation tool.* They are competent but not part of the culture. One bad egg can spoil the entire mixture, drain the organization of energy, create needless anxiety and lost work time, and blunt the collective thrust, thus weakening the company in relation to the competition. This does not preclude seeking out and benefiting from a culture of iconoclasts, for encouraging independence is a culture too. In fact, business results stipulate it.

You want people to feel good about coming to work. They will not when they are around quadrant three co-workers. Decisions about these people are often difficult. For workers to acknowledge the culture is a matter of good manners, realism, and respect for other people's values. Not to acknowledge the culture can be arrogant, self-centered, selfish, and inconsiderate of others. This is not to say that serious differences are not valued. In fact, a culture that is not based on differences is geared for failure.

Quadrant three is often where your greatest difficulties lie. These are your competent and smart people, jealous of you and not willing to cooperate in setting and maintaining the culture that is so dear and so important to you. They are frustrating. Many executives try to isolate them, so that they contribute without doing harm. Often this fails. The common thing is to give them a kind ultimatum and one more chance. It is a tragedy that some of the most talented people are not only not in the culture—which they manage through "eccentricity credits"—but that they outright sabotage the culture and take pride in undermining it.

The usual procedure is to let them go. It is these dismissals that occupy a great deal of executives' energy, time, and imagination—and expense. Regrettably, it is a great waste and does much damage. Prophylaxis is the best policy.

Those who fit into quadrant two—unable but willing, not competent but authentic—have possibilities. They need to be trained. In fact, you will find that most people are there. They are part of the culture, but not yet adequately trained. They are trainable. It is easier to enhance competence for those who are willing than it is to change culture among those who are not willing. Skills can be gladly learned; personality structure is irrationally entrenched.

Your eventual goal, of course, is to maximize membership in quadrant one—people who are both competent and authentic, able and willing—whether through internal growth or by recruiting. Above all, you want to create an environment in which the population of quadrant one is satisfied in having its needs met and its values recognized. You want to cultivate them. They will be your future. They will transform you into a great organization. Also, in this way you erect a workplace where all people want to move to quadrant one and who welcome help to get there. You want to keep the members of quadrant two, but quadrant one is the goal toward which you direct all the others.

Figure A.2 is a summary view of this useful matrix. It is a pragmatic prescription on how to address core culture issues in an organization. It is not unrelated to the system that General Electric and the Ford Motor Company, and others, have used to weed out yearly the bottom 10 percent of performers in their companies, keeping up quality consistently.

The Magic
The Subjective Perspective
If we now look at this situation from the perspectives of the individual quadrant populations, we create different strategies.

As discussed previously, you must always ask from whose point of view, from what subjective perspective, you are asking your leadership questions. As a manager, your job is to have a plan for the whole organization *and* a strategy for each member—be it member, partner, worker, student, or what have you. You must combine all the various perspectives. And these strategies may be in conflict because of the individual versus team polarity.

Quadrant fours are either alienated individuals or appear so because the company is an alienating organization. The individual subjective questions from their individual points of view are: "Do you get value out of his state of alienation?" "Do you wish/choose to continue it?" "Even to strengthen it?" "To justify, validate, and legitimize it?" or "To change it?" "What is in the way of change?" "What are the obstacles?" "What are the secondary gains for you of the status quo, that is, in not changing?"

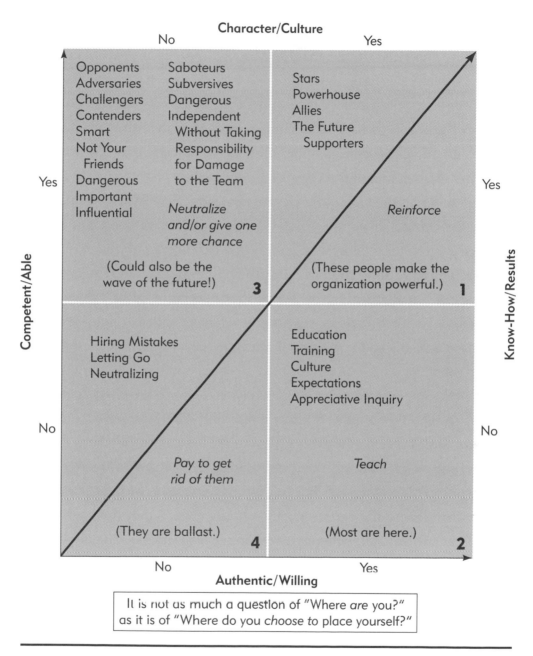

Figure A.2. Competence and Authenticity

Quadrant threes must be confronted with their asocial behavior. Or, more specifically, they need to hear that their indifference, even opposition if not outright sabotage regarding the culture, has consequences for which they must hold themselves responsible. Theirs may be highly moral postures, and that is commendable. But what is not mature is to disrupt and not know that you disrupt and not take personal responsibility for what happens to the team as a result of your actions and inactions.

Here is where the most difficult remedial work is needed. Often gratuitously, they create alienation. It can be a character deficiency. Or it can be moral courage. This is very far from honest differences of opinion, where at least people respect one another. The problem with quadrant threes—who can be exceptionally competent, which they may think gives them license to be arrogant ("eccentricity credits," as we have called them)—is their contempt and derision for the culture whose success your particular business has chosen.

The best way to confront these individuals is first to establish a coaching alliance in which you make it clear, honorably, after you point out their deviancy, that you are not unsympathetic to the logic of their behavior. They may feel the world is against them and need to defend their integrity. These are, of course, noble purposes, and you appreciate them as such, but they may be inappropriate to the current reality. On the other hand, their behaviors may be but atavisms, ancient ways of reacting against situations that no longer exist but which over time have become deeply ingrained habits in their personalities. This is neurotic behavior. But when compassion fails, it becomes a power play. And the person who has the power also has the responsibility, and firm action has to be taken.

There is a special caveat for quadrant threes. You may say, with justification, "I think of myself as a good leader and yet I feel that most of the time I find myself in this quadrant. Should I change?" That's a very good question.

From your point of view (and you may be totally right), you are a reformer, you are the wave of the future, you are the savior, but currently tucked away, in hiding, in the suspect third quadrant. At this point of insight and dialogue, however, the saboteur's image is transcended and the time has arrived for decent dialogue. There may still be a standoff at the end, but now it is a friendly one, a compassionate one, one of mutual understanding and respect.

You will also find that you now think of yourself as an outsider. And you think of the rest of the company as insiders. You feel excluded. It hurts. One day you will wake up with a strange feeling: Nothing has changed, it seems. Yet you are on the inside and the others on the outside. Overnight reality turns inside out. That is often how change feels. It comes over you on cats' feet, like the fog, as T.S. Eliot wrote. You go to bed on a clear night and you wake up in soupy fog. You heard nothing. Pure surprise. You must allow also for this eventuality in the third quadrant.

There is nothing wrong with being an independent thinker. Quite to the contrary, it is the mark of a leader. What does matter is motivation: concern for the whole or narcissistic exhibitionism. That determines the quality of the person.

Of course, those who deserve the most attention are quadrant twos, that is, people who are indeed willing but who need the teaching and the training in order to understand leadership better and know how to practice it.

From the personal and subjective perspective of people in the *first* quadrant, their issue is how to become even better at what they already do well, and to become the teachers of the rest. For people in this quadrant have the best chance to become top leaders during their lifetimes: They are both competent and authentic, bright and well-rounded, which means they have both the capacity and the desire to move forward in being leaders. This attitude, to begin with, is the ideal prescription for outstanding success. The better in leadership one is from the very beginning, the greater also are the prospects for dimensional growth.

The business application is not only to use the matrix for strategic design in your personnel policies, but as a teaching device. You invite people for "fun" to do self and peer diagnoses, so that the messages are internalized rather than imposed from outside.

> In the end, the full Diamond is closely tied to courage. For vision without courage is dreaming. The difference between ineffective and effective dreaming is that the latter includes *how to get there*!
>
> You are the *dreamer*. Your vision is the *dream*. And your courage is the *actions* that will breathe life into your dreams.

Final Words

Make it clear how people are to be classified on this matrix. In the last analysis, they are really doing it themselves, for they have a choice on how to be and who to be, and on how well they understand their social environment and how well they choose to integrate with it or how important it is for them to be independent. At minimum, membership in any one quadrant is co-created with the employee's surroundings. If the culture does not value you or does not understand you, if there is no empathy, then that may be unfair. But part of leadership is to learn to deal with unfairness. There are many options, all of which require both strategy and courage. You cannot develop your genius or your strategic thinking if you exist in an environment that is not congenial to you. Being in the quadrant where you do not want to be is indeed counterproductive.

◆ Activity

Focus on *vision* in this exercise.

For practice purposes, think of yourself as an OD specialist or consultant with the manager as your client. Create a diagnosis of your team members based on the authenticity-competence matrix discussed above. Using Exhibit A.1, indicate into which quadrant you would place each of your employees (substituting their names for those listed). State your reasons. And then design an action plan for each team member. How would you present your results to your client? How would you propose that this exercise be introduced to the team? What actions would you recommend?

An alternate practice exercise is to ask *each* team member to prepare a confidential matrix for each member of the whole team, including himself or herself. You then collate all of the results into one form and, not mentioning names, return the results to each member of the group—with the name order scrambled, given a number that only the bearer knows. (See Exhibit A.2 for an example.) A sensitively led discussion can be very constructive. Let each member know, privately, his or her code number. But keep this information confidential. Then you have both impact and safety.

Your Name:				
Team Member	Q1/ Stars	Q2/ Trainees	Q3/ Saboteurs	Q4/ Hiring Mistakes
Sean K.				
Leila F.				
Jane M.				
Sarah Z.				
Nicholas L.				
Sergei M.				
Hyun Joo K.				
Jürgen V.				
Xavier B.				
Björn S.				

Exhibit A.1. Sample Team Assessment 1

Your Name:				
Team Member	Q1/ Stars	Q2/ Trainees	Q3/ Saboteurs	Q4/ Hiring Mistakes
1		✓	✓✓✓✓	✓✓✓
2	✓✓✓	✓✓✓✓✓	✓	
3	✓✓	✓✓✓✓✓✓✓	✓	
4	✓✓✓✓✓	✓✓✓✓✓		
5	✓✓	✓✓✓✓	✓✓	✓✓
6	✓✓✓✓✓✓	✓✓✓	✓	
7		✓	✓✓✓✓✓	✓✓✓✓
8	✓✓	✓✓✓✓	✓✓	✓✓
9	✓	✓✓✓✓✓✓✓✓		
10	✓✓✓✓✓✓	✓✓✓✓		

Exhibit A.2. Sample Team Assessment 2

Next, have a constructive discussion about the meaning of these cross-evaluations, fully acknowledging both the value and the sensitivity of such an exercise, making clear that the purpose is to benefit from learning and not to cause career anxiety. This exercise has an advantage in that it is not one person's opinion but the opinion of the entire team. There is power in such assessment, but it also carries with it serious responsibility.

In the end, in a maturing and authenticating organization, people will feel free to vote openly, as part of a larger *integrating* process. Nevertheless, valuable as so much openness is, and central as it is to building a true team, great caution must be exercised to prevent tragic casualties.

APPENDIX B

Mastery Resources

THIS APPENDIX CONTAINS *the following additional activities to strengthen your insights into the Diamond and its uses:*

- The Rings/Arenas of Life: a self-assessment

- The Master Worksheet: a tool for evaluating yourself and your organization in terms of the six basic concepts used in Diamond Theory

- The Client Marketing Profile: a tool to help move your customers from the Shadow Diamond to the Leadership Diamond®

- The OD Practitioner's Checklist: twelve tips for OD strategists, their clients, and organizations

- The "Nay" Sayers: a useful summary of the Diamond for skeptics

- Your Twelve-Step Organizational Attitude and Implementation Audit: a case study plus useful organizational audit questions using Diamond criteria

- Q&A: questions and answers taken from an online Diamond course

The Rings/Arenas of Life

The best way to use this tool is to ask clients to rank themselves in terms of what they do and in terms of what matters, numbering from 1 through 8 on Figure B.1 (inserting other items as needed in the blank boxes and including them in the numbering system).

Now ask them what conflicts they are experiencing, such as between family and financial health—loving the family so much that they spend more money than is prudent. A very common conflict, of course, is family versus work. Some feel guilty about neglecting the family, not seeing the children grow up, in deference to the demands of the job. Others may have made a decision to favor the family, but at the expense of fast-track progress in their careers. They may feel guilty and inadequate seeing how others rise while they remain static, or worse.

Next ask: "What changes in attitude are required to effect changes in your arena configuration?" Here is where one can invoke the Diamond Reverse Engineering™ tool—start with a goal and work backward asking what else in Diamond terms must occur for the goal to be reached.

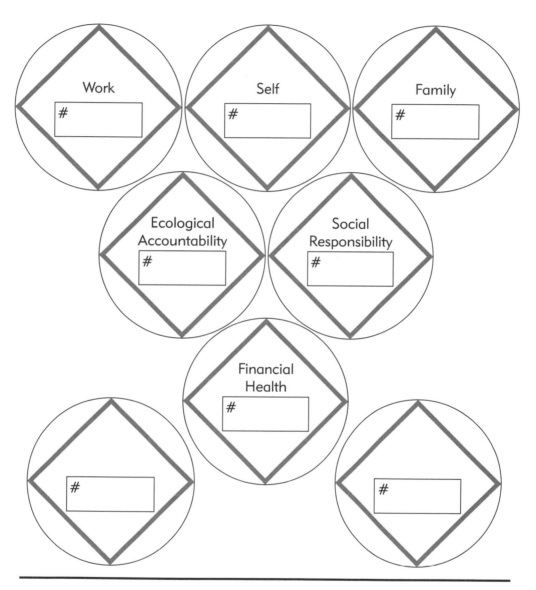

Figure B.1. The Rings/Arenas of Life

The Master Worksheet

The Master Worksheet that follows can be applied succinctly to cover all the Diamond insights. You may use it for individuals and for organizations, for diagnoses and for strategic designs, for generating business ideas and for marketing campaigns, for evaluating decision making and installing corporate cultures. In short, it is meant for CEOs and OD practitioners to master change and promote innovation.

Tell those who are filling out the form that, for each tool listed in the far left-hand column of Exhibit B.1, they are to complete the remaining columns as follows:

- Provide an example or model for each tool.

- Describe how the tool is relevant to their desired results.

- Using the scale at the top of the worksheet, rate themselves by responding to the statement, "I have mastered this leadership trait." Tell them to be prepared to explain and justify their profiles to their colleagues.

- Based on their rating for each tool, consider the implications for their careers.

The questions in the far right-hand column can be used to help stimulate their thinking on each of the tools.

This exercise lends itself well for intelligent leadership conversations at strategic invention moments.

Hand out additional paper as needed, along with copies of the exhibit.

Exhibit B.1. The Master Worksheet

For each tool, rate yourself using the following scale by responding to the statement, "I have mastered this leadership trait," and enter that number in the "Your Performance" column.

1-I strongly disagree   **2**-I partially disagree   **3**-I neither agree nor disagree

         4-I partially agree   **5**-I strongly agree

Tools	Your Example/ Model	Relevance to Results	Your Perfor- mance	Gain/ Loss and Career Implications	Heuristic Questions
Greatness/ Standards Hero • Passion • Maturity • Depth • Truth					• What is your vision of personal greatness? How do you think you came by it? How does it integrate/align with your organization's greatness needs? Is this true: P/VG = O/VG? • Name a time at which you were well led. What happened? How did you feel? Are you yourself that kind of a leader? • What gives you hope? Who has given you hope? How do you give hope to others?
Polarity/ Ambiguity Wizard • Reconcil- iation • Co-creation • Subjective Perspective • Prediction					• Describe one of the great conflicts in your life, such as keeping a job or changing jobs. How did you manage it? Did you like the results? What would you do differently today? • Restate one of your deepest concerns today in terms of polarity. Your job bores you; should you apply for an overseas assign- ment and disrupt your children's schooling? Do some polarity mapping, listing the pros and cons. • What are some of the principal polarities you find in business (examples: business vs. character; stability vs. change; part vs. whole; short-term vs. long-term; family vs. career; overtime vs. recreation; etc.)? • What worldwide uncertainties bother you the most? Political? Social? Economic? The stock market? Unemployment? Pollution? Terrorism? Flying? Can you see these un- certainties as here to stay, as normal? Can you adapt yourself and make a success of their existence? Have you learned to live with ambiguity, or do you need answers? • Which deep structure are you overempha- sizing at the expense of what other? Ethics at the expense of courage? What danger lies ahead? • What have you done recently for your com- munity? Just for yourself?

Exhibit B.1. The Master Worksheet *(continued)*

1-I strongly disagree **2**-I partially disagree **3**-I neither agree nor disagree
4-I partially agree **5**-I strongly agree

Tools	Your Example/ Model	Relevance to Results	Your Perfor-mance	Gain/ Loss and Career Implications	Heuristic Questions
Ethics/ Service Healer • Empathy • Principle					• What conversation do you still need to have with whom before it is too late? Write a psychodrama or script about it. • Sit with a colleague and answer these questions: "How can you help me?" "How can I help you?" "How can you hurt me?" "How can I hurt you?" Now reverse roles. *Notice how strongly you feel your interconnection!* • Set up this conversation: "What do you need from me that you are not getting? How can I make it emotionally safe for you to answer truthfully?"
Courage/ Initiative Warrior • Anxiety • Free Will					• Describe a critical decision point in your life. What did you do and how did you do it? What succeeded; what failed? What were the consequences? How do you feel about them today? What would you do differently today? • What acts of courage will life require of you in the next year? How will you respond? Will you be proud? • Describe a time at which you felt defeated. How did you recover? Did you feel wounded, alone, but strong and secure? What was missing? Give a voice to your scars. • How would you dialogue with a person who felt defeated and whom you wanted to help? • Name an overdue decision. Many people on their deathbed regret not having risked more, postponing for too long crucial decisions.

Exhibit B.1. The Master Worksheet *(continued)*

1-I strongly disagree   2-I partially disagree   3-I neither agree nor disagree

4-I partially agree   5-I strongly agree

Tools	Your Example/ Model	Relevance to Results	Your Perfor- mance	Gain/ Loss and Career Implications	Heuristic Questions
Reality/ Facts Merchant • Adaptation to Hardness • Image, Branding					• Use the arenas of life to do a reality check on your life. Where is your pride and where are your losses, your successes and defeats? How long has this diagnosis been in effect? Should you change it? Will you change it? What are the consequences? What will you actually end up doing?
Vision/ Big Picture Seer • Genius • Strategy					• Do an intelligence test segment* and describe the various states of your mind as it goes through trying to solve the problems. Remember that time/space/speed is a factor. How can you train yourself and others to do better? • Search out newspaper and magazine opinion articles, and books, that lay out grand connections: seeing past patterns and deriving from them current implications. What lessons does history teach you that will help you run your business better today? • What critical lessons for your business can you learn from the destruction of the World Trade Center? • What are some great visionary schemes today (e.g., the Euro and the European Union, the war on terrorism)?

Note: These can be found in SAT manuals in most bookstores. See also page 314, the Mensa activity.

Client Marketing Profile

Explain to the person you are consulting with that Figures B.2 and B.3 are images of customers—either individuals or organizations—and their basic needs and basic deficits, which it is the role of business to fulfill through prod-

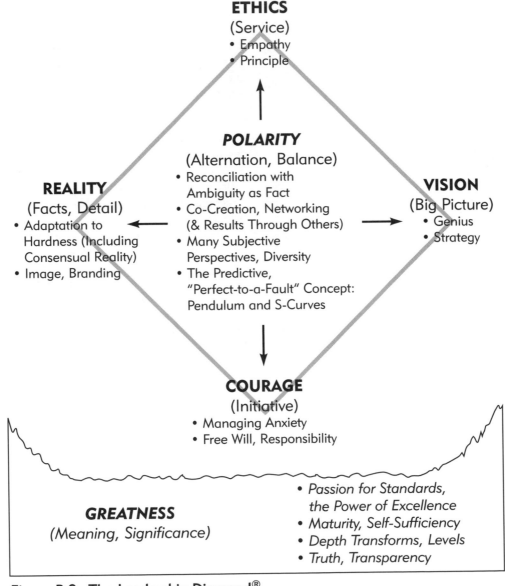

ETHICS
(Service)
• Empathy
• Principle

POLARITY
(Alternation, Balance)
• Reconciliation with
  Ambiguity as Fact
• Co-Creation, Networking
  (& Results Through Others)
• Many Subjective
  Perspectives, Diversity
• The Predictive,
  "Perfect-to-a-Fault" Concept:
  Pendulum and S-Curves

REALITY
(Facts, Detail)
• Adaptation to
  Hardness (Including
  Consensual Reality)
• Image, Branding

VISION
(Big Picture)
• Genius
• Strategy

COURAGE
(Initiative)
• Managing Anxiety
• Free Will, Responsibility

GREATNESS
(Meaning, Significance)

• *Passion for Standards,
  the Power of Excellence*
• *Maturity, Self-Sufficiency*
• *Depth Transforms, Levels*
• *Truth, Transparency*

Figure B.2. The Leadership Diamond®

ucts and services. Say that these needs are often met in symbolic form, such that an overly expensive car may fulfill deeper, underlying, and unconscious *greatness* needs. Help them to position themselves, their client, and their client's staff, the instruments for organizational change, on the model!

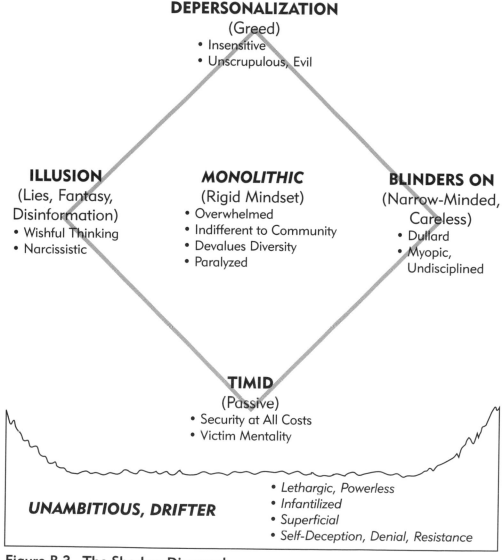

DEPERSONALIZATION
(Greed)
• Insensitive
• Unscrupulous, Evil

ILLUSION
(Lies, Fantasy,
Disinformation)
• Wishful Thinking
• Narcissistic

MONOLITHIC
(Rigid Mindset)
• Overwhelmed
• Indifferent to Community
• Devalues Diversity
• Paralyzed

BLINDERS ON
(Narrow-Minded,
Careless)
• Dullard
• Myopic,
Undisciplined

TIMID
(Passive)
• Security at All Costs
• Victim Mentality

UNAMBITIOUS, DRIFTER
• Lethargic, Powerless
• Infantilized
• Superficial
• Self-Deception, Denial, Resistance

Figure B.3. The Shadow Diamond

You can use the following text to explain this tool:

You are an *entrepreneur* in a *chaotic world*—greatness and polarity. Your self-discovery sequence is ethics, courage, reality, and vision: *people, drive, environment, and brains.* You need to adapt to ambiguities and uncertainties. And you are on an entrepreneurial journey, where there no longer are jobs, only contractors in a competitive world of customers and clients. Your Diamond inventory and profile (your Diamond's size and shape) co-construct your successes and your failures, what makes you proud and what troubles you. Your leadership prescription is to locate your *stuck points,* and then, through Diamond Reverse Engineering,™ trace it back to root causes, that is, your personal Diamonds. As you reconfigure your basic outlooks on life—which is something you *can* do—you also become the leader you have the potential to be. Here lie your individual and team power.

You see both an exalted image and a depraved image in the figures. The tasks of life, and in particular of running a business and consulting to a business, CEO and OD tasks, are to make a living by solving for others their problems of transition from Shadow to Leadership.

Where are you and where is your organization on this continuum of transformation?

Now show them Figure B.4.

After a thorough discussion of the terminology and the figures presented earlier, prepare to hand out the tool in Exhibit B.2, which is designed to be completed by the client about one of his or her customers. The goal is to figure out what the customer values and desires so as to be better able to market to and serve that customer. Explain in this way:

Let's say you are an OD professional supporting an insurance company. And the purpose of the exercise is to support your client, perhaps the sales man-

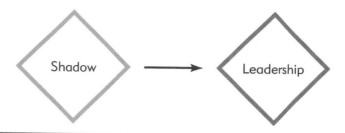

Figure B.4. From Shadow to Leadership

ager or the vice president in charge of marketing and sales, to increase productivity and margins. And this in turn requires that your client understand the leadership needs of the end customer, the insurance customer, the business, or the private party who buys the insurance products. To understand how to connect the insurance products and the sales and delivery relationship to the end customer is the ultimate hardcore business benefit of applying Diamond technology to commerce. This is the CEO's ultimate concern. The CEO or manager picks OD professionals and the OD professional coaches the CEO or manager in how to do better business.

This exercise is designed to teach others how to diagnose the end customer and how to design the full product, marketing, and sales strategy around meeting the deeper needs of that person. What docs the end customer need? The end customer actually is saying: "I want to satisfy my human needs through purchasing your product. I want the company to send people to me who are friendly (ethics), who take the initiative because they know what to do (courage), who know their business and my business and who are clear with the numbers (reality), and who can give me professional advice and good value when it comes to thinking about our future (vision). I want to do business with a company that understands how difficult life can be and how complexity is frustrating; in this I want their help (polarity). Above all, I want to feel that I am a better person, lead a better life, and provide better for my family because of my relationship with their insurance company (greatness)."

After you are certain that your client understands the points made above, give him or her copies of the profile shown in Exhibit B.2.

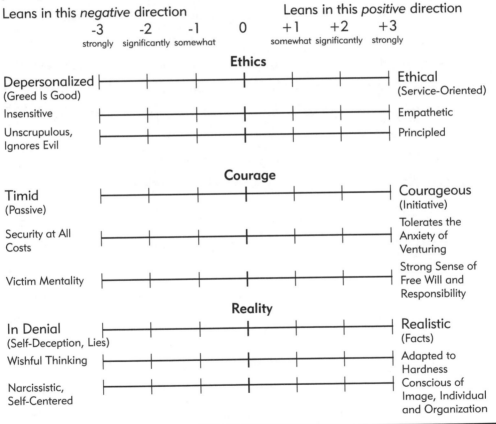

Instructions: Consider a current customer or customer organization. Looking at each scale below, evaluate your customer and place an "X" on the appropriate spot on each line. There is one response for each definition and each component. Personally tailored comments are important. This is confidential, only for your eyes.

Exhibit B.2. Customer Profile

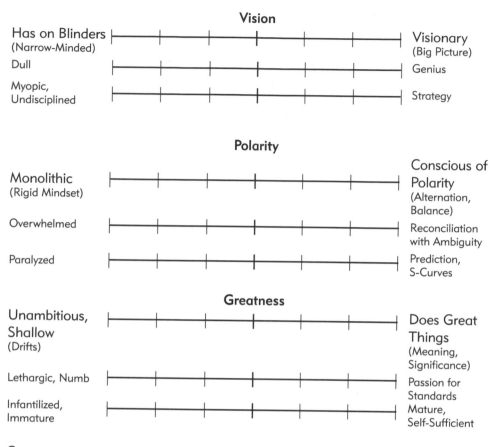

Vision

Has on Blinders (Narrow-Minded)		Visionary (Big Picture)
Dull		Genius
Myopic, Undisciplined		Strategy

Polarity

Monolithic (Rigid Mindset)		Conscious of Polarity (Alternation, Balance)
Overwhelmed		Reconciliation with Ambiguity
Paralyzed		Prediction, S-Curves

Greatness

Unambitious, Shallow (Drifts)		Does Great Things (Meaning, Significance)
Lethargic, Numb		Passion for Standards
Infantilized, Immature		Mature, Self-Sufficient

Comments:

Having assessed the end customer, prepare a proposal on how your client team can position their work so as to maximize the business and their reputation.

The OD Practitioner's Checklist

Twelve Questions for OD Strategists

These twelve questions and some discussion tips after each are for you, for your clients, and for your organization. As an OD practitioner, you can apply the Diamond to any of the areas listed below. All are discussed in one place or another in the book. The questions are intended to start impactful leadership dialogues.

1. For Which of Life's Arenas Will You Do Your Professional Work?

Select the life arena on which you want to work: *self, family, work, social responsibility, financial stability, or the environment.* Where are you stuck? Where do you want to see improvement?

Your stuck zone could be your job, your marriage, your demanding boss, an unreasonable client, the drop of your company's stock, managing an illness, coping with a profound loss, laying off someone, closing a department, helping to reorganize the team, and so forth. It could be more generic, such as not meeting your financial obligations, lacking marketing skills, not being as good at organizing tasks as some of your peers, doing a poor management job because you fear confrontation, not being creative enough to satisfy the demands of your work ("Why is it that the other person always comes up with the brilliant new ideas?"), and other more universal concerns. Or you may have more global concerns: for example, you go on vacation and find only polluted waters, you see lakes dried out where as a child you used to go boating, the trees are brown and dying, you can't see the mountains around your city because of smog, you cough on the freeways because of the fumes, and the like.

2. Are You Able to Make Translations into Leadership Language?

Reconstruct the language that you use from no-leadership to yes-leadership. Use the techniques of Intelligent Leadership Conversations (ILCs) and Strategic Intervention Moments (SIMs) as critical culture-building tools. Culture supports strategy. Culture is the secret of implementation. What we emphasize in our conversations is also the work that tends to get done.

3. How Good Are Your Diamond-Style Diagnoses?

Learn to diagnose in terms of the Diamond deep structures. Before you can have a plan of action, you need to understand where the long-term and underlying issues are. In medicine, for example, we diagnose by means of a blood analysis and a review of your medical history. In dentistry, we probe cavities and receding gums, and we talk about diets and preventive care.

In leadership, using the Diamond, the fundamental diagnostic principle is two-fold. The Diamond is a checklist to anticipate trouble spots. If you ignore one of the deep structures, then there is danger ahead. Your risk has increased; there is a discernible risk factor, which you can eliminate if you know the deficiency and if you summon the will to address it. So if you lack compassion, for instance, and understand not only the human ethical implications but also the business consequences, you can work on that simply by learning about it and choosing to change yourself. You would trace the roots of the personality structure that is alienated from compassion. Why do you think that works?

If you overdo *ethics* at the expense of *courage,* then you can catch yourself and correct both your language and your actions. This is certainly not meant to be simplistic, but you know the direction in which you must go in order to lower your risk of pathology in the leadership aspects of your life.

The second technique is the reverse. If you are stuck, it is because you ignore a deep structure—or several. At your work, people leave you. Why?

Because you are a courage/reality personality—tough and unpleasant, but results-oriented—and your people need an ethics/vision personality—understanding and connecting—who is kind and provides hope. Actualizing these particular clusters of deep structures means changing deeply entrenched habits of thinking, being, and acting. A personality change is required to alter results, to get past stuck. To bring about this deep change effectively requires much reflection and the willingness to arouse strong feelings. You can do it if you understand and if you set your mind to it.

4. Do You Have a Satisfactory Philosophy of Life?

Craft your own philosophy of life, your values, your belief systems. What do you think is the meaning of pain, of suffering, of frustration, of tasks? To what are you entitled, and what must you earn? What gives you significance? What is true love? Is anger good or bad? Is there a universal need for good manners? What must you still do before you die? In fact, what *is* death? Stress and illness are not just caused by environmental and biological factors, but *your philosophy of life is a major force in how healthy you are* in all of the six arenas of your life. Personalize your Diamond.

A surprising number of people are unaware of how central a good philosophy of life really is for their general health, happiness, and prosperity. But that is not why you develop a philosophy of life. You do it for the sake of truth and values.

A functioning philosophy of life has powerful side effects. You can say to your people: "There are business problems and there are character problems." And then ask: "Which are more important in your case? In the case of your organization?" What about leadership can be taught and what cannot be taught? You can teach and learn what to do. But can you teach and learn who you are? What—over the long haul—impacts your business the most?

5. Are Your Personal Values and Your Organization's Values Consonant with Each Other?

Align your personal vision of greatness and values with your company's vision of greatness and values. Both the company and you are responsible for working out this alignment. If the company does not cooperate or is not interested or suitable, then it is your responsibility, 100 percent, to make that happen. You do that either by personal adaptation (which is internal transformation) or by changing jobs (which is external transformation).

Conversely, if the employee is not willing or not interested, then it would be the company's task to assume 100 percent of responsibility to offer the employee this opportunity. Ask: "What is important to you? What really matters to you in life? Do we in our organization provide for you this chance to integrate your job with your personal fulfillment? Is this a good place to work?" And if we do not succeed with you, we may invite you to go elsewhere where you will be happier! These are the relevant questions.

6. How Well Do You Understand and Manage Your Debilitating Inner Conflicts?

Address your principal inner conflicts. Unattended, they drain you of energy. They cause paralysis. Either you resolve them, or you live with them. Either you make the hard choice and go one way—keep your job cheerfully or leave it courageously, confront your difficult customer or accept that person's intransigence—or you happily endure polarity as the normal way of life. Then be in dialogue with the two (or more) poles and reconcile yourself with the fact that you want to live and not die, yet this conflict is your fate: that you want to identify with your company, but their indifference and cold, calculating impersonality make a parody out of the meaning of loyalty. You instead make conflict itself your invigorating friend and not your debilitating enemy.

Addressed, inner conflicts may produce the anxiety of making difficult choices, accepting losses, giving up cherished hopes. But the reward is that you are indeed taking charge of how you are and how you live. And therewith you gain great pride, self-respect, and credibility. It is a feeling of being a substantial human being: grounded, both feet on the earth, influential, able to help others and earn their respect.

7. Do You Know How to Change Bad Stress into Good Stress?

Transform the bad stress of your *conflicts and frustrations* into the good stress of *challenge and growth*. This is a deliberate exercise in self-redefinition, the key to leadership growth. The question is not to distinguish between good and bad stress, but to know that when you feel bad stress it is because you do not have a philosophy of life that looks after you in defeat.

Redefinition means that to change results you have to change who you are. You avoid magic formulas. You make the tough decisions about yourself. Virtually anyone who loses weight on a diet regains it in a few years. Dieting is useless. Why? Because it is based on gimmicks and techniques, pills, behaviors, and even surgery. But the reality is much deeper. It is in the zone of your freedom to choose—and re-choose—who you are.

People like to eat and like to feel satiated, like babies, who after a feeding peacefully go to sleep. But dieting requires the mindset of a performer, an actor, a concert musician: feel a little hungry at all times, a little anxiety, a little on the edge. Then you have the energy, the alertness, of a predator, the permanently hungry animal. That is a conversion. That and only that will deal effectively with any weight problem.

8. Which Are Your Persistent Stuck Points?

Identify your stuck points. There is a superficial way of doing this, but also a deep way. The former would be, "I must meet this difficult deadline." The latter would be, "What can I do to overcome my habitual procrastination?" To deepen a stuck point means to move it from a one-time event to a characteristic pattern. We may ask: "Why were we acquired in an unfriendly takeover? Why was our company opportunistically dismembered? There was too much internal dissension at the top of our company. We should have fired our CFO during the early stages." This may be true, and the remedy correct. But there is a deeper side: History is going through you. What you experience and what happened to your company is simply one version of every business. Your CFO was not the problem. If you did not have that situation, then there would have been another player in the same role of saboteur. The saboteur is a necessary archetype in every organization, of every play. Once you know that, you realize you are not singled out for bad luck but you are facing the human condition, what is natural. Then you handle it with transformation and adaptation rather than problem solving and a meat ax.

9. Do You Continually Teach Leadership in All You Do, Especially in Your Relations with Your Clients and Customers?

You teach leadership as a way of doing business. Your internal and your external customers become better leaders in *their own* business organizations—using *your* product and services—as a direct result of doing business with you. That is the goal. Therein lies your competitive differentiation and advantage.

10. Do You Have a Clear Perspective on Your Real Strengths?

Know your strengths. Your strengths are what makes you distinctively marketable. However, it is more powerful to focus on where your weaknesses are, for they are likely to be what gives you trouble. Without being facetious, we can nevertheless say that one of your weaknesses may be that you do not know how to exploit your strengths!

11. Do You Have a Solid and Honest Grasp of Your Weaknesses?

Address your weaknesses. They cause your stuck point. This is as important to do as it is difficult to figure out. For your Diamond weaknesses are of the order of the "boiled frog syndrome." Depression can come over you ever so gradually. So can disorientation, when your judgment becomes flawed and gradually diminishes. You don't know it is happening, and suddenly you find yourself in a distraught condition. An account for which you are responsible gradually deteriorates, until one day it's canceled. The same can happen to the loyalty of a valued employee. The person says nothing, until one day this individual resigns, and you are faced unexpectedly with a big problem. You therefore need to maintain perspective on your behavior. Asking for feedback is helpful, realizing that deep feedback is sensitive and harder to come by and even hard to accept.

12. Do You Use the IdeaBank™ Concept and Other Tools?

There are additional tools that go with the Diamond. One of them is the Idea-Bank, discussed in Chapter 5, which is particularly suitable for innovation. It is a participative generator of new strategic concepts.

Another set of tools is to integrate the Diamond Leadership® *language* into the organization's principal means of communication and planning: e-mails, meetings, day planners, sales presentations, and memos. This can become a fine art and is a not uncommon strategy to address the pressing task of culture change.

A third tool is *measurement.* Experience shows that *discussing* how to measure the effectiveness of leadership coaching and culture building is even more beneficial than using the tools thus generated. Interactive discussions on measurement surface the deeper, underlying, leadership implementation prerequisites.

The "Nay" Sayers

Question

A client asks, "About two-thirds of our workshop participants are 'getting' it, but the other third cannot see the relevance of the Diamond to the things that are important to them and that matter at work and in their private lives. They say it's interesting and there is good will but they don't see the point. We are a pragmatic organization and deal with tough business issues all day long. Do you have any helpful comments?"

Answer

I am sure this is frustrating to you, and that is quite understandable. One, of course, appreciates your reference to good will, for if there are political or power issues in the background, then the personality conflicts would interfere with the learning.

Step one is to put aside any and all prejudgments you may have about what the Leadership Diamond® is and what it is meant to achieve. You are invited to approach the subject matter with a completely open and unbiased mind—otherwise we would not be communicating, but only talking to ourselves.

Many people have very good instincts and they operate according to Diamond principles already, but may not be conscious of it. This might indicate that they are not comfortable with the language and the vocabulary used to refer to inner space. The leadership messages are discoveries in inner space—such as free will, personal responsibility for the whole, anxiety and courage, sharpening the mind deliberately, coping with defeat—which we then move to outer space in order to become operational and bring business results. Some people do not have the language for these experiences and are not accustomed to exploring these important and powerful inner realities. So when we do get into that territory it seems very foreign to them. But it really isn't.

Moreover, some people fragment themselves so that their jobs and their true natures remain quite separate. They fail to see clearly the intimate connection between, on the one hand, who they are as people—their character, their personality structure, and their behaviors—and their business results on the other. Your personality characteristics have a major impact on how successful or unsuccessful you are in adapting to massively and rapidly changing political, social, and business environments. There are some people who have a really hard time understanding in their "gut" the connection between who they are as people and the effectiveness of the total organization of which they are members. Some people become upset because they feel that those who remain on the sidelines are not taking responsibility for the impact their attitudes have on the rest of the organization.

Some people are limited in their development. Their personal growth is one-sided—and they don't know it. They are all into *reality*, for example, blissfully unaware that they have little or no interest in *vision,* care little about *ethics,* that is, the ultimate fate of their customers and employees, and fail altogether to see the necessity of taking some truly *courageous* and anxiety-producing stands. They don't know what they are not doing. That is perfectly all right, since no one is entitled to enter their inward zones and "mess around" with their minds. But neither is anyone obligated to hire them and support them in their narrowness at the expense of the other members of the organization and the total viability of the enterprise. And if their one-sided personal development does not make them leadership material for the future of one particular company, then it must be made clear to them that they no doubt will be much happier elsewhere!

Finally, people who say they "don't get it"—or of whom others say they "don't get it"—may themselves have a very significant message, and it behooves us to pay attention to what they have to say and to the style in which they choose to say it. The only situation with which a rational approach usually fails is if there are in operation politically motivated hidden agendas. That is then the end of good will.

If you have these people in your organization, what do you do with them? This is how an OD consultant would coach the manager responsible:

1. You place them on the Competence-Authenticity Magic Matrix (see Appendix A) and help them understand how they are positioned in their current organization.

2. You let them know how others perceive them and the cost to them, as well as the benefit, of adapting to both the positive and the negative impact of being a nay-sayer.

3. You let people know, as a central feature of not only the company culture but also the more basic human nature, that they are responsible for the impact they make on others. They need to take care of not only their own feelings but also the feelings of others that are occasioned by their personality traits and their behavior. You cannot make problems for people without being aware of what you are doing and taking responsibility for it. This does not prescribe for them any specific action, but it does hold them responsible for the waves that they make and the consequences of these waves. One of the consequences is to disrupt the team. That needs to be translated into costs, lost revenues, and other financial measures.

4. As their leader, you are responsible for the disciplined behavior of your team. You need to summon your own intelligence of vision

and guts of courage to confront the nay-sayer with the fact that continuing this unsupportive behavior would probably make another position at another company very attractive to that person! With your toothiest grin you can say, "The present organization is no doubt becoming too uncomfortable for you."

More than once have I heard someone on a dysfunctional team exclaim to the others, "In order for *me* to succeed I need all of *you* to be a team! My father is dying. He has urged me all my life to become a manager. He has six months to live. I feel I have not received enough support from his team to do my job well. I need your help to do a good job before my Dad dies! Anytime there is a squabble in our team, even if it does not involve me, I am affected. Not only are my sales needs shunted aside, but I get upset and I am not able to be effective with my clients." The boss echoed the statement: "I can only succeed if you are a team. I need you to be a team—if for no other reason than my personal and professional responsibilities. I need you. I am dependent on you. It may not look that way to you, but it is the truth!" People don't know how much their behavior impacts other people, even at the deepest level of their self-concept. We call that unintended consequences.

Your Twelve-Step Organizational Attitude and Implementation Audit

Look at Figure B.5, an illustration of mindsets required for a culture change. Then do the following activity.

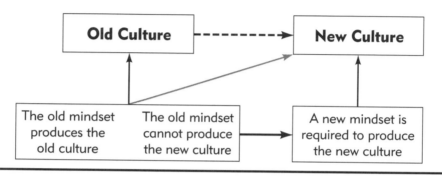

Figure B.5. Culture Change

Activity

You are a partner in one of the large consulting firms. Your client is the city manager of a major city. Your client's objective is to be named as one of the great cities of the United States. Here is your task:

> Your client city is being evaluated for the All-America City Award from the National Civic League. Your objective for the last five years has been to be recognized as one of America's ten best cities. You have a plan, but the key is the motivation of your team.
>
> Look at your own current organization. Look at the Diamond criteria. And review your objectives.
>
> How do you rate the leadership of your city manager's enterprise in terms of *awareness, organization, programs,* and *performance?*

Here are questions for journaling, as well as for focus groups. *Pick a few. Which to you are the most important questions?*

1. What is your organization's vision of greatness and of high standards?
    -   How much time and energy are spent on reflecting on this theme?
    -   How is that done?
    -   How integrated are these values into the activities of your total team?
    -   How powerfully are your people motivated toward excellence?
    -   What have you done to inspire them, and what remains to be done?
    -   In your organization, are your people alert or asleep? Energetic or lethargic? Ambitious or retired on the job?
    -   In making a commitment to the city, how much of that is for the organization, and how much of that is for themselves?

2. What are the dominant conflicts and contradictions plaguing your team and organization?
    -   How successfully does the organization manage these fundamental paradoxes, ambiguities, and conflicts? Can you cite a few examples?
    -   How can you deal better with paradoxes and polarities?
    -   Do people expect all conflicts to be resolved—like wanting to live and yet being destined to die—or are they getting experience in talking about conflicts in general and how one can live with irresolvable paradoxes?
    -   Do your people know that the democratic personality can live with contradictions, in fact, value them above single-mindedness?
    -   Can you be decisive and democratic at the same time?

- Can you accept that insisting on one view, and one view only, reflects an authoritarian personality?

3. Are you a compassionate organization?
   - What would be a good instance?
   - What is the level of trust that both the city council and the citizens of the community have in you and your staff?
   - In the perception of your client system, how high is the organization rated in fairness and integrity?
   - Would you say that the absolute minimum is that you be perceived as evenhanded and fair—favoring no one—in your four constituencies: the city council, the mayor, your staff, and the community?
   - Does the staff understand this point?

4. Do people in your organization, instead of looking for others to blame, willingly hold themselves accountable for results?
   - Is this attitude clearly and reliably entrenched in the culture?
   - Does the culture, and do people's peers, discipline effectively individuals who consistently "pass the buck"?
   - How, and how well, does your organization cope with *stress* and *burnout*?
   - Is yours essentially a *depressed* organization?
   - How are stress, burnout, and depression (a) recognized and (b) treated?
   - How much does FDR's famous "The only thing we have to fear is fear itself" apply to your organization?

5. Do your people really understand that, after all is said and done, their security is tied to their performance, and that the family feeling, beautiful as it may be, is nevertheless a cruel deception?

- Does your city have a realistic idea of how it is perceived in the community—or is it in denial and satisfied with illusions?
- How clearly does the city see itself in comparison with other cities, and what, in a more absolute sense, is really possible for them to achieve? How capable is it of seeing "gaps"?

6. What is the level of intelligence of the staff as a whole?
   - To what extent is there a critical mass of employees with high strategic thinking capabilities?
   - Is conceptual intelligence valued in your organization?
   - How much time do employees spend on just honing their thinking capacity, the sharpness of their intelligence?
   - There may be a workout gym on your premises, but is there also the equivalent of a "cerebral gym" to hone the mind's imagination for the complex tasks ahead?

7. Design your next steps, for yourself and for your organization, no matter where in the hierarchy you find yourself. This is the work for which you are paid. Here is where you are expected to perform.
   - Do your people remember this truism? Change and innovation start with you because being a self means also to be the center of your universe. And being free means that your choices help design the world in which you are destined to live.
   - Is your culture clear that there is no escape from freedom?
   - How can you give that message? How can you teach others to pass on that message?

8. Execution means to be able to have the right kind of leadership conversation with the right people at the right time and with the right depth. We talk in Diamond Theory about *Strategic Intervention Moments* for *Intelligent Leadership Conversations*: SIMs for ILCs. The

strategy is to deal with who, what, when, how, why, where, which, and whether?

- To what extent is this natural technique practiced in your organization?

9. What is in the way? What are the resistances? Why do things that look good end up not working?

- How will you and your organization change that and be different?

- Have you helped your people to understand that the most productive approach to culture change and innovation is to ask this one overwhelming question: Why are we not doing already today what we all know needs to be done? What are our defensive strategies, the clever rationalizations we place in the way of acting on what we fully know is our responsibility? What do we gain by denial?

    The answer, as old as the hills, is always the same. Running away from personal responsibility protects us, we think, from deep anxiety. Until we redefine the meaning of anxiety from negative to positive, there can be no leadership.

- Is that message given to the culture and by the culture of your organization?

10. Will you measure results? Is that possible? What's your solution, your answer, your decision to both the importance and the ambiguities of measurement?

11. What connection do you see between these audit questions and the Leadership Diamond® shown in Figure B.2 on page 394?

12. And then ask, what is the connection between this conversation and achieving your objective of being one of the ten best cities?

After this exercise, raise the question, "Was our time well spent? How so?"

Questions and Answers

As part of the seminar/workshop, the facilitator in a Diamond program invites students to post questions to the author on a website. This is a routine design feature toward the end of the program.

Prior to participating in the course, class members received the following memo:

> Thank you for your interest in the Diamond Model. Participating in this program and raising questions are sound investments in your own personal leadership, your marketability within and outside of your company, and especially in the end quality of the leadership of _____ Company and its culture. Your commitment will lead your company to become a better place to work, a company with growing reputation and respectability, and a business with rising profitability and stock values. All these are results expected from increased attention to leadership coaching, leadership teaching, leadership conversation, and leadership behavior, and to the continued formation of a leadership culture. You are helping your company in a major way to become a better enterprise than it already is.
>
> The Diamond is the result of extensive historical research on what the basic, various, and fundamental answers have been to these three underlying questions:
>
> - "What is leadership?"
> - "How can I become a better leader?"
> - "How can we become a stronger leadership organization?"

The participants receive a speedy response to their online questions, timely enough to discuss the answers at the end of their Diamond program. Below is a sample of questions that have been received and the author's responses.

1. Where does the term "sustained initiative" come from? It has to do with courage, which requires initiative. Sustainable means you do not choose once but continuously, in an ongoing fashion. You do not just merely pick a project and that is it. You make a commitment to do a good job, and that means you choose daily to do a good job, and moreover, every day you choose all day long to do good work. This is sustained initiative and this works for results. Nothing else does.

2. How long is long enough to sustain "sustained initiative"? It never ends. That is how it feels to be alive, to have joy, to experience hope, and to be instrumental in helping others to become happier and more prosperous.

3. How do we measure personal responsibility? This is a hard question. The big problem is, how do you measure those things that exist before measurement, like life itself, love, ambition, faith, happiness?

Are you married? How do you measure the success of your relationship? Who has the rules? Who knows what really matters in life? Is it entertainment? Being humored? Loyalty and commitment? Learning? Pleasure? Duty? Pride? Who is to say? What do you think? Are these not bigger-than-life questions and perhaps also bigger-than-life measurements? We can measure all we want. No problem. But let's respect the sanctity and the integrity of the subject matter. Being responsible is the nobility of the soul. Do we dare poke at it with a measuring stick?

4. This sounds idealistic. Where is the meat? Strange question! Idealism *is* meat, unless you want to relegate the highest human values to the dustbin of history.

You probably mean "All this is fantasy." The Diamond has taught you that leaders exhibit *both* vision *and* reality in their mindsets and in their organizations. And the Diamond teaches you to pay attention to *polarity*, which means that leaders have the skill to bring vision and reality into a single orbit. People who are only visionary live in the clouds. And people who are only realistic have no values. We need both. *Either-or* is NOT leadership. *Both-and* IS leadership. Who are you?

5. **If we're really free, are we free from the laws of physics, ethics, and sociological norms?** There are common but also colossal misunderstandings about the meaning and the nature of freedom. Freedom is what you find when on the path to self-discovery you look inward and find that in your soul you have free will.

And that discovery leads you immediately to the overwhelming awareness that you are responsible for all your actions and inactions—and that there are consequences to how you choose. You recognize that you and no one else becomes the consequences of these free choices. It is like having a child. You are responsible for the pregnancy and the life of the child that develops. And you are accountable. And that is an enormous responsibility. And there is no escaping from the consequences of your free choices. Responsibility is a fact, not just a value. It is the way the world is wired, and you too. Accountability—resonating to how your world reacts—has enormous survival value. That's heavy! And that's the human truth.

And the world will hold you severely accountable for the consequences of your free choices, for you are not only your free choices but you are also the consequences in the world of these free choices. If in the heat of frustration you frighten a subordinate by losing your temper and yelling at that person, you will not be excused for such unprofessional conduct. You are a co-creator in this unprofessional emotional scene.

You had a choice. You could have acted otherwise. You gave in to your impulses. All of these are choices, and they are *your* choices. There may be nothing wrong in your mind with how you chose. You are of course free to choose as you please. But the world exacts consequences from your actions in that you are accountable for these repercussions. For you are the you that exists in the cubicles and the hallways of your employer's business, the waves you have made, the initiatives you have taken, the effect that you have had. That is you. And you created your own you. That is the social actuality, that is how leaders think, and that is how you are responsible.

Understanding your freedom to co-create a culture at your company and organization can fill you with anxiety and with guilt. Leaders choose to be held accountable, for it honors them and gives them credibility as leaders.

This point makes or breaks a leader. Freedom is not license, by any stretch of the imagination. Freedom is to know that you, like God, create the world in which you live and are therefore responsible for the character of that world. You do not create it alone, no—but you are fully responsible and should be, and want to be held accountable, for your contribution to what this world is and for what it does.

This point is not merely overlooked, *it is deliberately repressed,* because we are all anxious and guilty over the consequences of our freedom and free will. In avoiding responsibility we think we avoid the anxiety of being free, choosing constantly. The truth is the reverse: Not holding ourselves responsible is the attrition of our humanity—and the end of sustainable business.

To see the world in this responsible way and to live accordingly, that is leadership. You measure the quality of a person first and foremost by the degree of responsibility that person takes for the consequences of his or her free choices! That is the core preparation for leadership.

6. Isn't there an inherent conflict between serving people and the reality of the marketplace and providing value to the shareholders? Yes. And it is your job and mine to manage this conflict with statesmanship. That is why leaders are paid. The market is brutal and exploitative, materialistic and opportunistic—a jungle. Decent human beings demand a principled and compassionate environment. That leads to a clash, which politely is called a polarity. To be a leader is to help people make profitable organizations, successful on the market, which also foster the highest values for which humanity stands—and for which many have died. This is the toughest assignment in life, and you as a leader are entrusted to make it work. We need to stick together here, for we are all the victims and the perpetrators, and instead we must make all of us the beneficiaries. We will not solve this problem in our lifetime, but we can address the "inherent conflict between serving people and the reality of the marketplace" with understanding and good will, rather than become co-conspirators and collude with the forces of ethical breakdown.

7. How can I use this to transcend the politics, systems, and so forth needed to do the job? Leaders educate and re-educate themselves and their organizations in Diamond technology. The Diamond serves as a catalog for time-tested leadership essentials that are then taught and incorporated in people's conversations, behaviors, systems, and culture—for results. Make sure that concepts such as vision, reality, ethics, and courage appear in your vocabulary at leadership moments. And make certain they are expected to become behaviors as well. You will gain credibility with your colleagues and, more importantly, with your clients.

8. It seems that I can have a balanced Diamond personally, but when customer needs, organizational requirements, and so on are overlaid, it becomes distorted. How do I handle this, or is this a flaw in the model? This is a good insight. And it is true. You state the problem well. Leadership is the solution. That is why leadership exists and why it is practiced.

Here is the process: Leadership starts with understanding and teaching ethics—the commitment to create a more serviceable work community.

Then it requires courage, the capacity to claim your freedom and understand the meaning of these three leadership phrases found in leading teams: (1) We create an organization of our own choosing; (2) We learn the art of co-creation; and (3) We choose to be held accountable.

This is how leading organizations differentiate themselves from the rest.

Then it requires realism, the decision to face the hardness of the business environment.

Finally leaders use their intelligence to the maximum. In Diamond technology it is called vision: analysis, systems thinking, promoting creativity and innovation, and making the decision to always start from the overarching perspective and guard ourselves against thinking small.

You can make these choices. Your team can make these choices. Spreading the Diamond language is to install in organizations the discipline of leadership thinking and acting.

9. Does the leadership model change from situation to situation, and if so, how do we know how/when to change ourselves? The Diamond describes the universal leadership mind. This is your operating system. Specific situations require specific solutions—applications. They are designed for a specific need: accounting, word processing, design, communication, and so on. The applications you design by installing in your team a *sense of responsibility for the whole.* That requires conversations about:

- *Ethics,* which means you work for people and through people—and only through people;

- *Courage,* which means you take the initiative and also that you can recover from defeat;

- *Reality,* which means you know at all times that you face the market as a company and not as an individual; and

- *Vision,* which means you know the thrust of it all and that you have bought into the strategy that will bring you results—if there is commitment and intelligence to back it up.

10. You talk about vision being "universal." From a practical standpoint, isn't vision more limited? Vision is a universal need. In its application, you are right, it is always specific.

11. Isn't the real value in this our ability to incorporate elements of the model that are important to use personally rather than try to be a perfect 10 at each corner? All I have to say is, congratulations, you are "getting it"!

12. Should our goal be to learn and use the model as it is or to deliberately select/reject the elements as they fit or don't fit us personally? Good point. Once you understand the model, you take responsibility to create your own. You are the leader and it is your task to build your model.

13. Should this all come to us naturally or is this something we will need to work at constantly? What comes naturally to leaders is that they are constantly alert about the quality of leadership thinking, talking, and acting that they demonstrate to the world. They take charge, deliberately and constantly, to do the easiest thing in the world, that is, to activate all the corners of their leadership minds, as appropriate to the circumstances that they find.

14. How does this fit with the model that Stephen F. Covey teaches? He represents one application of the universal leadership mind. The Diamond gives you the foundation. Covey and others give you possible uses. The Diamond is the operating system. Covey and others are the applications.

15. I'm fifty and doubt that I can really be taught to be "visionary." Can it really be learned and developed? At the time of the midlife crisis you ask if your life is what you want it to be. Then you make a decision about greatness:

"What was my childhood ambition?" and "What happened to it?" Now that you are mature, you ask, "What is the meaning of my life?" "What are my core values?" and "How can I connect my personal values with the values and strategies of the company in which I work?"

Those are exciting questions. They open for you a cornucopia of possibilities while you are at the very pinnacle of your life. You are today more mature than you have ever been, wiser and better informed, and more experienced. What a great place to be!

16. Does my attempt to use the model to define my leadership in fact limit my freedom? This is how you choose to use your freedom. If you find more in the mind than the universal model of leadership suggests, then grab it, for you have struck gold.

17. Is greatness defined through sociological norms or do I define it for myself? Great question! Greatness is defined by you, and, strictly speaking, you have nothing to go on, for you choose your own criteria of measurement. In our culture, greatness is tied to sports, the arts, religion, politics, the military, big business, and leadership. What is your preferred symbol for greatness?

18. Does the model help me be more aware of others and their capabilities, and therefore make me a better leader? Absolutely yes. You got the point and it is delightful to witness!

19. How do you rate your model versus other well-known leadership models? The Diamond is philosophy. Other models are behavioral science. The Diamond is the operating system. Other models are applications. Philosophy and the behavioral sciences are not in competition. Quite to the contrary, they need each other. A reinforced cement block is your house's foundation. You live above the foundation in a delicate studio apartment. The latter rests on the former. You don't want to live in the cement block, nor do you want your delicate apartment to rest on thin air. This is how a philosophy-based leadership approach and psychological and religious leadership models support each other. It's a beautiful synergy.

20. Is there a single element or characteristic whereby I can recognize a successful authentic leader when I meet one? Yes. The person exudes credibility, and you feel he or she cares about you. When a non-Diamond manager runs a meeting, then everyone enters cheerful and leaves upset and stressed. Whereas when a Diamond manager runs a meeting, people enter depressed and anxious and leave full of joy and hope. When you have a conference with a non-leader, you leave exclaiming, "This is one bright person!" But when you have a conference with a true leader, then you depart exclaiming. "I had no idea I was so smart!"

What kind of meetings are yours?

BIBLIOGRAPHY

Bartlett, J. (1992). *Bartlett's familiar quotations* (16th ed.). Boston, MA: Little, Brown.

Bennis, W. (1993). *An invented life.* Reading, MA: Addison-Wesley.

Bennis, W. (1994). *On becoming a leader* (2nd ed.). Cambridge, MA: Perseus.

Blake, W. (1805). *Auguries of innocence.* Poems from the Pickering manuscript.

De Saint Exupéry, A. *The little prince.*

Fritsch, P. (2001, July 3). Life on the lam is good for Mr. Ross, in a Belizean paradise. *Wall Street Journal,* p. 1.

Fromm, E. (1994). *Escape from freedom.* New York: Henry Holt.

Good grief: Don't get taken by the trauma industry. (2001, October 25). *Wall Street Journal,* p. A21.

Johnson, B. (1992). *Polarity management.* Amherst, MA: HRD Press.

Keats, J. (1848). *Life, letters, and literary remains of John Keats.* (R.M. Milnes, Ed.). London: E. Moxon.

Kohn, A. (1993, September-October). Why incentive plans cannot work. *Harvard Business Review,* p. 54.

Putnam, R.D. (2001). *Bowling alone.* New York: Simon & Schuster.

Rauch, S. (2001, July 4). The fear of losing jobs. *Monterey County Herald,* p. E1.

Rigby, D. (2001, June). Moving upward in a downturn. *Harvard Business Review.*

Rilke, R.M. (1923). *Letters to a young poet* (J.B. Greene & M.D. Herter, Trans.). New York: W.W. Norton.

Rilke, R.M. (1939). *Duino elegies.* (J.B. Leishman & S. Spender, Trans.). New York: W.W. Norton.

Roan, S. (2001, October 27). Response to terror. *Los Angeles Times,* p. A1.

Sartre, J.-P. (1992). *Huis clos et les mouches [The flies].* Cambridge, MA: Schoenhof's Foreign Books.

Serebriakoff, V. (1995). Self-scoring IQ tests. Derived from *How intelligent are you.* Robinson Publishing.

Shakespeare, W. (1964). *The tempest.* New York: Dover.

Tanouye, E. (2001, June 13). Untitled. *Wall Street Journal,* p. B1.

Welch, J. (2001). *Jack: Straight from the gut.* New York: Warner.

Welch, J.R., Jr., Collingwood, H., & Coutu, D. (2002, February). Jack on Jack: The HBR interview. *Harvard Business Review.*

Whyte, D. (1996). *The heart aroused.* New York: Currency/Doubleday.

ABOUT THE AUTHOR

PETER KOESTENBAUM'S primary concern over his lifetime has been to become a respectable philosopher and apply this ancient discipline to people's major life concerns. For one generation he has applied philosophy to the practical needs of business, developing in the process his well-known and widely used concept of the Leadership Diamond®.

He was a professor of philosophy for thirty-four years at San Jose State University in California, and has spent a generation traveling the world and consulting with major companies and individuals in high levels of responsibility. A few among his major clients have been the Ford Motor Company, CitiBank, Electronic Data Systems, Exxon/Mobil, Ciba Geigy, American Medical International, Volvo, and many of the city managers in the United States. He has been a frequent presenter at the World Economic Forum. He spends much of his time in individual leadership coaching and in helping to set up companies along the lines of the Leadership Diamond® principles.

He is a frequent lecturer and conducts seminars in both culture building and strategic marketing. He has done so in over forty countries and on every continent. The Koestenbaum Institute is in Stockholm and in Los Angeles (where it is connected with Quantum Leadership Solutions).

He was born in Germany and raised in Venezuela, arriving in the United States right after WW II. He went to school at Stanford, U.C. Berkeley, Harvard, and Boston Universities, receiving his B.A., M.A., and Ph.D. degrees, all in philosophy. He also studied physics and music, and worked intensively with psychologists and psychiatrists applying philosophic insights to the healing arts. While teaching, he was named Outstanding Professor in the State of California.

His other business books are *The Heart of Business* (Saybrook), *Leadership: the Inner Side of Greatness* (Revised, Jossey-Bass/Pfeiffer), and *Freedom and Accountability at Work* (with Peter Block, Jossey-Bass/Pfeiffer).

Peter Koestenbaum can be reached at his e-mail, *Peter@Koestenbaum.com,* and on the web, *http://www.PiB.net.*

Index